*David Reid*
■
■
■

# SUSTAINABLE DEVELOPMENT

## *An Introductory Guide*

■
■
■

EARTHSCAN

**Earthscan Publications Ltd, London**

First published in 1995 by
Earthscan Publications Limited
120 Pentonville Road, London N1 9JN
Web site-http://www.earthscan.co.UK
Email – earthinfo @earthscan.co.UK

Reprinted 1996, 1997

ISBN: 1 85383 241 3

Copy-edited and typeset by Selro Publishing Services, Oxford
Printed in England by Clays Ltd, St Ives plc

Earthscan Publications Limited is an editorially independent
subsidiary of Kogan Page Limited and publishes in association
with the International Institute for Environment and Development and the World Wide Fund for Nature.

"God has lent us the earth for our life; it is a great entail. It belongs as much to those who are to come after us, and whose names are already written in the book of creation, as to us; and we have no right, by anything that we do or neglect, to involve them in unnecessary penalties, or deprive them of benefits which it is in our power to bequeath."

(John Ruskin, *The Seven Lamps of Architecture*, 1849)

"We use land because we regard it as a commodity belonging to us. When we see land as a community to which we belong, we may begin to use it with love and respect."

(Aldo Leopold)

"Any fundamental human need that is not satisfied reveals a poverty."

(Manfred Max-Neef)

"Call a thing immoral or ugly, soul-destroying or a degradation of man, a peril to the peace of the world or to the wellbeing of future generations; as long as you have not shown it to be "uneconomic" you have not really questioned its right to exist, grow and prosper."

(E F Schumacher)

"When any environmental issue is probed to its origins, it reveals an inescapable truth — that the root cause of the crisis is not to be found in how men interact with nature, but in how they interact with each other; that to solve the environmental crisis we must solve the problem of poverty, racial injustice and war; that the debt to nature, which is the measure of the environmental crisis cannot be paid person by person, in recycled bottles or ecologically sound habits, but in the ancient coin of social justice."

(Barry Commoner)

"When we try to pick out anything by itself, we find it hitched to everything else in the universe."

(John Muir)

"What kind of development?"

(telephone receptionist at the Scottish Office)

"Sustainable what was it?"

(librarian, Scottish Agricultural College)

IN MEMORY OF MY LATE PARENTS,
DAVID MACDONALD REID AND HELEN MARGARET JOHNSTONE;

and for their grandchildren,
Juniper, Brendan, Anna, Kirsty and Jenny,
my strongest links with future generations.

# Contents

# Acronyms

| | |
|---|---|
| ADR | average disparity ratio |
| BP | British Petroleum |
| CAP | Common Agricultural Policy |
| CAT | Centre for Alternative Technology |
| CFC | chlorofluorocarbon |
| $CO_2$ | carbon dioxide |
| CSD | Commission on Sustainable Development |
| DDT | dichloro-diphenyl-trichloro-ethane (an insecticide) |
| ECCO | enhanced carrying capacity options |
| ECOSOC | Economic and Social Council (of the UN) |
| EDR | extreme disparity ratio |
| ETC | Education and Training Consultants |
| FAO | Food and Agriculture Organization (of UN) |
| FOE | Friends of the Earth |
| G7 | the group of seven "leading" industrial nations |
| GATT | General Agreement on Tariffs and Trade |
| GDP | gross domestic product |
| GEF | Global Environmental Facility |
| GNP | gross national product |
| ICC | International Chamber of Commerce |
| ICDSI | Independent Commission on Disarmament and Security Issues |
| ICIDI | Independent Commission on International Development Issues |

| | |
|---|---|
| IIED | International Institute for Environment and Development |
| IEEP | Institute for European Environmental Policy |
| IIASA | International Institute for Applied Systems Analysis |
| ILO | International Labour Organization/Office (of the UN) |
| IMF | International Monetary Fund |
| IPCC | Intergovernmental Panel on Climate Change |
| ISEW | Index of Sustainable Economic Welfare |
| IUCN | International Union for the Conservation of Nature and Natural Resources |
| LETS | local exchange trading system |
| LGMB | Local Government Management Board |
| MIT | Massachusetts Institute of Technology |
| MTO | Multilateral Trade Organization |
| $N_2O$ | nitrous oxide |
| NAS | National Academy of Sciences (US) |
| NEF | New Economics Foundation |
| NEPP | National Environment Policy Plan |
| NGO | non-governmental organization |
| NOX | oxides of nitrogen |
| NSDS | national sustainable development strategy |
| OECD | Organization for Economic Cooperation and Development |
| Oxfam | Oxford Committee for Famine Relief |
| PCB | polychlorinated biphenyl |
| PEC | primary environmental care |
| PRA | Participatory Rural Appraisal |
| SANGEC | Scottish Academic Network for Global Environmental Change |
| SERA | Socialist Environment and Resources Association |
| SPCK | Society for Promoting Christian Knowledge |
| TNC | transnational corporation |
| UK | United Kingdom |
| UN | United Nations |
| UNA | United Nations Association |

| | |
|---|---|
| UNCED | United Nations Conference on Environment and Development |
| UNCHE | United Nations Conference on the Human Environment |
| UNCTAD | United Nations Conference on Trade and Development |
| UNDP | United Nations Development Programme |
| UNECA | United Nations Economic Commission for Africa |
| UNECE | United Nations Economic Commission for Europe |
| UNEP | United Nations Environment Programme |
| UNESCO | United Nations Educational, Scientific and Cultural Organization |
| UNICEF | United Nations (International) Children's (Emergency) Fund |
| UNRISD | United Nations Research Institute for Social Development |
| UNSTAT | United Nations Statistical Office |
| USA | United States of America |
| WCED | World Commission on Environment and Development |
| WCS | *World Conservation Strategy* |
| WHO | World Health Organization |
| WRI | World Resources Institute |
| WWF | World Wildlife Fund |
| WWI | World Watch Institute |

# Acknowledgements

This book is a product of two years spent at the Centre for Human Ecology, which is part of the Institute of Ecology and Resource Management at the University of Edinburgh. It owes a large intellectual debt to the ideas of the many writers to which the Centre introduced me or gave me further access. The references and quotations in the text attempt to acknowledge my indebtedness to particular writers. The book also owes much to the staff, associates and postgraduate students of the centre — all "teacher-students" or "student-teachers" in Freire's words, who have clarified and enlarged my understanding of sustainable development.

I am grateful to the following for permission to reproduce copyright material: Oxford University Press, New York; Michael Carley and FAO; Michael Colby and Elsevier Science; Robert Costanza and Elsevier Science; and the Merlin Press.

I am particularly grateful to a number of individuals: to Gareth Edwards-Jones of the Scottish Agricultural College, for first suggesting that the original version merited wider readership than a board of examiners; to Alastair McIntosh, development director at the Centre for Human Ecology, for the idea of "a book" and for catapulting me into what has been a happy relationship with Earthscan; to John Kirkby of the University of Northumbria for important comments at an early stage; to Ulrich Loening, director of the Centre for Human Ecology, for many stimulating suggestions; to Jackie Roddick of the University of Glasgow for a discussion on the Rio Summit; to the members of the administering board of the Kerr-Fry Trust, for their financial support; to Alex Sproule and Jane Rosegrant, for reading nearly all of the book in draft and making many valuable suggestions; and to Elspeth, my wife, for her patience, encouragement and practical help.

Whatever success this book may have in helping to promote a wider understanding of the most important issue of our time is largely theirs; its shortcomings are entirely mine.

# Author's Note

In referring to groupings of countries it is hard to find general terms which do not mislead. Here the terms "North" and "South", adopted by the Brandt Commission, are used to refer to industrialized countries with high average GNP and countries with little industrialization and/or low GNP respectively. Although these terms require readers to remember that Australia and New Zealand are part of the "North", and perhaps fail to give sufficient recognition to the newly industrializing countries of South-East Asia, they seem preferable, for reasons which I hope will become clear, to such terms as "developed countries", "developing countries" and "the Third World".

# Introduction

"Sustainable development" has become one of the catchphrases of the 1990s, yet in its short existence it has frequently been damned with faint praise — for example, "moral convictions as a substitute for thought" (Redclift, 1987, p2); "a 'good idea' which cannot sensibly be put into practice" (O'Riordan, 1988, p48); "how to destroy the environment with compassion" (Smith, 1991, p135). Such censures seem oddly directed at one of the buzz-words of the decade.

The term "sustainable development" first came to prominence in the *World Conservation Strategy* (WCS) published by the World Conservation Union (IUCN) in 1980.[1] It achieved a new status with the publication of *Our Common Future*, the Brundtland Report, in 1987 and has gained even greater attention since the United Nations Conference on Environment and Development (UNCED) held in Rio de Janeiro in June 1992. Now the concept engages governments and non-governmental organizations (NGOs), civil servants and environmental activists, local government officials and community groups, development agencies and grassroots organizations, planners and commercial developers, industrialists and environmental agencies, established bureaucracies and *ad hoc* networks, as well as a host of

---

1. Credit for the invention of the term has been variously accorded to Eva Balfour, founder of the Soil Association, the International Institute for Environment and Development (IIED), and Wes Jackson, the American geneticist and biodynamic farmer.

academics representing a wide range of fields from atmospheric science through political economy to gender studies.

In the wake of UNCED — the "Earth Summit" — the member states of the international community are preparing and publishing national sustainable development plans and strategies, and submitting these to a specially created commission of the UN (the Commission for Sustainable Development). In the United States a presidential council deliberates on the principles of sustainable development. The UN Development Programme (UNDP) promotes "sustainable human development"; the International Monetary Fund (IMF) and the Organization for Economic Development talk of "sustainable economic growth"; the World Bank is committed to "sustainable development and equitable development" and the European Union, since Maastricht, has explored the notion of "sustainable economic and social development". Meanwhile local authorities have adopted criteria of sustainability and sustainable development[2] in reviewing and creating policy, and a host of funding agencies in both North and South wish to be satisfied that new projects will not perpetuate the impacts of unsustainable development in the past.

Many factors have contributed to this surge of interest. Brundtland's concept of sustainable development — with its concern for both social justice and ecological health — offers hope and encouragement both to those who are appalled by the amount of extreme poverty in the world today and to those who do not accept that economic "success" can be satisfactorily gauged by a quantitative economic indicator such as gross national product (GNP). Therefore sustainable development appeals to values that have been traditionally regarded as fundamental, as Roger Levett has suggested (LGMB, 1993a, p16): "There is no mystique or obscurity about the central meanings of sustainable development.

---

2. A review of the literature shows that "sustainable development" and "sustainability" are used with a range of meanings. "Sustainable development" usually refers to the process "developing" in a sustainable way, to be defined as the book proceeds, and also to the "goal" of that process; "sustainability" refers to the concept of sustainable development, and also — confusingly — both to a state of sustainable resource use, not necessarily the same as sustainable development, as in "ecological sustainability" and to a state in which the goals of sustainable development have been achieved.

They are rooted in perennial themes of responsibility to others, providing for the future and dependence of life on the natural environment . . . since time immemorial." In contrast, the phrase also appeals to many others, members of societies that have been content for several decades, if not centuries, to live by a generally unexamined belief in progress. For those for whom the want of unmistakable signs of imminent disaster appears to vindicate the rapid and irreversible degradation of resources, sustainable development appears to encourage a belief in the possibility of perpetuating the conventional model of development. If such "development" can be maintained "sustainably", without thought of tomorrow, without having to heed the doom-laden predictions of environmentalists, or without having to worry about the long-term availability of resources, so much the better.

Thus the idea of sustainable development has attracted groups with very different interests. It has been able to do this largely through the vagueness and even ambiguity of the term itself. Much of this imprecision stems from the fact that the term "development" is used over a wide range of contexts ranging from the world of commerce and industry to the realms of social and human welfare. We talk and hear talk of "economic development", "development opportunities", "development funding", "development aid" and "development assistance", "overseas development", "regional development", "social development", "community development" and even "human development". "Sustainable" is by comparison a newcomer, and has not yet acquired its own range of overlapping and sometimes conflicting associations. However, it is clearly a good thing. Who would ever argue for the "unsustainable" version of their particular development interest?

This vagueness and ambiguity are also present in Brundtland's definition of sustainable development. For Brundtland sustainable development is development that "meets the needs of the present without compromising the ability of future generations to meet their own needs" (WCED, 1987, p8). These now famous words have a "beguiling simplicity" (O'Riordan, 1988), offering no hint of what sustainable development involves in practice, what commitments it requires and what the costs will be. Some see an advantage in this imprecision. Herman Daly, the American economist who has argued for a "steady state economy" for over 20 years, has suggested that "it has allowed a considerable consensus to evolve in support of the main idea that it is both morally and economically wrong to treat the world as if it were a business in liquidation" (Daly, 1992a, p248).

Others agree that despite its vagueness — indeed, perhaps because of it — the Brundtland definition makes an important statement. Bert de Vries, a Dutch scientist, has pointed out that it has more of the character of a moral principle than a precise definition: "Sustainability is not something to be defined, but to be declared. It is an ethical guiding principle" (quoted in Peet, 1992, p209). In this sense sustainable development is rather like democracy or justice. People are generally in favour of it, while retaining their individual definitions of what it actually means, and conceding that they might be hard pressed to agree with others on how we might actually achieve it. No one openly advocates unjust practices — any more than people come out in favour of unsustainability. Nevertheless, some act unjustly, many are caught up in social and economic systems that are unjust, and the majority, as the combined effects of their consumption patterns, social priorities and voting preferences reveal, tolerate injustice in society at large if they themselves are not too directly or too drastically affected by it.

In addition to its vagueness, the language of Brundtland's definition has a rhetorical quality, particularly in the second part of the definition, which gives it a powerful emotive appeal. In reminding us of the need to respect the limits of the planet's resources, the words — "without compromising the ability of future generations to meet their own needs" — avoid the negative prognostications of doomsday scenarios and the bluntness of dire warnings that we are fast approaching "limits to growth". Instead, they seem to strike two chords. First, they touch on our sense of guilt about what we have done to the planet, and second, and particularly relevant here, on a very deeply-rooted human desire to make sure our children's futures are provided for.

However, it is difficult to be sure that an emotive appeal, even to deep-seated feelings about the welfare of our own descendants, is an adequate basis for meaningful commitments to the welfare of an unspecified number of generations of humanity *en masse*.

Why, it may be argued, should we be more affected by the plight of future generations than by the predicament of those generations alive today? Why should we be so moved by the argument for *inter*-generational equity when we do so little about *intra*-generational equity, able as members of the international community to condone the persistence of human deprivation on massive scales while also allowing the numbers of the homeless, the malnourished and the unemployed to increase in our own midst?

The appeal of the desirability of passing on advantages to children and grandchildren works against the insistence on need (also vague to the point of ambiguity) in the first part of the definition (sustainable development "meets the needs of the present ..."). Thus the emotive quality of the language helps to conceal the demand for equity which, we shall see, is implicit in meeting needs. On this level Brundtland's words make a strong though implicit appeal to those inclined to favour the status quo.

Several commentators fear that the ambiguities and resonances of the Brundtland definition allow the notion of sustainable development to be hijacked by those wishing to cloak unsustainable activity in its respectable garb. For example, Daly (1992a, p249) fears that "the term is now in danger of becoming an empty shibboleth". Tim O'Riordan, professor of environmental sciences at the University of East Anglia, has argued that its imprecision may lead to abuse. Both environmentalist and "developer" may evoke it in support of their own ends, which may be diametrically opposed. Thus a term coined to create a bridge between environmentalists and developers is in danger of being discredited.

Despite these misgivings Henryk Skolimowski (1995, pp69–70) of the Politechnika Lódzka in Poland insists on the force of the idea:

> *Yet something was new: the very idea of Sustainable Development. It struck a middle ground between more radical approaches which denounced all development, and the idea of development conceived as business as usual. The idea of Sustainable Development, although broad, loose, and tinged with ambiguity around its edges, turned out to be palatable to everybody. This may have been its greatest virtue. It is radical and not yet offensive.*

Palatable it may be, but can the idea do more than create a benign consensus? Can the "idea of Sustainable Development" be translated into principles on which practicable and effective policies can be based and which will reverse current unsustainable trends of ecological degradation and human oppression? To class it as significantly more than an inoffensive idea, we have to have answers to a number of questions:

- Is it meaningful to talk of sustainable development when we may not be able to tell with certainty what the needs of future generations may be, which particular ecological, social and economic conditions represent the "sustainable state", and how close to such conditions we may be?
- Is it possible to devise a set of operational guidelines which would, if implemented, satisfy the twin criteria of "meeting the needs of the present" and "not compromising the ability of future generations to meet theirs"?
- Is any national or international programme for sustainable development likely to win political approval? Or is sustainable development merely an idea, which provides a basis for many theoretical studies but which cannot survive in the world of economic "realities", short-term political priorities, North–South suspicions, growing inequities, political oppression, and the prevalence of corruption, which in more or less blatant forms afflicts both North and South?
- Is the concept of sustainable development so open to mis-interpretation that established interests can ignore its radical implications and be content with minor adjustments to their practices to allow them to claim they are following a sustainable path?
- Is it possible that the more radical implications of any set of operational guidelines can survive their mediation through the institutional machinery of mainstream development, staffed by an international desk-bound elite who have allowed bureaucracies to proliferate, but who have failed to arrest either the continuing degradation of the ecological systems of the planet or the deterioration in the welfare of many people throughout the world?

The seriousness of these questions should not be under-estimated. As later chapters make clear, earlier models of development have largely failed "to meet the needs of the present" in both North and South over the past 50 years. Is it then realistic to suppose that sustainable development can not only achieve the goals its predecessors failed to meet but also solve the additional problems created by the population growth and ecological damage which have occurred over the last half-century? Is then the call to consider the needs of future gener-ations a realistic aspiration, or merely an example of the pious but vacuous rhetoric to which, some critics would allege, UN agencies are prone? Is it an expression of an ever more ambitious but imprecise idealism unchecked by a sense of reality, goaded on rather than deterred by past failures?

Or does sustainable development incorporate some new features, the absence of which explain the failures of the past? Does it point to a sufficiently coherent, compelling and practic-able way forward to guarantee not just lip-service but action, commitment of funds, negotiation of binding agreements and enactment of the legislation that will be necessary? Can sustainable development avoid the pitfalls of development in the past and meet the needs of the present without leaving future generations with less than their fair share of the resources they will require to achieve similar ends? This is the crux of the matter: from now on, development, if it is to be sustainable, is faced with a rather tall order — to work within constraints *it has so far failed to observe*, to achieve goals *it has so far failed to meet*.

To answer these questions we need to examine sustainable development in the context of the linked histories of develop-ment and the environment in the second half of the twentieth century.

Part I of this book describes the global crisis and responses to it over the last four decades.

Chapter 1 provides a brief review of the global crisis — the interconnected problems of development and environment, which have become particularly acute over the past 20 or 30 years. Chapters 2 and 3 review the environmental and the developmental response to the deepening crisis and to a growing awareness that the path of development has produced problems which, it is hard to believe, have been outweighed by the actual benefits.

Part II re-examines the implications of Brundtland's definition of sustainable development. Chapter 4 considers the implications of meeting human needs. Chapter 5 formulates principles for the sustainable use of resources without which sustainable development cannot be achieved, and Chapter 6 explores the contribution improved efficiency and effective use of economic instruments can make to extending current limitations on practical options for sustainable development.

Part III discusses the obstacles to the rapid implementation of sustainable development (Chapter 7) and the ways in which these may be overcome (Chapter 8).

Part IV looks at recent progress on sustainable development. Chapter 9 is an account of UNCED — the Earth Summit in Rio. Chapter 10 is a survey of progress towards sustainable development in the years since 1992. Chapter 11 considers how much remains to be done.

# Part I

## The Global Crisis and Responses to it

# Chapter 1 | THE GLOBAL CRISIS

In recent years we have become used to talking about global problems, although environmental concern — or more properly concern about problems caused by development — first arose on a local scale in the expanding industrial economies of the North, where such problems as Love Canal and, later, Seveso were seen as local, despite their seriousness.

It was not long, however, before environmental problems were acknowledged to have an international dimension and significance. Before the end of the 1960s it was clear that radioactive fallout from nuclear tests was not the only pollutant to ignore national boundaries, as the effects of acidification on Swedish lakes and forests and the presence of DDT in fish in both the Arctic and Antarctic proved. Anxiety about the extent and insidiousness of the impact of economic activity was heightened by the first space shots which portrayed the Earth — its soft greens and blues set in whorls of white cloud against the black void of space — as a single, precious and rather vulnerable entity.

Two decades later, James Lovelock's Gaia hypothesis, with its view of the planet as a single system regulated by homeostasis, raised fresh questions about whether planetary equilibrium and the opportunity it affords humankind might be at risk. Could the stability achieved over aeons of geological time be destroyed within a few generations, with no guarantee that any new balance would offer our descendants an ecological niche?

In the mid-1990s, some 30 years after evidence of trans-border pollution began to accumulate, it does indeed seem appropriate to talk in terms of a global crisis. A considerable amount of evidence is now available to prove that if unsustainable development continues, it will be at the cost of even greater human suffering worldwide, and will create even more serious and pervasive ecological damage to the biosphere.

Such evidence is documented in great detail in a range of publications.[1] From the mass of statistics three issues stand out:

### (1) The Increase in Human-Related Activities and their Impacts, and an Accompanying Decrease in the Resources of the Planet

Since 1900 the world's population has tripled and global industrial production has increased 50 times. Some 80 per cent of the increase in industrial production has occurred since 1950 (MacNeill, 1989). In 1991 the annual 'product' of the global economy was valued at $29,000 million — which meant it produced in a mere 17 days the equivalent of the entire annual global product in 1900 (Brown et al, 1991, p95). Throughout much of the century there have been accelerating increases in the consumption of both renewable and nonrenewable resources. Agricultural production has risen dramatically (but so have desertification, soil erosion and the salinization of productive lands). It has been estimated that humanity now consumes about 40 per cent of total terrestrial photosynthetic production (Vitousek et al, 1986). Energy generation, industrial processes, transport, high-input agriculture and domestic consumption continue to make bigger and bigger demands of the capacities of the earth and the atmosphere to absorb $CO_2$, sulphur, NOX and methane emissions, CFCs, and a range of toxic chemicals — for example, PCBs, dioxins and other carcinogens, including radioactive wastes — which threaten widespread endemic pollution. The impacts of such emissions now extend globally, not only through their dispersal in the oceans and the atmosphere but also as a result of the export of hazardous wastes to the South.

Over recent decades these increases have been accompanied by accelerating rates of deforestation, decline in fish stocks, loss of

---

1. See UN agency reports (for example from UNEP, UNDP and FAO), World Bank Reports, and also the World Watch Papers and State of the World Reports published by the WWI and the publications of the WRI.

agricultural land, loss of soils, depletion of fresh water, loss of habitats, loss of species and loss of biodiversity — one scientist estimates the rate of extinctions at 100 species a day.[2] These losses in natural resources are paralleled by a loss of human diversity on many scales and in many areas (for example cultural diversity). While many of the impacts of these changes appear to be most graphically illustrated in the poorer countries,[3] they are by no means confined to tropical regions. These unsustainable trends can be represented by the annotated sketch graphs in Figure 1.1.

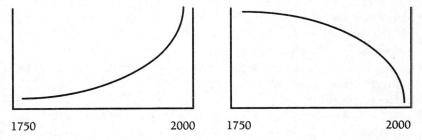

| 1750 | 2000 | 1750 | 2000 |

*Increases in:* human population, consumption of fossil fuels, consumption of other resources, industrial production, agriculture, desertification, salinization, pollution, military expenditure (until 1987).

*Decreases in:* forests, fish stocks, farmland, soils, habitats, species, biodiversity, environmental services, human diversity.

*Source*: Loening, 1992.

*Figure 1.1 Rates of change on the planet*

These accelerating trends have been punctuated by dramatic single events, such as Bhopal, Chernobyl, the *Exxon Valdez* disaster, the setting alight of the Kuwait oil wells during the Gulf War and, recently, the Siberian oil pipeline disaster. (The impact

2. See Lovejoy (1980) and Ryan (1992). UNEP estimates there may be as many as 30 million species in the biosphere, of which only 1.5 million have ever been described, and that up to 25 per cent of the total may face extinction.
3. The impression that resource depletion and degradation are most conspicuous in the South may be partly due to our habit in the North of regarding deforested and over-exploited landscapes as 'natural'.

of these "macro" events is, however, probably exceeded by the continuous succession of "micro" impacts of "routine" emissions and waste discharges.) No less dramatic have been the "natural" disasters (floods, drought, disturbance of weather patterns and famine) which seem to follow each other with increasing frequency. During the 1970s the death toll from such events increased sixfold over the preceding decade (WCED, 1987, p4).

Even more serious is the evidence that the combined effects of resource depletion on a massive scale and the global diffusion of waste emissions (particularly greenhouse gases and CFCs) represent another order of ecological damage. Their joint impact threatens the stability of the complex biogeochemical systems, which maintain the conditions on which life on the planet depends — conditions such as the composition of the atmosphere, planetary temperature regulation, climatic and weather patterns, the salinity of the oceans, the hydrological cycle and the other chemical cycles.

The accumulated evidence makes it increasingly plain that environmental problems have been problems of development all along. The sheer weight of the evidence of ecological damage leads more and more people to doubt seriously whether the end justifies the means. Why, as one commentator (Rolston, 1990) remarks, should we destroy a relict wilderness in order to obtain molybdenum to make electric carving knives? However, ecological damage is not the only impact of unsustainable development.

*(2) Growing Inequity Between Rich and Poor — Between Rich and Poor Nations and Between Rich and Poor within some Countries*

The global situation is represented by the graph in Figure 1.2 which shows the distribution of world income at the beginning of the 1990s. The disparities in income are matched by many other inequities, including the inequitable consumption of resources, as shown in Table 1.1 (see also the UNDP's annual reports). These inequities mean that, for the poorest, life is a daily confrontation with a reality which is hardly imaginable to most Northerners but which nevertheless exists on a massive scale. It is estimated that over a billion people (approximately 20 per cent of the world's population) exist in conditions of extreme poverty, lacking

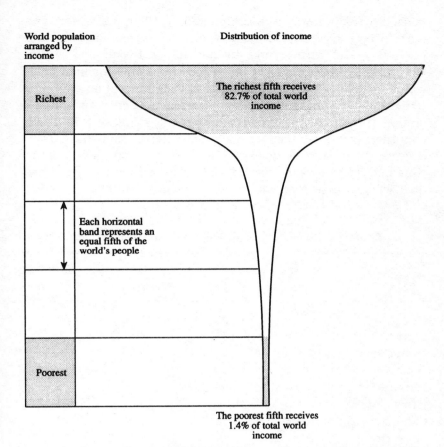

World population
arranged by
income

Distribution of income

Richest

The richest fifth receives
82.7% of total world
income

Each horizontal
band represents an
equal fifth of the
world's people

Poorest

The poorest fifth receives
1.4% of total world
income

*Note*: The diagram shows the global distribution of income. The richest 20 per cent of the world's population receives 82.7 per cent of the total world income while the poorest 20 per cent receives only 1.4 per cent. Global economic growth rarely filters down.

*Source*: UNDP (1992).

*Figure 1.2 The distribution of world income*

adequate nutrition, access to safe drinking water, sanitation, health care and housing. Children are at particular risk from these deprivations. A child born in the South is on average about 15 to 20 times less likely to survive beyond the age of five than a child in the North. About four million of the children who die before the age of five in the South each year die of diseases caused by lack of safe water and sanitation (Elliot, 1994, p22). More and more people try to grow staple foods on unsuitable soils, and have to travel further and further for fuelwood and water. Declining yields, exhausted soils and the increasing marginalization of the landless poor mean increasing rates of migration to settlements around cities. Even in the remotest areas indigenous groups find their livelihoods threatened. Moreover, in some countries, repressive regimes deny their citizens human rights or deprive them of civil liberties. This is not, however, a static situation. The plight of the poorest, relative to the richest, has been worsening over recent decades. The gap continues to widen as Table 1.2 indicates.

*Table 1.1 Consumption of selected items, North/South*

|  | share (per cent) | | ADR | EDR |
|---|---|---|---|---|
|  | North | South | North/South | North/South |
| Meat | 64 | 36 | 6 | 52 |
| Cereals | 48 | 52 | 3 | 6 |
| Round wood | 46 | 54 | 1 | 6 |
| Paper, etc | 81 | 19 | 14 | 115 |
| Fertilizer | 60 | 40 | 5 | 6 |
| Iron and steel | 80 | 20 | 13 | 22 |
| Cars | 92 | 8 | 24 | 320 |
| Electricity | 81 | 19 | 13 | 46 |
| $CO_2$ | 70 | 30 | 8 | 27 |

*Notes:* The average disparity ratio (ADR) is the ratio of per capita consumption levels in North and South. For example, on average a person in the North eats six times as much meat as a person in the South. The extreme disparity ratio (EDR) is the ratio between the richest and poorest countries, using the USA and India. Thus on average an American eats 52 times as much meat as an Indian. The eastern European countries are included in the North, and the newly industrialized countries of Asia are included in the South. The ADR is therefore smaller than the real disparities between many European countries and the low income countries of Asia and Africa.

*Source:* Parikh et al (1991), quoted in Rowley and Holmberg (1992, p335)

The poorest sections of the populations of Northern countries are spared the most acute forms of hardship suffered by their counterparts in the South, but in the North too there has been an increase in social inequities as the human and social costs of unsustainable trends continue to grow. In both Britain and the USA the number of people living in poverty has increased in the last two decades, and there have been corresponding increases in homelessness, poor nutrition, poor health, child neglect, crime, drugs and racial violence (see, for example, Rowntree Foundation, 1995; Commission for Social Justice, 1994).

Development in the North has not been able to guarantee employment either. In December 1994 there was a total of just over 18.4 million registered unemployed in the European Union. Indeed unemployment appears to have become a structural feature in Northern economies as political leaders attempt to compete in international markets with the low-wage economies of poorer countries. Advances in technology allow companies to make workers redundant even as they announce record profits. The power of the transnational corporations (TNCs) and the lack of restrictions on the movement of capital from one country to another mean that wages are driven down and that legislation intended to promote safety at work and guarantee basic levels of welfare is threatened.

*Table 1.2 Ratio of income of richest 20 per cent to poorest 20 per cent of world population*

| | |
|---|---|
| 1960 | 30:1 |
| 1970 | 32:1 |
| 1980 | 45:1 |
| 1989 | 59:1 |
| 1991 | 61:1 |

*Sources*: UNDP (1991) and UNDP (1994)

### (3) Population Growth

The world population of almost six billion is now rising by over 90 million a year. It has more than doubled since 1950 and may double again. It is estimated that, because of the phenomenon known as "demographic momentum" (for a brief explanation see Ehrlich and Ehrlich, 1990, pp59–61), world population will not stabilize till the year 2040 at a figure of somewhere between eight billion (the UN's low projection) and 14 billion (the UN's high projection) (WCED, 1987, p4). Despite significant falls in the rate of increase in some countries (for example, Colombia), "ahead lie four decades of the fastest growth in human numbers in all history" (Harrison, 1992, p270).

It is almost impossible to contemplate such figures without relating them to the question of food supplies. While it is accepted that at present the world produces enough food to feed the present population (despite an estimated one billion suffering from chronic malnutrition), there will have to be at least a doubling of the food production in 1993 if the population of 2040 is to be adequately fed. Yet per capita food production has declined in many countries since 1980; world per capita grain production continued to increase till 1990, since when it has dropped (Brown, Flavin and Kane, 1994); and it seems doubtful if increased applications of nitrogenous fertilizers will increase yields by the amount required (although other developments, for example in biotechnology and genetic engineering, may have this potential).[4] Such considerations have led Paul and Ann Ehrlich, co-authors of *The Population Explosion*, to assert that "Arresting global population growth should be second only in importance to avoiding nuclear war on humanity's agenda" (Ehrlich and Ehrlich, 1990, p18).

The combined effects of development, inequity and population growth now extend across the entire surface of the earth, affecting virtually every human community and extending to a vast range of human activity as the box opposite indicates.

Also pervasive, but less easy to quantify, is a widespread feeling of powerlessness in the face of prevailing social and economic forces. Neither the efforts of the individual nor the community's power to act in its own interest seem able to reverse trends. Recent years have seen a healthy scepticism about politics change into a corrosive cynicism about the motives of politicians, the

---

4. Even if increased applications of nitrogen do increase yields significantly, they would also almost certainly mean more serious problems of runoff, unless application technologies become very much more efficient.

THE EXTENT OF THE GLOBAL CRISIS: RANGE OF ISSUES IN
SUSTAINABLE DEVELOPMENT

(a) Global pollution of atmosphere and oceans; national
consumption patterns of fossil fuels contributing to climate change
and sea-level rise; fresh water pollution; soil degradation and
erosion, chemical pollution from excessive use of fertilizers and
pesticides, and soil salinization from improper irrigation.

(b) Concern about intergenerational flows of natural and man-
made capital in a "full world" where natural capital is the limiting
factor of production; loss of biodiversity and degradation of agro-
ecosystems arising from deforestation, fuelwood collection, erosion
and urbanization; loss of genetic diversity in modern farming
systems; the trend towards commoditizing exploitable natural
resources, genetic material and genetically-altered organisms.

(c) Growing inequality between the world's rich and poor, and the
need to address poverty and basic needs on a global scale; the need
to secure food security in the face of rising population; the breakdown of traditional, ecologically-sound systems of resource management under commercial and population pressure; displacement by
economic processes of the resource-poor to marginal lands or to
rapidly growing cities, resulting in under-employment.

(d) Concern about powerful trends which could contribute to
unsustainable development: industrialization and integration of
finance, and marketing and advertising in the global marketplace;
the growing aspirations for Western-style consumption patterns
fuelled by satellite television; the explosion of capitalist energy in
Asia and South America; the massive suburbanization in land use
patterns, and the expected doubling, by the year 2025, of motor-
vehicle numbers from the current 500 million.

(e) Issues of governance and mediation in development and the
need for long-term, holistic planning; the need for economic growth
on a global scale; reconciling market mechanisms and short-term
political objectives with longer-term development needs; concern for
international equity among nations to recompense for past
unstainable resource extraction and pollution; the need to develop
national policies, human resources, management systems and
mechanisms for participation, which define sustainable processes of
development.

(*Source*: Carley, 1994)

potential of the political process, and the effectiveness of political mechanisms and institutions. The more affluent detect a decline in the quality of life even as conventional indicators of material prosperity continue to rise. According to Manfred Max-Neef (1991, p3), director of the Development Alternative Centre in Chile, "we are losing, if we have not already lost, our capacity to dream", "drowsy managers of a crisis which we feel is impossible to solve by our own means".

## THE *PROBLÉMATIQUE*

Many of the problems that constitute the global crisis are connected with each other, as the Brundtland Report (WCED, 1987, p4) acknowledges: "the various global crises ... are not separate crises: an environmental crisis, a development crisis, an energy crisis. They are all one." Recognizing these connections, the Club of Rome, a group of industrialists, coined the term "global *problématique*" to refer to the complex of global problems and the dynamic interactions which exist between them: not only are problems linked in complex ways, but they change even as their contexts are changing.

These connections may not always be very obvious or easy to trace: for instance, the building of the Aswam High Dam in Egypt has reduced the nutrients reaching the Mediterranean via the Nile delta and adversely affected fish stocks; the mysterious decline of the albatross population on Possession Island is directly linked to the fishing techniques of Japanese vessels operating hundreds of miles to the north; and the stimulation of the winter demand for cut flowers in Northern cities may have contributed to the numbers of landless poor in Kenya.

Problems that appear radically different may in fact be directly linked. For example, in Thailand the problem of "overdevelopment" in Bangkok, and the problem of "underdevelopment" in the hilly country in the northeast appear very different, but each is really the obverse of the other.[5] Many "modern" cities in the South are surrounded by shantytowns and squatter townships where the impoverished majority live, dispossessed of their land

---

5. I am indebted to John Kirkby of the University of Northumbria for this example and for several other suggestions on scale and meta-problems.

and the livelihood it guaranteed — again two facets of the same development process. (The contrast is less extreme in Northern cities.) Such linkages exist on various scales — within regions, within cities, and even within towns and villages.

The linkages and the knock-on effects may be harder to trace on larger scales. A newly-equipped industrial fishing fleet may have a wide range of impacts, including the impoverishment of "subsistence" fishermen and the malnutrition of their families in areas far from its home port. The fleet itself may partly be a response to a rising demand for protein in countries with rapidly growing economies, where there has been an influx of capital that has been withdrawn from high-wage production on the other side of the world. Thus the role of the fishing fleet and its impact must be seen in the context of the destabilization of two economies — the weakened industrial one and a local economy on which many livelihoods have depended.

Or take the example of a river catchment in a forested area. Clear felling may lead to soil erosion, which in turn has several impacts. The forest ecosystem may be unable to re-establish itself on the denuded slopes. Silt may muddy the streams, spoiling the fish stocks on which local people may depend. Increased rates of rainwater run-off may lead to serious floods, which in turn cause erosion on a new and more serious scale. Areas of cropland are damaged and their fertility impaired. New flood defences are needed. It is suggested that their maintenance will need funds that can only be raised from cash-crop revenues. Attempts to convert local agriculture to cash-crop production may lead to a new range of problems. Loans may be available for inputs, but debts begin to accumulate. Richer and more successful farmers survive; others are forced to sell, become labourers, or move on. Social tensions mount. There may be a polarization between rich and poor, and a loss of social diversity and harmony. The rich are drawn into patterns of economic activity controlled by forces that operate from far beyond the region. Some may find these come to dominate them and many will feel that their lives are shaped more by alien economic pressures than by local factors. Over the years the local economy is transformed. Profits no longer circulate locally; there is a loss of local autonomy and of distinctive social and cultural traditions. Such a simple outline can trace only the major relationships, but the connections are numerous and complex, and operate on many different scales.

Linkages may extend worldwide over time. The following outline pinpoints a few facts in a highly complex picture. European imports of soya bean animal feeds rose from 49,000 tons in 1949 to 5 million tons in 1972 (plus another 13 million tons of unprocessed beans). Interestingly, this rise was triggered by the European farmers' need for supplementary foodstuffs after they adopted American varieties of corn (maize), which gave higher yields but less protein. In response to predictions of a rising demand for soya bean animal feeds in the South, the Brazilian government encouraged the production of soya, which became Brazil's biggest export by the end of the 1970s. However, soya production needed fewer labourers and meant smaller crops of staples such as corn, black beans and rice. The shortage of corn also sharply affected prices of beef and chicken. By the early 1980s the proportion of the Brazilian population suffering hunger had doubled from one-third to two-thirds, and the numbers of landless peasants increased to over ten million. Finding their claims for land often brutally opposed by landowners, many of the poor followed the government's encouragement to find new land in the Amazon, thereby adding to the destruction of the rainforest by the large ranchers granted concessions by the Brazilian government (see George, 1976, pp92–3, 148–9; Lappé and Collins, 1988, pp32–3, 77).

*Scale*

Connections can also be obscured by differences in scale. Thus activities may appear innocuous until their accumulated impacts manifest themselves on a much larger, even global scale. As Lester Brown of the World Watch Institute (WWI) points out (Brown et al, 1991, p93), we are living "in an age when tropical [or boreal] deforestation in one country reduces the entire earth's biological wealth, when chemicals produced in one country can cause skin cancer in another, and when $CO_2$ emissions anywhere hasten climate change everywhere".

Differences in scale also account for the fact that problems that appear quite different may have the same underlying causes. For example, the difference in GNP between North and South, the gulf between the members of the Indian middle classes and the 350 million Indian peasants, and the domination of a poor village in a poor district by a few individuals (say a landowner, money-lender, or a few rich peasants) are all manifestations of unequal access to resources and opportunities. This problem also manifests itself at the scale of the individual household or family, where in many societies gender determines access to income or material possessions.

We should also be aware of scale when making general comments. It is a convenient shorthand to be able to talk of the "rich North" and the "poor South". However, this becomes misleading if it distorts our view of reality. In fact, there are, as we have seen, large and growing differences (on more than one scale) between rich and poor in the North, and similarly widening differentials in the South. The distinction is useful for discussing problems in general terms, but there is reason to suppose that the frequency with which it is used reflects, confirms or helps to create a reluctance to address the size of the problem of inequity in both North and South. This has important implications for sustainable development: as we shall see later, the perpetuation, not to mention the increase, of inequities in the North is a serious impediment to the reduction of inequities between North and South.

## Meta-Problems

Some commentators use the term meta-problem to refer to a cluster of very closely interconnected problems. For example, in some tropical countries soil erosion, decline in soil fertility and productivity, lack of labour, the consequent failure to maintain, say, soil terraces or irrigation channels, poor management of water resources and encroaching desertification are all really part of one larger problem of inappropriate — or unsustainable — rural development. Each aspect of the problem is so closely related to the others that any attempt to solve it is unlikely to be successful unless the others are treated simultaneously.

The term meta-problem is also a useful way of referring to very large underlying problems. These usually represent powerful forces, which generate a number of problems on different scales and in different guises. It is possible to identify a number of meta-problems, for example, rates of population growth in the South, overpopulation in the North, poverty, unequal access to resources, systems of land tenure and ownership, lack of democratic rights and the Western model of development.

## Perspective

It is also important to be aware of the perspective from which we view the global crisis. Within the context of North–South relations both North and South tend to focus more attention on distant problems than on local ones. The problem is well illustrated by the words of Gerald Ford, president of the USA (1974–76), then as now the nation with the highest per capita consumption of oil: "No one can foresee the extent of the damage nor the end of the disastrous consequences if nations refuse to share nature's gifts for the benefit of all mankind" (quoted in Higgins, 1980, p173). Sadly, he was referring, not to America's reluctance to be content with its fair share but to the "selfishness" of the oil-exporting countries.

Until very recently, at least until evidence of the global impacts of some waste emissions became available, the North has tended to see the global crisis in terms of environmental destruction in the South (the loss of rainforests, desertification, decimation of wildlife, loss of habitats) and of population pressures rather than in terms of the activities of the "developed" world. The South on the other hand tends to emphasize, with some justification, the high levels of resource consumption in the North and the unfairness of the international economic order, and claims that the North's interest in the South stems at least as much from self-interest as from altruistic concern. Leaders in the South have rather less to say about lack of democracy and failure to deal with problems of land-ownership and access to resources.

The images of the South with which people in the North are most familiar are those that periodically dominate our television screens — images of the victims of famine, floods or other natural disasters, of refugees, of shantytowns, of threatened forest tribes, of encroaching desert, denuded hillsides, devastated forests. They reinforce prejudices and stereotypes that portray the South as less "developed". The view that the South has not travelled as far along the path of "progress" as the North appears to be confirmed by virtually all the commonly available indicators — capital accumulation, material standards of living, the extent of the transition from rural, predominantly subsistence, cultures to industrialized societies, vulnerability to natural disaster and development of the political institutions that have suited the countries of the North. Such evidence confirms Northern "success" and the importance of science, technology and economic power, ignoring the destructiveness of their impacts both on natural environments and human welfare in the South.

Thus there is a largely unexamined assumption that the problems of the South are different in kind from the problems of the North. However, closer examination makes it hard to maintain the widespread perception in the North that it has successfully avoided the problems of the South. The North's advantages — temperate climates, good soils, adequate rainfall and, for the most part, freedom from debilitating diseases — have tended to obscure the fact that North and South share many similar problems and that many of these have similar origins. Any suggestion that the North is free of those types of environmental degradation *about which the North is most concerned in the South* is erroneous. For example, for a number of reasons the North is concerned about the felling of large areas of tropical forests. Yet in both Britain and the USA there remain only tiny fractions of virgin forest. Despite protests, clear-felling of virgin forest continues in western Canada, and vast areas of virgin forests in Siberia are also threatened. Similarly, the processes connected with desertification, loss of agricultural land, loss of soil fertility and decline of fisheries are at work in the North as well as in the South. In both the North and the South small farmers are being forced to abandon their land as both the Green Revolution and the European Union's Common Agricultural Policy (CAP) have produced widening differentials between rich and poor farmers.

There is, however, an even more important point at issue than the element of complacent superiority in Northern attitudes to the South — the North owes much of its present level of development, its current wealth, to the South. There are at least three reasons for this. First, much of the North's current wealth — its accumulated capital — is due to the appropriation of resources during colonial times. Between the seventeenth century and the present the North commandeered resources that might otherwise have funded social development in many parts of the South. Such resources helped England to alleviate the problems associated with its landless poor, problems which emerged after the enclosure of common lands in the sixteenth century. Second, in a less crowded world, Britain and other European nations were able to alleviate the problem of surplus population by the simple expedient of exporting people. Third, and most important in the current crisis, material resources such as metals and timber, which the North acquired from the South in a system of one-way trade, helped to build the economies that continue to deplete and degrade global resources, many of which are still to be found in the South. What appear to many in the North as unexceptionable *norms* — standards of living, levels of consumption, techniques of production, patterns of trade, expectations of further rises in material standards of living — are in fact problems because they make life, and attempts to improve it, more difficult for people in the South. Thus not only has the North derived much of its wealth from the South, but it has done so at the expense of the South.

The trade, aid and debt policies of the international economic system have enlarged long-established inequities between North and South. Under the ideology of free trade, international trading has developed from a network of many relatively independent national economies, which traded to their mutual advantage, into a competitive system dominated by a few economically powerful nations and TNCs, 600 of which control 75 per cent of world trade. The free movement of capital means nearly all industrial nations, including the richest, have to compete for their market share. F E Trainer, an Australian sociologist writing in 1987, describes the predicament of a country no longer able to trade "freely" despite the ideology of free trade:

> Over the last ten years we have allowed market forces to cut our manufacturing capacity in half to shift it to Southeast Asia, where wage rates are one tenth. Previously we allowed market forces to build us into depending on mineral and agricultural exports, and now their prices have dropped. We have a massive trade deficit and national debt largely because we have to import lots of things we could be producing for ourselves and once did. Not so long ago

*nations only traded surpluses; now we have all been drawn into trading necessities, which means that when the global economy doesn't want your bananas or wheat you've had it. Now we search frantically for sunrise industries to earn export income to go on buying all the things we could be making for ourselves, had we developed the right industries. In this global economy you are only safe so long as you keep running the fastest. Unless you are constantly finding new markets, more efficient ways, new things to flog, you will be beaten and trampled.*

(Quoted in Smith, 1991, p159, emphasis in original)

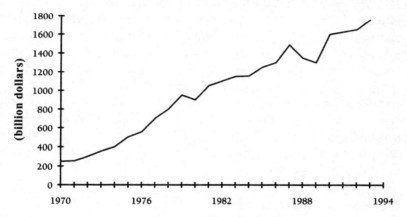

*Source*: French (1995, p178) from World Bank figures.

**Figure 1.3** *External debt of developing countries*

Over $60 billion of international aid a year is given to countries in the South to help them develop their economies, but only a small proportion of this actually benefits those most in need.[6] Although some official aid does benefit local communities in the South, a substantial proportion is spent on boosting the domestic economy of the donor country, furthering its foreign policy interests, or paying the salaries of development professionals who

---

6. The figure of $60 billion includes all official bilateral aid (aid donated by one government to another) and all multilateral aid (aid donated by an international organization, usually a UN agency or the World Bank), but excludes NGO aid.

enjoy a standard of living in marked contrast to that of those with whom they are professionally concerned. In addition, hundreds of billions of dollars have been misspent on unproductive projects; on importing luxuries and prestige projects; on arms (arms spending has risen faster than GNP in many countries in the South); and on "capital flight" — a euphemism for the embezzlement of aid funds which end up in private bank accounts in countries far from those supposed to benefit from the aid (see Hancock, 1989 and Ekins, 1992a, pp24–6).

The story of aid is not just one of national self-interest, inefficiency, waste and corruption. Much international aid is given in the form of loans on which interest has to be paid. New levels of lending in the 1970s and rises in interest rates on world markets in the 1980s meant huge increases in debt service payments. As a result, the total external debt of the South has grown seven times in the last 20 years. In 1993 it stood at over US $1.7 trillion (see Figure 1.3). The total of the debt-service payments made by the South — US $160 billion — is two and a half times the flow of capital from North to South in the form of official development assistance.

However, the full extent of the crisis becomes apparent only when the increases in debt repayments are set against the falls in prices of exports from the South (see Figure 1.4). These came about through the operation of the law of supply and demand as Southern countries put increased emphasis on the production of raw materials in an attempt to earn the revenues to meet larger debt repayments — which meant not only larger exports but faster depletion of resources and greater destitution for the people who should have benefited from them, as Susan George (1988) has documented in *A Fate Worse than Debt*.

The systems of trade, aid and debt are part of an economic order many see as profoundly unfair. Paul Ekins of the University of London (1992a, pp28–9) describes the effects of current arrangements:

> *At present powerful Northern (creditor) institutions are reaping handsome returns on loans that never get any smaller; Northern industry and consumers are getting Southern commodities at rock bottom prices; Northern arms manufacturers are selling nervous*

*Third World elites large quantities of weapons; and, perhaps most important, Third World countries are being effectively tied in to Western models of development, with Western countries guaranteed a permanent technological lead. The old economic order is doing industrial countries very nicely economically and politically. Third World resources are as cheaply available as in colonial days without the costs of foreign administrations. A prosperous Third World would assuredly revive the talk of the 1970s of "self-reliance" and "culturally appropriate development" which would not be at all in perceived Northern self-interests.*

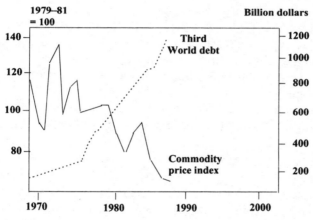

*Source*: Brown et al (1990, p144).

*Figure 1.4 Commodity prices and Third World debt, 1970–89*

Equity demands that we assist the South, on a far grander scale and in a far more effective manner than development agencies have managed so far, to tackle simultaneously the linked problems of meeting human needs and arresting environmental degradation. The unsustainable impacts of current development trends mean that it is no longer possible to hold the view that the South's salvation lies in following the developmental path of the North. Such a path entails an enormous cost, in both human and ecological terms, which the North has imposed on the South — hence the South's need. Moreover, there is no further world from which the South can draw resources to build up its wealth and improve the welfare of its people to Northern levels. As Gandhi pointed out, "It took Britain half the resources of the planet to achieve its prosperity; how many planets will a country like India require?" (quoted in Goodland, 1992, p15).

## CONCLUSION

The notion of a global *problématique* may make the global crisis seem even more daunting. There is, however, a consolation. Though it may be difficult to trace all the connections, especially on a small scale, many important linkages can be identified. It is possible, if the appropriate interventions are made at the right points in the system, to reverse the general trends of events, even in a "turbulent" world in which the impact of action cannot always be accurately predicted. It would be far more discouraging to learn that such afflictions as growing child poverty in Britain and the crises of Ethiopia, Somalia and Rwanda were entirely random, arbitrary and unconnected.

The importance of the concept of sustainable development is that it is built on a realization of the need to alleviate the global crisis in a systematic way that integrates human, ecological and economic factors. This awareness has led to the Brundtland Commission's definition of sustainable development; its report, "hailed, despite its contradictions, as the most radical document to come out of a grouping consisting of the world's elites" (Ekins, 1992a, pviii); and Agenda 21, an action plan for the twenty-first century which stresses the importance of the participation of ordinary people, including the poorest, in decisions affecting their welfare and that of their children and their children's children. To assess these responses to the global crisis, it is important to look at earlier ones from which the idea of sustainable development emerged. The next two chapters attempt to highlight some of the more important of these by concentrating on three strands:

- conservationist and environmentalist responses to the growing impacts of industrialization, including global "environmentalism", and culminating in the World Conservation Strategy (WCS) published in 1980;
- The UN's responses to the impact of development on the poor, up to and including the first Brandt Report, also published in 1980; and

- attempts since 1980 to find a new way forward based on the integration of environmental and developmental concerns.

We look first, in Chapter 2, at the environmental response.

# Chapter 2 | ENVIRON-MENTAL RESPONSES

During the 1950s and 1960s increasing material flows in the economies that had maintained economic growth since the end of the Second World War revived questions about the continued availability of resources. It was anxieties about these that had led to "conservation" movements in the USA, which aimed to maintain material well-being. In the 1930s, it has been claimed, conservation was "really organized resource exploitation and regional economic planning" (O'Riordan, 1981, p37). During the 1960s increasing trade, improving communications, superpower rivalry, the race to the moon, all contributed to a new awareness of the earth as "one world". For example, Adlai Stevenson, the US ambassador to the UN, spoke of the earth as a spaceship "dependent on its vulnerable supplies of air and soil" (Ward and Dubos, 1972, p31). "Only One Earth" was to become the motto of the United Nations Conference on the Human Environment (UNCHE) held in Stockholm in 1972. Together, the two concerns helped to stimulate a new interest in global approaches to environmental issues.

## SPACEMEN AND COWBOYS

In 1966 Kenneth Boulding, an English-born professor of economics in the USA, used the image of the spaceship in addressing the question of material growth in a paper entitled "The Economics of the Coming Spaceship Earth". He contrasted two models of the economy. The first, the prevailing one, viewed more and more production as a good thing and judged economic success by the amount of "throughput" made up of the inputs (raw materials and energy) and the amount of output into what he called the "reservoirs of pollution". Such a measure of success was plausible "if there are infinite reservoirs from which materials can be obtained and into which effluvia can be deposited". This was "open system" economics, which exploited abundant resources, used vast amounts of energy and accelerated production with little thought of tomorrow. Boulding called this the "cowboy economy", which reflected "the reckless exploitative, romantic, and violent behaviour, which is characteristic of open societies" (Boulding, 1992, p31).

In its place Boulding (1992, p31) offered "the spaceship economy", which operates within a closed system with finite limits — the biosphere — in which stocks are maintained by cyclical flows and which is ultimately dependent on solar energy: "the economy has become a single spaceship without unlimited reserves of anything, either for extraction or for pollution, and in which, therefore, man must find his place in a cyclical ecological system which is capable of continuous reproduction of material form even though it cannot escape having inputs of energy".

The spaceship economy had a very different view of throughput and regarded capital *stock* rather than consumption *flows* as the indicator of economic success:

> In the spaceship economy, throughput is by no means a desideratum, and indeed it is to be regarded as something to be minimized rather than maximized. The essential measure of success of the economy is not production and consumption at all, but the nature, extent, quality and complexity of the total capital stock, including in this the state of the human bodies and minds. . . . The idea that both production and consumption are bad things rather than good things is very strange to economists, who have been obsessed with the income-flow concepts to the exclusion, almost, of capital-stock concepts.
>
> (Boulding, 1992, pp31–2)

Despite the elitist and technocratic associations of the spaceship metaphor, the two ideas of resources being part of a system with finite limits and of conserving capital stock found ready acceptance in several quarters. As a result, with the depletion of resources and the production of wastes continuing to increase, the early 1970s saw a wave of critiques of economic growth. For many in the North, the simultaneous rapid increase in the size of the world's population gave the issue of limits a special urgency.

## THE ENTROPY LAW

A few years later, an American economist, Nicholas Georgescu-Roegen, wrote a book entitled *The Entropy Law and the Economic Process* in which he developed his thesis that "the basic nature of the economic process is entropic and that the Entropy Law reigns supreme over this process and over its evolution" (Georgescu-Roegen, 1971, p283). Technological progress, which preferred to exploit fossil fuels rather than refine the technology of the era of the sailing ship and watermill, "has meant a shift from the more abundant resource of low entropy — the solar radiation — to the less abundant one — the earth's mineral resources" (Georgescu-Roegen, 1971, p304). These should not be valued lightly:

> We need no elaborated argument to see that the maximum of life quantity requires the minimum rate of natural resources depletion. By using these resources too quickly, man throws away that part of solar energy that will still be reaching the earth for a long time after he has departed. And everything that man has done during the last two hundred years or so puts him in the position of a fantastic spendthrift. There can be no doubt about it: any use of the natural resources for the satisfaction of nonvital needs means a smaller quantity of life in the future. If we understand well the problem, the best use of our iron resources is to produce plows or harrows as they are needed, not Rolls-Royces, not even agricultural tractors.
>
> (Georgescu-Roegen, 1971, p21)

Georgescu-Roegen points out that economic activity speeds up the entropic process, adding to the constant automatic "shuffling" of entropy in the environment. In addition to this background movement to a lower state of order in which energy is no longer available for work, a "sorting activity" takes place during economic production and consumption. Economic activity must therefore be directed to significant ends:

> And, since sorting is not a law of elementary matter, the sorting activity must feed on low entropy. Hence, the economic process is

> *actually more efficient than automatic shuffling in producing higher entropy, i.e. waste. What could then be the raison d'être of such a process? The answer is that the true "output" of the economic process is not a physical outflow of waste, but the enjoyment of life.*
> (Georgescu-Roegen, 1971, p282)

If we are not aware of these facts, we cannot "discover the real source of economic value which is the value that life has for every life-bearing individual" (Georgescu-Roegen, 1971, p282).

Applying the laws of thermodynamics, Georgescu-Roegen (1971, p281) points out that the economic process neither "creates nor consumes matter or energy, but only transforms low into high entropy". Economic development requires better use of low entropy, and therefore depends on improved economic efficiency. Economic expansion — economic growth — will increase the scale of the transformation of low into high entropy, but not its efficiency. It cannot therefore properly be called economic development if there is no increase in the benefits to be gained from the use of low entropy:

> *If divested of all the obstructive garb donned on it by all the growth models now in vogue, economic development boils down to only two elements: development proper, i.e., the innovation of finer sieves for the sifting of low entropy so as to diminish the proportion of it that inevitably slips into waste, and pure growth, i.e., the expansion of the sifting process with the extant sieves.*
> (Georgescu-Roegen, 1971, p294)

## ETHICAL QUESTIONS IN A FINITE WORLD

Georgescu-Roegen was quick to point out that acceptance of the notions that any use of energy has an entropic "cost" and that any economy has finite limits should immediately raise questions of priority in a world of scarcity or potential scarcity:

> *The reality that our system is finite and that no expenditure of energy is free confronts us with a moral decision at every point in the economic process, in planning and development and production. What do we need to make? What are the real long-term costs of production, and who is required to pay them? What is truly in the interests of man, not in the present only, but as a continuing species?*
> (quoted in Daly, 1992c)

Answering Georgescu-Roegen's question involves some consideration of policy, of social goals, finally of what Daly calls the "ultimate end", by which we justify consumption of the "ultimate means", the resources of the planet and the stocks of low entropy they represent:

> *Is the nature of the Ultimate End such that, beyond some point, further accumulation of physical artefacts is useless or even harmful? Are some of the intermediate ends now being served, and those newly proposed, really desirable or less than worthwhile, in the light of the Ultimate End? Could it be that one of our wants is to be free of the tyranny of infinite wants? Second, will we not at some point run out of ultimate means or reach limits to the rate at which ultimate means can be used? Are ultimate means limited in ways which cannot be offset by technology? . . . The nature of the Ultimate End does in fact limit the* desirability *of continual economic growth, and the nature of the ultimate means does in fact limit the* possibility *of continual growth.*

(Daly, 1992a, p21)

Georgescu-Roegen underlined the point in concluding his statement to the Stockholm conference: "Even the clear formulation from the economist's perspective of the choices before us is an ethical task, not a purely analytical one, and economists ought to accept the ethical implications of their work" (quoted in Daly, 1992c).

In this way Georgescu-Roegen and Daly added a moral — indeed spiritual — dimension to the debate about the long-term availability of natural resources on a global scale, which reached a new height in the early 1970s. There were several contributions on the theme of limits to growth in 1972 alone, the year of the Stockholm conference (UNCHE). Among these there recurs the notion of the eventual collapse of economic and social systems brought about by the ever more serious impacts of rising resource consumption and rapidly growing world population. Such thinking is often labelled neo-Malthusian, after Thomas Malthus (1766–1834), an English aristocrat and mathematician, who argued that population growth would inevitably outstrip increases in food production and would, unless checked, lead to widespread famine.

## THE TRAGEDY OF THE COMMONS

For Garret Hardin (1968), an American ecologist, increases in resource consumption gave a new urgency to the old problem of the commons. If each individual with a right of access to a common resource, whether it be a forest, a fishery or grazing land, continues to increase the yield he takes from it in pursuit of his own interest and to the exclusion of all considerations of mutual interdependence, eventually the stock will be depleted and all those who depend on the common resource will be impoverished. The analogy with economic growth needs no elaboration. Such an outcome can only be prevented by the establishment of some kind of authority for the management of the common resource in the interests of all. Hardin reaches the conclusion that there must be limits to individual freedom and that the survival of the global commons depends on "mutual coercion mutually agreed on", for no other system of regulation can emerge spontaneously. Such "coercion" will be the responsibility of an administrative elite. In the "complex, crowded, changeable" world of the late twentieth century, any administrative elite will draw on technical expertise and be able to apply special powers of enforcement in supervising the management of the commons. Such supervision raises the old question of *quis custodiet custodes?* — Who supervises the supervisors? As we shall see (Chapter 9), these issues — particularly the scientific "authentication" of such an authority and the question of who insists on its establishment — have a new relevance in the 1990s.

## BLUEPRINT FOR SURVIVAL

In 1972 the British magazine *The Ecologist* published *Blueprint for Survival*, drawing on data provided by a research team at the Massachusetts Institute of Technology (MIT) headed by Dennis and Donella Meadows. *Blueprint for Survival* took as its starting point the view that the continuation of the trends then prevailing would lead to "the breakdown of society and the irreversible disruption of the life-support systems on this planet, possibly by the end of the century". Such an outcome would be the inevitable consequence of adherence to deeply rooted beliefs in continuous growth. The more economies grew, the more governments had an incentive for further growth, because economic growth tended to create the need for more economic growth. *Blueprint for Survival* (*The Ecologist*, 1972, pp30–1) listed six reasons why this should be so:

- technology damaged natural ecosystems and created a "need" for more technology to overcome the damage;
- industrial growth led to population growth which created a demand for more jobs which — current social values demanded — meant more growth;
- governments relied on economic growth to avoid the problem of unemployment;
- the need for businesses to make surpluses for future investment favoured growth;
- governments are commonly judged by their ability to raise the standard of living or increase GNP; and
- without economic growth there could be an erosion of confidence in the economy, which could lead to social collapse.

In contrast, a stable society required (*The Ecologist*, 1972, p34):

- the minimum of disruption of ecological processes;
- maximum conservation of materials and energy — or an economy of stock rather than flow;
- a population in which recruitment equals loss; and
- a social system in which people are able to enjoy rather than have to endure the conditions in which they live.

Working out these ideas in more detail, *Blueprint for Survival* proposed a "steady state" economy featuring resource self-sufficiency, energy conservation, resource recycling, low-impact technologies, biotic rights, and a decentralized society made up of rural communities in which people would show more interest in the quality of life than in increasing the number of their material possessions.

## LIMITS TO GROWTH
Within a few months of the appearance of the *Blueprint for Survival*, the Meadows' team published *Limits to Growth*, in the form of a report to the Club of Rome. The "green" radicalism of

*The Ecologist's* work had caused a stir in Britain, but *Limits to Growth* attracted enormous attention, provoked intense debate and became a bestseller in several languages. It described the use of a computer-based systems model, *World 3*, to study the implications of continuing exponential growth in five interconnected trends "of global concern" — industrialization, population growth, widespread malnutrition, depletion of nonrenewable resources, and ecological damage. The results of the study were as clear as those of *The Ecologist's* analysis. If the trends continued unchanged, "the limits to growth on this planet will be reached sometime within the next one hundred years", the report declared (Meadows et al, 1972, p23). Even if the model incorporated "the most optimistic estimates of the benefit of technology", continued growth would lead to breakdown. This would come about through resource shortages, which would cause a sharp fall in industrial output and food supplies around 2010, and a rapid decline in population about 40 years later. Even with different scenarios that assumed more resources or greater food production, or both, the model still indicated that serious social breakdown would occur. There was, however, an alternative: "It is possible to alter these growth trends and to establish a condition of ecological and economic stability that is sustainable far into the future" (Meadows et al, 1972, p24). In marked contrast to *Blueprint for Survival* though, *Limits to Growth* makes no attempt to specify how such stability might be achieved.

Several reasons have been suggested to explain why *Limits to Growth* attracted such interest — widespread scepticism about the ability of economic growth to deliver promised material riches; public despair at social changes that seemed to detract from the quality of life; and growing public uncertainty about the effectiveness of political solutions. The public mood seemed to respond to the "pessimism" of the report, its apparent "simplicity" (with no details of possible solutions to blur the clarity of its striking conclusion) and its antipolitical overtones. Critics, including a group from the Science Policy Research Unit at the University of Sussex, questioned its authority, pointing out that the findings of such a model were neither superior to the mental models on which it was based nor any less subjective than the ideological assumptions these embodied. Similarly, neither the prestige of MIT nor the exclusiveness of the expert world of computer-aided systems analysis should delude people into uncritical acceptance of its findings. There were also specific criticisms of the adequacy of the available data, the appropriateness of using global averages, the choice of deterministic rather than probabilistic projections, and the modellers' failure to take sufficient account of social and political factors.

However, it was the Malthusian projection of inevitable catastrophe that caused most concern. One member of the Sussex group, Marie Jahoda, accused the modellers of having deliberately ignored the political process, of having "chosen to be unconcerned with politics, unconcerned with social structures, unconcerned with human wants and needs" (Cole et al, 1973, p212). Another, H G Simmons, argued that the feedback between electorate and politician is different in kind from other forms of feedback in the model, and that the political process is not about setting a fixed course for an unchanging goal, but a continual process of mediation in which "goals and objectives are constantly shifting, where values are frequently in conflict, being called into question or even inarticulate" (Cole et al, 1973, p202).

The plain fact was, Jahoda continued, that Jay Forrester, who developed the original model, knew that exponential growth can be influenced by action, but had not "built this knowledge into his model, nor shown that he understands the continuous process by which scarcities lead to substitutions, new inventions and changing ways of life which, in turn, change the physical properties with which the model deals" (Cole et al, 1973, p213).

Thus the assumptions and deterministic features of the model were seen to discount both the adaptive abilities of individuals and societies and the potential of the political process (however slow and cumbersome it might be). The report was accused of being subtly undemocratic and opposed to the interests of the people of the South — for a genuine concern for their welfare would have led, it was argued, to an exploration of the possibilities of at least modifying existing trends.

The prominence of the projected collapse attracted other criticisms. *Limits to Growth* was also seen as a dangerous enticement to despair at the hopelessness of a worsening situation and the futility of attempting to ameliorate it. Furthermore, the Sussex team claimed, it distracted the attention of both decision makers and the general public from what could be done, there and then, to solve urgent existing problems, such as issues of distribution. "Man's inventiveness in changing social arrangements", Jahoda declared in a closing barb, "is without limits, even if not without hazards" (Cole et al, 1973, p215).

The authors of both *Blueprint for Survival* and *Limits to Growth* insisted that their principal aim was not to forecast the future but to stimulate debate. This they certainly did. Many environmentalists argued a "zero growth" case, while others, including many economists, argued that such thinking was quite wrong-headed. John Maddox, editor of *Nature*, dismissed the pessimism of the report in his book *The Doomsday Syndrome*, published in 1972. He claimed that human welfare was increasing; resources were more plentiful; the problem of energy scarcity had been solved through human ingenuity; and countries afflicted with famine would produce surpluses of food by the 1970s and 1980s. His optimism now seems sadly misplaced.

The value of human ingenuity was also stressed by Julian Simon, an American professor of economics, in a book entitled *The Ultimate Resource* in which he suggested that population growth meant an increase in "crucial" resources as well as greater consumption of material resources. Other economists cast doubt on the validity of the *Limits to Growth* projections, arguing that prices give no indications of impending resource scarcity and that technology would find substitutes when such signals were received. Robert Solow, another American economist, who won a Nobel prize for economics, went so far as to declare that probably "the world can, in effect, get along without natural resources" (Daly, 1992a, p117).

Such critics apparently overlooked the fact that even if the *Limits to Growth* model could be criticized on points of detail, the basic assumption had to be right, namely that growth that depended on the consumption of more and more resources could not continue indefinitely in a finite world. Nor were they receptive to a further conclusion, which emerged as the Meadows' team explored its basic projection, that pollution rather than a shortage of energy or scarcity of resources would be the key factor in bringing about eventual collapse.

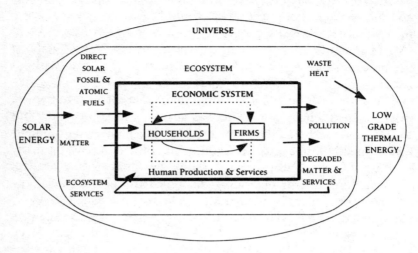

Source: Colby (1991).

**Figure 2.1** *Economic production from a biophysical perspective*

The impossibility of unending growth in a finite world led Daly (1973 and 1992a) to propose the "steady state economy", reviving an idea put forward by John Stuart Mill in his essay *On the Stationary State* published in 1848. For Daly the steady-state economy is founded on the recognition that the human economy must be a subset of the global ecosystem, drawing resources from, and emitting wastes to, other subsystems of the global system. Thus Daly suggests the appropriate model of economic activity is not the neoclassical circular flow of exchange, but rather linear entropic throughput within the biosphere (and the geosphere), in which continuous inputs of low-entropy fuels and resources are converted into high-entropy heat and matter in the form of wastes (see Figure 2.1). The scale of this activity will be determined by the finite limits to the capacities of the ecosystems it makes use of. Thus there will be a maximum level of throughput which must not be exceeded. There will also be an optimal level, allowing a margin of safety against the effects of "random interferences" which "in a complex ecosystem nearly always disrupt the functioning of the system" (Daly, 1992a, p247). This level will ultimately be determined by ecological and ethical considerations. Daly (1992a, p182) rejects the notion that the steady state would mean a static, closed society: "The end of physical accretion is not the end of progress. It is more a precondition for future progress in the sense of qualitative improvement". Other commentators, too, for example Meadows (1992), emphasize that a society based on a steady-state economy will be an evolving one — as did Mill almost 150 years ago.

As recently as 1992 the Meadows team published *Beyond the Limits* in which they reviewed and updated their work of 20 years before. Their conclusions have varied only slightly. They discovered that "in 20 years some options for sustainability have narrowed [many resource and pollution flows now being beyond sustainable limits], but others have opened up". They conclude (Meadows, 1992, pxvi):

1. . . . . *Without significant reductions in material and energy flows, there will be in the coming decades an uncontrolled decline in per capita food output, energy use and industrial production.*

2. *This decline is not inevitable. To avoid it two changes are necessary. The first is a comprehensive revision of policies and practices that perpetuate growth in material consumption and in population. The second is a rapid, drastic increase in the efficiency with which materials and energy are used.*

3. *A sustainable [global] society is still technically and economically possible. It could be much more desirable than a society which tries to solve its problems by constant expansion.*

## INTERNATIONAL POLLUTION

The rise in global environmentalism coincided with the realization that it could no longer be assumed that the environmental impacts of industrialization would be confined to the country in which they originated. However, the fact that the new international scale of the impacts of waste emissions was in line with the Meadows' projection that pollution would be the cause of collapse of exponential growth trends seems to have been generally overlooked. This was not for want of evidence that pollution ignored boundaries. Sweden, for example, could point to damage to lacustrine ecosystems from acid rain, pollution in the Baltic, and the accumulation of pesticides and heavy metals in birds and fish at the top of the food chain. Its concern about these and other impacts of "imported" pollution played a large part in bringing about UNCHE, which was held in Stockholm in 1972.

## THE UN CONFERENCE ON THE HUMAN ENVIRONMENT

The Stockholm conference was not the first attempt by the international community to reach agreement on environmental matters. However, it was the first major attempt to involve the nations of the world in a concerted, constructive response to environmental problems, which now clearly had an international dimension, and to look beyond the immediate problems to deeper issues. For this reason it is generally regarded as a milestone in the development of global responses to environmental issues, despite the fact that it was prompted by the concerns of Northern nations.

For the nations of the North the issue was clear. The concept of global resource management offered hope of a solution to the problem of pollution, which was now no longer either "easily" disposed of locally or "harmlessly" dispersed through tall chimneys or long pipes. However, many of the countries of the South were less happy with this approach, regarding action aganst pollution as a luxury to be considered only when the more pressing problems of raising living standards had been solved. The phrase "the pollution of poverty" indicated priorities in many countries in the South, which saw global solutions as a threat not only to development through industrialization but also to sovereignty: the North should accept responsibility for solving problems of its own creation — a theme which was to be heard again two decades later.

A preparatory UN seminar on environment and development held at Founex in Switzerland in 1971 prevented an open split between the North and the South. The North came to realize that the South was motivated as much by resentment of the international economic order, which denied them economic independence (which would give substance to newly-won political independence in many countries), as by the fear that conservation might restrict economic development. The North accepted the proposition — which was important to the South — that lack of development could be as important an agent of environmental damage as development. The meeting also reached agreement around the notion that development and the environment could be managed to the advantage of both, but gave no indication of the means by which this might be achieved.

The Stockholm conference itself (see Clarke and Timberlake, 1982) was attended by representatives of 119 countries and 400 NGOs. It published two documents. *The Stockholm Declaration on the Human Environment* is part of the UN constitution, alongside the *Declaration of Human Rights*, but "almost no one knows it exists" (Douthwaite, 1992, p173). It states 26 principles and reviews those forms of human activity causing most environmental concern. Some of the 26 principles attempt to meet the South's reservations: given "integrated development" or "rational planning", development could proceed without being impeded by measures to protect the environment; indeed, development could provide the means to improve the environment. As at Founex, however, these assurances were unsupported by precise indications of how they could be implemented. W M Adams (1990, p39), of the Department of Geography at the University of Cambridge, comments: "The suggested solutions, 'rational planning' or 'integrated development' were words without substance".

The second document, *Action Plan for the Human Environment*, made 109 recommendations under the three headings of global assessment, environmental management and supporting measures. Only eight of the recommendations, however, dealt with the relationship between environment and development. These focused principally on ways of reducing the costs of protecting the environment and have been described as "extraordinarily negative" (Clarke and Timberlake, 1982, p12). Otherwise the *Action Plan* had little to say either about development issues or about an approach to environmental issues that placed them in a context of development activity.

Some environmentalists have been dismissive of these attempts to integrate environment and development. One commentator described the conference as having a "remedial focus" intended to limit environmental damage or have it made good, but not to check development: "the principal strategy was to legalize the environment as an economic externality" (Colby, 1991).

However, the Stockholm conference did succeed in placing environmental problems, especially pollution, on the international political agenda. It also led to the establishment of the United Nations Environment Programme (UNEP). With headquarters in Nairobi, Kenya, UNEP became the first UN body to be based in the South. It was given a triple remit: to act as a governing council for environmental programmes within the UN; to create wider awareness of the environment and draw together environmental action within the UN; and to adminster a fund for environmental programmmes. UNEP has done much to encourage many countries to develop environmental policies and to set up government departments and other agencies, which have produced a considerable amount of environmental legislation, especially in the industrialized countries of the North. UNEP also played a part in the preparation of the *World Conservation Strategy* published in 1980 by the IUCN.

## THE WORLD CONSERVATION STRATEGY

If the words "sustainable development" were not actually used at Stockholm, the idea was certainly in the air. By 1980, when the IUCN published its *World Conservation Strategy* (WCS), the term had been coined, and the concept had become an important part of conservationist and environmentalist thinking, as the WCS's definition of its goal (Section 1.2) illustrates: "the integration of conservation and development to ensure that modifications to the planet do indeed secure the survival and well-being of all people". Prepared with financial backing from UNEP and the WWF and the benefit of comment from FAO and UNESCO, the WCS had a clear practical objective: "to stimulate a more focused approach to the management of living resources and to provide policy guidance on how this can be carried out" (IUCN, 1980, pvi). The strategy defines development as "the modification of the biosphere and the application of human, financial, living and non-living resources to satisfy human needs and improve the quality of human life" (Section 1.3). However, such modification of the biosphere is a threat unless resources are effectively conserved. Hence there is a strong emphasis on conservation, which is defined as "the management of human use of the biosphere so that it may yield the greatest sustainable benefit to present generations while maintaining its potential to meet the needs and aspirations of future generations" (Section 1.4).

Conservation has three main objectives:

- to maintain essential ecological processes and life-support systems,
- to preserve genetic diversity and
- to ensure the sustainable utilization of species and ecosystems.

Each of these is supported by a list of priority requirements (Sections 5–7) selected according to criteria of importance, urgency and irreversibility.

The next seven sections (8–14) discuss what action should be taken by individual countries. This should be based on national strategies, which should consist of four main stages:

- a review of development plans in the light of the three conservation objectives listed above, and a statement of the priorities for conservation,
- an account of the obstacles to attending to these priorities and a statement of cost-effective proposals for surmounting them,
- a statement of the ecosystems and the species whose conservation should receive high priority, and
- the preparation of a practical plan of action.

National strategies (Section 8.6) should be based on "strategic principles":

- *Integrate*: abandon sectoral approaches and integrate conservation and development;
- *Retain options*: manage ecosystems in such a way as to safeguard options for utilization in the future;
- *Mix cure and prevention*: attend to impending problems which could be worse than current ones; and
- *Focus on causes as well as symptoms*: prevent the need for conservation by tackling causes of ecological degradation and remedy damage when symptoms become apparent.

WCS concludes with a discussion (Sections 15–20) of various

international initiatives to promote conservation across natural boundaries. Its concept of sustainable development is founded on the notion that conservation and development are "mutually dependent" (Section 1.10) rather than antithetically opposed. Only effective conservation will ensure that the "modification of the biosphere", which development entails, will achieve the "social and economic objectives of development" (Section 1.12).

For this to happen, conservation must be given high priority at an early stage in development, and planning must be done in such a way as "to integrate every stage of the conservation and development processes, from their initial setting of policies to their eventual implementation and operation" (Section 9.1). Conservation must therefore be applied "cross-sectorally", and not be seen as a separate "activity sector in its own right". There is a need to develop anticipatory environmental policies, which may have high costs, but which are more cost-effective than "the measures taken once a problem has arisen when they may require redesign, restructuring, the banning of a product or the abandonment of a partially completed project" (Section 9.7), and also for national accounting systems, which will include non-monetary indicators of success in conservation (Section 9).

WCS closes with a section entitled "Towards Sustainable Development". This emphasizes that development and conservation operate in the same global context and that the underlying problems, which must be overcome if either is to be successful, are identical. It identifies the main agents of habitat destruction as poverty, population pressure, social inequity and terms of trade that work against the interests of poorer countries. It gives a check list of priority requirements, national actions and international actions, and calls for a new international development strategy aimed at redressing inequities, achieving a more dynamic and stable world economy (to allow all countries to participate more fully and more equitably), stimulating "accelerating" economic growth and countering the worst impacts of poverty.

WCS points out that sustainable utilization does not conflict with a "needs-based" approach to development, which had received new impetus since Stockholm (see pp70–2): "Conservation is entirely compatible with the growing demand for "people-centred" development, that achieves a wider distribution of benefits to whole populations (better nutrition, health, education, family welfare, fuller employment, greater income security, protection from environmental degradation); that makes fuller use of people's labour, capabilities, motivations and creativity; and that is more sensitive to cultural heritage" (Section 20.6).

Nevertheless, WCS remains environment-oriented. It shows its debt to the global environmentalism of a decade earlier in its interest in "global strategies both for development and for conservation of nature and natural resources" (IUCN, 1980, pi), its concern with population growth and its application of the concept of carrying capacity (taken from ecological approaches to wildlife management) to human populations: "Human beings, in their quest for economic development and enjoyment of the riches of nature, must come to terms with the reality of resource limitation and the carrying capacities of ecosystems" (IUCN, 1980, pi). But it fails to consider how other factors, particularly social and economic forces, affect human beings' attempts to "come to terms" with the utilization of resources. In particular, it fails to explore the very considerable potential of an integration of sustainable utilization and needs-based development.

WCS reflects both the utilitarian and moral strands of environmentalist thinking of the 1960s and 1970s. It takes a practical, utilitarian interest in the economic potential of ecosystems and the application of scientific knowledge to their management. As a result it is able to make many detailed suggestions for sustainable utilization so that resources continue to be available "almost indefinitely" (Section 4.1). To this is allied a precautionary approach stemming from the insights of ecology — "We cannot predict what species may become useful to us" (Section 3.2). It also acknowledges a conservation ethic founded on respect for the intrinsic, as opposed to the utilitarian, value of the biosphere: "we have not inherited the earth from our parents, we have borrowed it from our children" (Section 1.5). The strategy stresses humanity's special responsibility in view of its recently-acquired ability to affect the course of evolution: "human beings have become a major evolutionary force ... we are morally obliged — to our descendants and to other creatures — to act prudently" (Section 3.3).

There is, of course, a practical advantage in asserting both arguments, as Adams (1990, p48) points out: "This dualism is extremely useful. On the one hand, the utilitarian argument allows conservation to be packaged in a way which is expected to be attractive to the materialism which is seen to underlie thinking about development. On the other, moral arguments can be employed where they are more effective, for example among environmentalists in industrialized countries."

Despite its achievements in proposing sustainable utilization schemes, promoting national strategies and giving wide publicity to the notion of sustainable development, WCS has attracted serious criticism. For example, it has been dismissed as "repackaged 1970s environmentalism", being seen by development agencies in both North and South as very much in the tradition of setting limits to development. So widespread was this perception that the IUCN stressed in its next major statement, *Caring for the Earth*, published in 1991, that it had not been opposed to development in the WCS.

Its most serious limitation, however, is its lack of attention to the social and political obstacles to integrated development. Despite its proposal for a new international development strategy, it does not discuss the political and economic changes needed if there is to be any prospect of progress towards either cross-sectoral conservation or sustainable development. It shows little awareness that, far from being "above ideology", conservation values reflect cultural and social views of nature and natural resources. Adams (1990, p51) sums up this critique by commenting on WCS's declared goal, quoted above: "This is pious, liberal and benign, but it is — inevitably — ideological. Furthermore, in the context of development and social theory, it is disastrously naïve."

Both world conservation and global environmentalism offer "solutions" that can be applied on a global scale. They tend to be presented as the obviously right thing to do, and therefore non-controversial. However, far from being apolitical, they reflect Northern bias. Their perspective is that of Northern interests — whether conservationist or exploitative — in largely Southern resources; their diagnoses are validated by Northern science on whose findings they are based, and their implementation would require Northern technology and expertise.

To suggest solutions based on such "self-evident" principles as "population increase must be halted" and "carrying capacity must be respected" without considering the political realities affecting the chances of their being implemented is to ignore the rights of local people, neglect the impact of social and economic forces on their access to and use of resources, and deny the reality of the effort needed to surmount the many political difficulties associated with negotiating "improvements" that have any recognizable similarity with "obvious" global solutions.

Such proposals can appear to Southern eyes as part of an undemocratic attempt to impose solutions that assume North-directed global management, serve Northern interests and entail Southern compliance at a disproportionately high cost. Samir Ghabbour (1992, p172) of Cairo University expresses a widespread Southern response on the publication of *Caring for the Earth*, the IUCN's sequel to WCS in 1991:

> *Working towards sustainable living is welcome, if it is taken globally, but building a sustainable society, with the present global configuration of nation states, is definitely unwelcome for the majority of the human race, suffering as they do from abject poverty and rampant diseases. Making Third World societies aware of the need and the tools for caring for their environments is welcome, but convincing them to accept their suffering and be content with their squalor is definitely unwelcome.*

Plainly environmental responses to the global crisis need to be informed by an awareness of development issues. The next chapter continues the survey of the last three decades, adjusting the focus to examine the efforts of international development agencies to address the most urgent issues of human need arising from the global crisis.

# Chapter 3 | DEVELOP-MENTAL RESPONSES

When in 1962 the UN published *The Development Decade: Proposals for Action* for the first development decade (1960–70), optimism about the development efforts of the 1950s was still high. Rapid industrialization was the key to progress in the poorer countries, for it would lead to improvements in standards of living, so the argument ran. Growth in GNP was a measure of success in industrializing the economy and with it would come improvements in social welfare. However, for those in the South whose prime concern was to reduce poverty and provide basic social services similar to those available in the North, such improvements could not be left to chance. *Proposals for Action* thus tried to insist on a balance between economic and social development, pointing out that: "The problem of the underdeveloped countries is not just growth, but development. ... Development is growth plus change. Change, in turn, is social and cultural as well as economic, and qualitative as well as quantitative. ... The key concept must be improved quality of people's lives" (quoted in Esteva, 1992, p13). A year later the UN created its Research Institute for Social Development (UNRISD) as part of an attempt to ensure that economic planning did not go ahead without considering social objectives.

Within a few years, however, this attempt to insist on the importance of social objectives had failed. Economic growth had continued, but the need to reduce hunger and malnutrition, end poverty and bring about improvements in health (especially rates of survival in infancy) was greater than before, as the UN itself had to acknowledge. The report of a meeting in 1969 of experts on social policy and planning stated: "The fact that development either leaves behind, or in some ways even creates, large areas of poverty, stagnation, marginality and actual exclusion from social and economic progress is too obvious and too urgent to be overlooked" (quoted in Esteva, 1992, p13). The economic dimension of development had dominated; other measures of progress were clearly needed.

UNRISD's publication of the *International Development Strategy* in 1970 was intended to herald a new form of integrated development which took account of the global interaction of resources, technology, economic forces and other factors leading to social change. A UN resolution published about the same time called for nations to adopt a unified approach to development and planning in an attempt to ensure several laudable objectives:

- all social groups should benefit from development,
- all nations and all groups within each nation should be provided with the means, in the form of structural change, to take part in development,
- development should promote social equity, and
- development should fulfil human potential.

The success of these proposals with their implied critique of the past achievements of development agencies depended on their receiving an enthusiastic welcome and being accompanied by a clear practicable strategy for implementing them. Neither, however, was forthcoming. Meanwhile other issues were coming to the fore, as we have seen in the previous chapter.

## THE MID-1970S: A NEW EMPHASIS ON HUMAN DEVELOPMENT

By the mid-1970s the debate on the integration of economic and social development had moved on. Continuing dissatisfaction with the dominance of the conventional model of economic growth and its seeming inability to reduce destitution led to the participants in a UNEP–UNCTAD symposium on the "Pattern of Resource Use, Environment and Development" (held in Cocoyoc in Mexico in 1974) issuing what came to be known as the Cocoyoc Declaration. This stated that the point of development "should not be to develop things, but to develop man", and went on to say that: "Any process of growth that does not lead to the fulfilment [of basic needs] or, even worse, disrupts them — is a travesty of the idea of development" (quoted in Esteva, 1992, p14). The declaration was also critical of development's destructive impact on the diversity of local and traditional economies and cultures. It emphasized the need for the poorer countries to pursue the goal of self-reliance and called for radical economic, social and political changes to allow them to do so.

The Cocoyoc Declaration was followed in 1975 by *What Now? Another Development*, published by the Dag Hammarskjöld Institute in Uppsala, Sweden (see Chapter 4). The thinking revealed in the two documents helped to formulate the basic needs approach, which was an attempt to find a more effective way forward than the rather vague scheme suggested in the *International Development Strategy* of 1970. An ILO conference in 1976 surveyed the evidence of the previous two decades: the years of economic development, far from eliminating hunger and hardship, had coincided with an increase. More of the same kind of development would almost certainly increase the number of people, estimated at more than a billion, suffering from extreme poverty. The new approach would concentrate on the urgent task of meeting the basic needs of the poorest people, rather than trusting in the conventional development process to bring about some improvement in their lot. The approach won the approval of both the World Bank, which had begun targeting the rural poor and small farmers, and a wide range of governments. It also found favour with development experts because it allowed flexibility in responding to local conditions. However, practical projects were handicapped by the difficulties created by economic forces and by the failure to achieve targets, which seemed to affect so many aid projects.

## THE SEARCH FOR A NEW ECONOMIC ORDER

The steep rise in the price of oil in 1973 increased the seriousness of the economic situation of many countries in the South. In May 1974 a conference of the Organization of Nonaligned States met in Algeria and adopted a *Declaration and Plan of Action for the Establishment of a New International Economic Order*. This stressed several points, including the need to protect prices of primary commodities; the right of less developed countries to expropriate foreign enterprises; and the need for international regulation of foreign firms. The UN General Assembly almost immediately adopted the declaration and also approved a *Charter of Economic Rights and Duties* proposed by Mexico, which emphasized sovereignty, autonomy and non-interference as the esssentials of a new international economic order.

By the late 1970s the crippling effect of the burden of interest payments on development loans became a major issue for many Southern countries. The debt crisis gave a new focus to the resentments expressed at Stockholm about the inequity of the international economic system, which appeared to discriminate against the fledgling economies of recently independent nations.

The worsening financial plight of the poorer countries and the increasing suffering of their populations led the UN to appoint three independent commissions to report on aspects of the crisis: the Independent Commission on International Development Issues (ICIDI) (the Brandt Commission), set up in 1977; the Independent Commission on Disarmament and Security Issues (the Palme Commission), set up in 1980;[1] and the WCED (the Brundtland Commission), set up in 1984.

## THE BRANDT REPORTS

The first independent commission to report, within a few months of publication of the WCS, was the Brandt Commission, made up of "elder statesmen and men and women of stature" from both North and South. It published its first report, *North–South: A Programme for Survival*, in 1980, and a second, *Common Crisis*, in 1983, when the scale of the debt crisis became evident. *North–South* accepted that development based on economic growth had failed: "the hope that faster economic growth in developing countries by itself would benefit the broad masses of

---

1. The Palme Commission argued that national military strength cannot guarantee genuinely peaceful security and called for a halt to the arms race and nuclear weapons. Such security is obviously an important element in a sustainable world. However, reasons of space preclude any further discussion of the Palme Commission's report here. For a brief account, see Ekins (1992a, pp16–23).

poor people has not been fulfilled" (ICIDI, 1980, p24). It went on
to declare: "No concept of development can be accepted which
continues to condemn hundreds of millions of people to star-
vation and despair" (ICIDI, 1980, p50). The situation was not
simply one of crisis, but possibly of survival. If a solution could
not be found, the accumulated impacts of hunger, economic failure and environmental disaster might lead to terrorism, war and
chaos. *North–South* also rejected development based on "a guiding philosophy which is predominantly materialistic". In words
reminiscent of the Cocoyoc Declaration it explained (ICIDI,
1980, p12) how much more was involved in development than
simply making economic progress:

> *World development is not merely an economic process. . . . The
> new generations of the world need not only economic solutions, they
> need ideas to inspire them, hopes to encourage them, . . . they need a
> belief in man, in human dignity, in basic human rights; a belief in
> the values of justice, freedom, peace, mutual respect, in love and
> generosity, in reason rather than force.*

Development showed too little concern for the quality of
growth, and too little respect for different cultures and traditions:

> *Statistical measurements of growth exclude the crucial element of
> social welfare, of individual rights, of values not measured by
> money. Development is more than the passage from poor to rich,
> from a traditional rural economy to a sophisticated urban one. It
> carries with it not only the idea of economic betterment but also of
> greater human dignity, security, justice and equity*
> (ICIDI, 1980, p49)

However, *North–South* contained no suggestion of how the
goals of "human dignity, security, justice and equity" might be
achieved. Instead, its authors insisted that economic growth and
industrialization — the very processes which had led to an
increase in human degradation, insecurity, injustice and social
inequity and which had led to so much criticism of the development model — were essential if the living standards of the poor
were to improve.
Nevertheless, the Brandt Commission was clear about the

prime cause of the failure of development. Some nations in the South might have created problems for themselves by over-ambitious development planning or economic mismanagement, but the major reason was external forces, which worked through world recession, high interest rates, the falling prices of primary exports from the South, and protectionism in the North. All these were beyond the control of the South: "The unfavourable external environment has exacerbated their problems beyond measure, and is forcing most countries, even many of the well-managed ones, into excessive retrenchment. 'The developing countries', as the World Bank President put it, 'are being battered by global economic forces outside their control' " (ICIDI, 1983, p20).

The Brandt Commission argued that the impact of such forces both restricted the growth of Southern economies and contri-buted to the stagnation of industrialized economies in the North, no longer able to take advantage of expanding markets in the South. An effective solution required a form of structural adjust-ment, based on a thorough rethinking, in which the then Soviet Union and China should be involved, to create a new type of economic relationship which could include all nations. The key to such a new relationship was to recognize "that the legitimate self-interests of nations often merge into well-understood common interests". Poorer nations could only be helped "through more purposeful collaboration between North and South, and much more systematic assistance from the North" (ICIDI, 1980, p58). Countries with economies in surplus should organize their surpluses for the benefit of the poorer countries, transferring funds at concessionary rates. This suggestion was made even more strongly in the second Brandt Report, *Common Crisis*, published in response to the deepening debt crisis.

Brandt's strategy was to redirect and revive the world economy by increasing aid to the South and making adjustments in the North to reduce the advantages the North enjoyed at the expense of the South. The two reports put forward a number of proposals designed to counter external economic forces by increasing finan-cial flows from North to South. These included measures to increase growth in both the North and the South; transfers of capital and technical assistance; better trading agreements, including the removal of some tariffs; a fairer monetary system and measures to reduce other inequities between North and South. The proposals contained some imaginative suggestions such as initiating a programme of additional aid extending over 20 years; increasing the aid contributions of Northern governments to 1 per cent of GNP (still not generally achieved in 1995) (see p226); introducing an international taxation scheme to help poorer countries; and giving the poorest countries a more effective voice at the World Bank and the IMF. There were also proposals to guarantee food supplies and develop energy in the South. These proposals would combat poverty, which had to be reduced and eventually eliminated if there was to be a solution to the problem of population growth, which Brandt saw as affecting the North at least as much as the South.

Together, many of these proposals amounted to an impressive statement of what was required for a more equitable deal for the South. However, the international community made little effective response to the Brandt proposals, very few additional transfers of funds were made and the Brandt Commission was disbanded shortly after the submission of its second report to the UN General Assembly.

There are a number of reasons for its failure to win support for its proposals for a more equitable world founded on a new international economic order. One of these was its publication at a time when the larger economic powers in the North (both in the east and west) were reluctant to consider additional aid commitments. Others stem from the assumptions of *North–South* itself. Perhaps the most important of these was its concept of the mutuality of the interests of North and South. Unfortunately this idea did not stand up to close examination. It is doubtful whether Northern economies required growth in the South to escape stagnation. Nor can it be assumed that an expansion of trade would necessarily benefit all countries.[2] The arguments for a new economic relationship based on a mutuality of interest — that the North's exports to the South would increase as the South became more prosperous and that the world's financial system might

---

2. See Ekins (1992a, pp34–6) for a summary of why trade does not necessarily benefit all parties.

collapse without some reform — made little impact in the North, where governments and banks were benefiting from the flow of interest repayments and low commodity prices.

One critic (Jones, 1983) claims that the members of the Brandt Commission adopted the single rather idealistic premise of the mutuality of the interests of North and South at the very start of their work before holding wider consultations. Perhaps this helps explain the weakness of their approach to several other issues. Aware that governments in the South were insufficiently concerned about distributing any new wealth ("only if governments are committed to enabling the poor to benefit from increasing growth can the plea for increased international assistance and co-operation command moral strength"), they called for a frank discussion in both South and North of the abuse of power by elites. However, they neither discussed the issue in the report nor succeeded in starting a discussion elsewhere. Moreover, though aware that much development funding was swallowed up by unproductive investments, prestige projects, luxury imports, arms purchases and capital flight to private bank accounts abroad, the authors of *North–South* failed to discuss the means by which these deep flaws in the development process might be corrected: for example, by making aid conditional, setting more rigorous criteria for selecting projects, devising ways of blocking misappropriated funds, implementing rigorous monitoring, and reviewing the success of projects. This is a crucial deficiency in a report which stresses the need for more growth and more industrialization: without an overhaul of the system, more development aid to achieve these ends would simply mean more of the same problems. For this reason it has been accused of ignoring the practicalities of implementing its chosen solution: "the peculiarity of institutions, the complexity of issues, the logic of negotiation, the imperfection of communities, the mutual inconsistency of objectives, the private ambitions of public figures, and a host of domestic constraints on foreign policy — are either ignored or dismissed as technicalities and details" (Jones, 1983, p93). There is a similar naïvety in its assumptions about the readiness and ability of the political leaders in the North, to whom it was addressed, to support its proposals. As Adams (1990, p64) points out, "It assumes that political and economic interests in the North are uniform, explicitly articulated and susceptible to rational debate".

*North–South* has also been criticized for conducting its analysis almost exclusively in terms of nation states, international relations, and the international financial institutions that dominate development. Despite its opening section on the quality of development and other sections on such topics as basic needs, women's role in development, the environment, human rights, people's organizations and the "informal" sector, the report fails to press the case for more participation in development by those most affected by it — for example, by extending human rights, by involving people's organizations, by allowing participation at community level, or by attempting to integrate development and the environment. Significantly, there is very little reference to these issues in either report's summary of recommendations.

By any practical measure the Brandt Commission failed to achieve its aims. It did not persuade the North that mutuality of interest existed. There were no new major transfers of funds on special terms. This was not surprising, in Ekins's (1992a, p29) view: "The Brandt Commission ... was composed of top people, thinking top down, as such people normally do. The problem with their top-down recommendations was that other top people [in both North and South], who would have had to implement them, were and are doing very well out of the status quo."

*North–South* marks a transitional stage in responses to the global crisis. It gave publicity to ideas about human needs, about respecting local cultures, about self-reliance and about extending participation in developments, which had not been given prominence in other UN statements since Cocoyoc. If only by its failure to do more than pay lip service to these, it may have helped to stimulate interest in their potential. However, it is misleading to talk of the end of an era, for it repeats the emphasis of the 1960s and 1970s on economic growth — which was to remain a dominant theme in the 1980s. Moreover, despite its gestures towards the need for the integration of economic and social development, it failed to consider the concept of sustainable development, which had emerged during the 1970s and was to become the dominant development theme of the 1980s. Only a year after the second Brandt Report, the UN General Assembly appointed the Brundtland Commission to formulate a new synthesis of environmental and development thinking and to suggest realistic proposals for effective action.

## THE IUCN OTTAWA CONFERENCE

In June 1986, while the Brundtland Commission was still at work, the IUCN followed up the WCS with the Ottawa Conference on Conservation and Development. The introduction to the published proceedings attempts to supplement the WCS's insistence on the importance of the health of the biosphere with a coded acknowledgement of the importance of other issues: "The overriding requirement emerging from this critique of the World Conservation Strategy was that we must view life and earth as an integrated system. If we analyse elements of that system in isolation, we seriously compromise any useful understanding of how to achieve sustainable development" (Jacobs et al, 1987, p17). The conference stressed, as Brundtland would too, the need for a radical change from the old model of development: "we need an alternative society, another type of development that is linked with structural transformation; the ability to practise design and management for sustainable development will require substantially different paradigms, institutional structures and methodological tools than have been considered adequate before" (Jacobs et al, 1987, p19).

The conference followed the WCS in stressing both the practical and the moral arguments. Sustainable development is derived from "two closely related paradigms of conservation": that nature should be conserved, which is "a reaction against the *laissez-faire* economic theory that considered living resources as free goods, external to the development process, essentially infinite and inexhaustible"; and a second "derived from the moral injunction to act as steward, and a response to the warnings of Aldo Leopold, *Silent Spring* and *Limits to Growth*" (IUCN, 1986, p18).

However, the conference's list of five requirements for the "emerging paradigm" of sustainable development draws on wider support than arguments for conservation:

• integration of conservation and development,

- satisfaction of basic human needs,
- achievement of equity and social justice,
- provision for social self-determination and cultural diversity,
- maintenance of ecological integrity.

These were seen as "so strongly interrelated it is difficult, and indeed unhelpful to arrange them in a hierarchical or priority order. The first could be seen as synonymous with sustainable development, and as encompassing all the others" (IUCN, 1986, p20).

## CARING FOR THE EARTH: A STRATEGY FOR SUSTAINABLE LIVING

In 1991 IUCN published a second major policy statement, *Caring for the Earth*, which reflects the impact of contributions to the Ottawa conference. The focus has shifted from conservation to "sustainable living", which is based on respect for ecological integrity and a new critique of development. Nine principles are announced. The first is the founding principle: "respect and care for the community of life" (which is seen as one great interdependent system). Principles 2–5 imply the criteria by which the success of the application of the first principle can be judged:

- improve the quality of human life,
- conserve the earth's vitality and diversity,
- minimize the depletion of nonrenewable resources, and
- keep within the earth's carrying capacity.

The last four principles state the directions to be followed at all levels (IUCN, 1991, pp9–12):

- change personal attitudes and practices,
- enable communities to care for their own environments,
- provide a natural framework for integrating development and conservation, and
- create a global alliance.

*Caring for the Earth* clearly reflects its debt to the development thinking of the 1970s. Improving the quality of human life concerns more than just material welfare and will be achieved if certain "virtually universal" goals are met: a long, healthy life, education, access to resources for a decent standard of living, political freedom, guaranteed human rights and freedom from violence. There is a firm insistence that development is only meaningful if it encompasses all these ends: "development is only real if it makes our lives better in all these respects".

Local communities are seen as the focus for many of the changes needed to achieve sustainable living, but it is also emphasized that they can do little without the power to act and must, therefore, be given the authority to manage the resources on which they depend. There is no attempt, however, to examine why many local communities do not have such power, or to describe what sort of changes would enable them to acquire it.

*Caring for the Earth* shows some awareness of the political dimension of development, which was largely lacking in the WCS, and an awareness of the importance of an integrated approach to environmental and developmental issues. However, it has been overshadowed by events, especially the publication of the Brundtland Report and preparations for the Rio Conference.

## THE BRUNDTLAND REPORT

In 1987, a year after the IUCN conference in Ottawa, the WCED published its report, *Our Common Future* (the Brundtland Report), after three years of work, including hearings on all five continents. The commission had been asked by the UN General Assembly to "propose long-term environmental strategies for achieving sustainable development by the year 2000 and beyond", and hence formulate "a global agenda for change" (WCED, 1987, pix). In preparing such an agenda, it was given three objectives: "to re-examine the critical environment and development issues and to formulate realistic proposals for dealing with them; to propose new forms of international co-operation on these issues that will influence policies and events in the direction of needed changes; and to raise the levels of understanding and commitment to action of individuals, voluntary organizations, businesses, institutes and governments" (WCED, 1987, pp3–4).

Their investigations led the members of the commission to

focus on "one central theme": "many development trends leave increasing numbers of people poor and vulnerable, while at the same time degrading the environment. How can such development serve next century's world of twice as many people relying on the same environment?" (WCED, 1987, p4). They also became aware "that a new development path was required, one that sustained human progress not just in a few places for a few years, but for the entire planet into the distant future" (WCED, 1987, p4). Thus *Our Common Future*'s starting point is a concern for people. It expresses anxiety about the impact of the prevailing pattern of development on them and declares the need for· an equitable and sustainable form of development.

Recognizing that what happens to the environment happens as a result of forces that cause inequity and hardship, the commission had rejected the option of considering the environment in isolation and committed itself to an integrated approach to issues of environment and development: "It is therefore futile to attempt to deal with environmental problems without a broader perspective that encompasses the factors underlying world poverty and international inequality" (WCED, 1987, p3).

*Our Common Future* goes on to trace the relationship between environment and development: "Many forms of development erode the environmental resources on which they must be based, and environmental degradation can undermine economic development." There are also reciprocal links between poverty and the environment, poverty being recognized "as a major cause and effect of global environmental problems" (WCED, 1987, p3). These linkages can be represented diagramatically as in Figure 3.1. It is the high levels of consumption of resources, largely in the North but also among the elites in the South, that account for development's impacts on both planet and people, and that forces the poor in the South to exhaust resources and destroy ecosystems in their attempts to maintain their existence. For development to be sustainable it must, as we have seen, "meet the needs of the present without compromising the ability of future generations to meet theirs" (WCED, 1987, p8). Thus, sustainable development must first of all meet human needs. Significantly, perhaps, *Our Common Future* devotes only a few paragraphs in some 350 pages to discussing human needs directly. It appears content with a few general statements: meeting essential human needs depends partly on achieving "full growth potential", and also on "ensuring equitable opportunities for all" (WCED, 1987, p44) and not over-exploiting the environment; the essential needs are for livelihood, food, energy and the "linked basic needs of housing, water supply, sanitation and health care" (WCED, 1987, p55). It therefore fails to consider the nature of human need or its implications for development, despite its assertion of their importance: "The satisfaction of human needs and aspirations is so obviously an objective of productive activity that it may appear redundant to assert its central role in the concept of sustainable development" (WCED, 1987, p55). Such reluctance to risk being seen to state the obvious may seem a little precious in view of the frequency with which the objective of satisfying human needs fails to be met.

Sustainable development is also about acknowledging, and where possible extending, the limits which affect the welfare of both present and future generations. These limits are not the

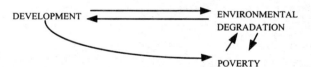

*Figure 3.1 Linkages between development, environmental degradation and poverty*

absolute ecological limits of the global environmentalists, but "limitations imposed by the state of technology and social organization on the environment's ability to meet present and future needs" (WCED, 1987, p8). This is not to deny the existence of absolute limits but to be wary of applying such a notion too simplistically: "Growth has no set limits in terms of population or resource use beyond which lies ecological disaster. . . . The accumulation of knowledge and the development of technology can enhance the carrying capacity of the resource base" (WCED, 1987, p45). An imposed programme of objectives for ecological sustainability would be politically impracticable: "A development path that is sustainable in a physical sense could theoretically be pursued even in a rigid social and physical setting. But physical sustainability cannot be secure unless development policies pay attention to such considerations as changes in access to resources and in the distribution of costs and benefits" (WCED, 1987, p43). The goal of ecological sustainability cannot therefore be achieved without the existing limits on development being extended by, for example, more equitable access to resources as a result of land reform, more equitable distribution of wealth and the greater availability of cleaner technology to poorer countries.

The two key concepts of sustainable development are linked by their dependence on equity: human needs cannot be adequately met unless resources are shared out fairly, and even the limited goal of physical sustainability requires equity, both intergenerational (equity between generations) and intragenerational (equity within each generation). Essential for the achievement of sustainability will be the removal of inequities that bring ecological limits closer: "But ultimate limits there are, and sustainability requires that long before these are reached, the world must ensure equitable access to the constrained resource and reorient technological developments to relieve the pressure" (WCED, 1987, p45). The commission later acknowledges that "our inability to promote the common interest in sustainable development is often a product of the relative neglect of economic and social justice within and among nations" (WCED, 1987, p49).

Sustainable development is therefore not a "fixed state of harmony", but "a process of change in which the exploitation of resources, the direction of investments and the orientation of technological development and institutional change are made consistent with future as well as present needs. We do not pretend that the future is easy or straightforward. Painful choices have to be made. Thus, in the final analysis, sustainable development must rest on the political will" (WCED, 1987, p9).

The report goes on to specify and discuss the "critical objectives for national environment and development policies that follow from the concept of sustainable development". These include (WCED 1987, p49):

- *reviving growth;*
- *changing the quality of growth;*
- *meeting essential needs for jobs, food, energy, water, sanitation;*

- *ensuring a sustainable level of population;*
- *conserving and enhancing the resource base;*
- *reorienting technology and managing risk; and*
- *merging environment and economics in decision-making.*

The list includes both environmental and developmental objectives. However, the objective most closely related to integrating environment and development is placed last, while "reviving growth" and "changing the quality of growth" are at the top of the list. As in *North–South*, the pathway to the desired solution seems to lead back to the broad highway that has led to crisis: "It is essential that global economic growth be revitalized. In practical terms this means more rapid economic growth in both industrial and developing countries, freer market access for the products of developing countries, lower interest rates, greater technology transfer, and significantly larger capital flows, both concessional and commercial" (WCED 1987, p89).

As *Our Common Future* points out, a new era of economic growth would have very serious ecological implications. It estimates that "given population growth rates, a five- to tenfold increase in manufacturing output will be needed just to raise developing-world consumption of manufactured goods to industrialized world levels by the time population growth rates level off next century" (WCED 1987, p15), and also that "to bring developing countries' energy use up to industrialized levels by the year 2025 would require increasing present global energy use by a factor of five" (WCED 1987, p14). It plainly accepts that such an increase in energy use could not achieve the goal of sustainable development: "The planetary ecosystem could not stand this, especially if the increases were based on nonrenewable fossil fuels" (WCED 1987, p14). However, the report evades the question of how to reconcile growth with ecological limits (see Chapter 2) with a bland insistence that "the Commission's overall assessment is that the international economy must speed up world growth while respecting environmental constraints" (WCED 1987, p89). This has led one critic (Hueting, 1990, p112) to comment that the report is "either blind to present day realities or is speculating on as yet uninvented technologies, while putting at risk the basis of our existence."

Clearly *Our Common Future* sets much store by a different form of growth, referring both to "changing the quality of growth" and "a new era of growth". However, it offers very little explicit guidance on how this might be achieved. If we interpret "changing the quality of growth" to mean targeting production to meet the most pressing human needs, some of the difficulty disappears. The report does suggest that growth must be regulated by ecological criteria and equity: "Living standards that go beyond the basic minimum are sustainable only if consumption standards everywhere have regard for long-term sustainability. . . . Sustainable development requires the promotion of values that encourage consumption standards that are within the bounds of the ecologically possible and to which all can reasonably aspire" (WCED 1987, p44). Thus *Our Common Future* suggests not just a halt to rises in the material standard of living in the richer nations (consumption standards must have regard for long-term sustainability), but, more radically but rather hesitantly, a decline in such standards to levels "to which all can reasonably aspire". It would appear that the kind of economic activity Brundtland advocates here has as much to do with distribution as production. However, this rather tentative interest in the reorganization of economic activity to meet prioritized human needs is swamped by the frequency of references to what appears to be conventional economic growth.

*Our Common Future* contains the following list of global requirements or "goals that should underlie national and international action on development" (WCED, 1987, p65):

- *a political system that secures effective citizen participation in decision-making,*
- *an economic system that is able to generate surpluses and technical knowledge on a self-reliant and sustained basis,*
- *a social system that provides for solutions for the tensions arising from disharmonious development,*
- *a production system that respects the obligation to preserve the ecological basis for development,*
- *a technological system that can search for new solutions,*
- *an international system that fosters sustainable patterns of trade and finance, and*

- *an administrative system that is flexible and has the capacity for self correction.*

Their magnitude and scope — in effect a major overhaul of established systems ranging from national politics to international trade and finance — are matched only by the absence of any guidance as to how they might be achieved.

In Chapter 3 of *Our Common Future* Brundtland examines "international economic exchanges", which must be equitable and based on a sustainable use of resources if all parties are to benefit. Because patterns of trade meet neither of these criteria, many countries in the South require flows of capital without which "the prospects for any improvement in living standards are bleak. As a result the poor will be [are already?] forced to overuse the environment to ensure their own survival" (WCED, 1987, p68). The report proceeds to call for the improvement of economic policies in areas "where scope for co-operation is already defined: aid, trade, transnational corporations, and technology transfer" (WCED, 1987, p76) and specifies:

- increased capital flows to the Third World directed to promote sustainable projects,
- new agreements on commodity trade (which will do away with protectionism, and pay particular attention to the "hidden" pollution costs of industrial processes in developing countries),
- more "responsible" transnational investment, to be achieved by strengthening the bargaining position of the South and negotiating new codes of conduct for the larger corporations,
- broadening the technological base, through the transfer of environmentally sound technologies, and technological capacity building.

Brundtland goes on to look at a wide range of "common challenges" in the light of this analysis. The report sets out in considerable detail what is required in several "policy directions". Dealing with the "population problem" will require ending poverty and promoting education. This is "not just a demographic issue": making it possible for parents to choose the size of their families is "a way of assuring — especially for women — the basic human right of self-determination". In agriculture there must be a reduction of subsidies in the richer countries and an improvement of the terms of trade for farmers in the poorer countries. Food security could be improved by land reform and integrated rural development, which would create more jobs in the countryside. Conservation of natural resources is urgently required: the cost of arresting the decline in biodiversity and resource stocks will be high, but will have economic advantages in the long run. Sustainable development also requires "a safe and sustainable energy pathway". Until one is found there is a pressing need for energy efficiency and an increase in the production of the fuelwood on which half of humanity depends. Governments should take a long-term view when weighing the costs and benefits of various measures to encourage energy efficiency. Industrial growth, which is required if "many essential human needs are to be met", should aim for "higher productivity, increased efficiency and decreased pollution". By the year 2000 half the world's population will be living in urban centres. Good city management, including decentralization to local authorities and close liaison with the urban poor, will be vital.

The report closes with a section entitled "Common Endeavours", which discusses the management of the global commons, reduction of arms spending, tighter control of the testing of weapons of mass destruction and many recommendations for institutional and legal changes. Consistent with its concern for meeting human needs, *Our Common Future* also discusses the role of nongovernmental groups in development, a theme of the Brandt Report. However, Brundtland gives much more emphasis than its predecessor to people's organizations, people's rights of participation in decision-making, and decentralization of decision-making to give local people and small producers more say in policies for allocating resources.

Rather, like the idea of sustainable development itself, the Brundtland report can be seen as eclectic, drawing on a range of earlier insights and approaches. The resulting synthesis makes it a more comprehensive analysis of global problems than most of its predecessors. It avoids repeating the warnings of the early 1970s of catastrophic breakdown and makes relatively little reference to notions such as carrying capacity which receives more emphasis in the WCS's conservation-oriented approach. Instead it prefers to consider the sustainable management of ecosystems in the light of social and economic factors.

However, some commentators, for example Adams (1990) and Middleton et al (1993), question its synthesis on the environment, equity and economics. They point out that more environmentally sound practices and multilateral co-operation and dialogue can only achieve so much. Capital flows for sustainable projects, reforming TNC investment and even ending protectionism will not in themselves remedy the structural flaws in the economic system.

Though aware of the inequities to which these flaws give rise, Brundtland criticizes national and international institutions only in terms of their being "established on the basis of narrow preoccupations and compartmentalized concerns" and of "governments' failure to make the bodies whose policy actions degrade the environment responsible for ensuring that their policies prevent that degradation" (WCED, 1987, p9). Like its predecessor, *North–South, Our Common Future* does not include a thorough analysis of the reasons for these inequities and of the part played by the economically more powerful nations, institutions and corporations in allowing them to persist:

> *The fact that poor countries are caught in the vice of falling commodity prices on the one hand and the need to service the past loans that they have contracted with governments, bilateral agencies and private financial institutions on the other, is recognized. At the same time the culpability of the lending agencies ... in maintaining the levels of debt, of the international bourses, of the great financial and industrial corporations, of the wealthy who own shares in poverty goes largely unmentioned"*
> (Middleton et al, 1993, pp20–1)

*Our Common Future* states that reforms will be required if the world economy is to stimulate ecologically sound growth in the South that will not simply be a "general acceleration of global economic growth" — which would "mean a mere perpetuation of existing economic patterns" (WCED, 1987, p89). In Brundtland's opinion, such reforms will require a "deep commitment by all countries to the satisfactory working of multilateral institutions, such as the multilateral development banks; to the making and observance of international rules in fields such as trade and investment; and to constructive dialogue on the many issues where national interests do not immediately coincide but where negotiation could help to reconcile them" (WCED, 1987, p90). Thus no radical analysis is necessary in the eyes of those who accept the basic soundness of the existing system and who feel able to assume the goodwill of all parties.

Regretting the "recent decline in multilateral co-operation in general and a negative attitude to dialogue on development in particular" (WCED, 1987, p90), Brundtland reveals a faith not only in multilateral co-operation and dialogue, but also in Brandt's mutuality of interest: "At first sight the introduction of an environmental dimension further complicates the search for such co-operation and dialogue. But it also injects an additional element of mutual self-interest, since a failure to address the interaction between resource depletion and rising poverty will accelerate global ecological deterioration" (WCED, 1987, p90). The section ends on a serenely complacent note: "The Commission feels confident that the mutual interests involved in environment and development issues can generate the needed momentum and can secure the necessary international economic changes that will make it possible" (WCED, 1987, p90).

By the end of the report the commission's concern for the people who most require its support seems to have slipped from the forefront of its attention. The integration of environment and development turns out to be less about "meeting the needs of the present" (beginning with the most immediate needs of those people and countries impoverished by the world economic system) along pathways now largely defined by ecological criteria, and more about another form of development which, despite calls for a new quality of growth, maintains economic growth and preserves and boosts the world economy: "There is a real sense that developmental issues, including the essential issues of local participation, have been subsumed under economic and environmental imperatives" (Middleton et al, 1993, p17).

Thus the comprehensiveness and detail of *Our Common Future* is overshadowed by the inadequacy of its treatment of human need and its bias towards economic growth. Its proposals for growth will stimulate "trickle-down" justifications and render less likely the changes in social organization the commission hoped would ease constraints on attempts to meet human needs. Without clear specification of a new ecologically sound growth, the emphasis on growth will also in effect counter the potential of technological change to push back the ecological limits.

Moreover, the bias is not just towards economic growth, but also towards international business as usual. Gains for the poor are conditional on the maintenance and reform of the system that disadvantages them, as Neil Middleton et al (1993, p20) point out: "Social justice has become a matter only to be approached through humanizing the workings of the market. Yet those workings are clearly, themselves, dependent on maintaining something approaching the status quo."

By trusting in growth and multilateral co-operation and dialogue to amend the existing economic order Brundtland follows Brandt in what Adams (1990, p65) calls "rather comfortable Keynesian reformism". In doing so, in passing over the opportunity to discuss human needs or needs-based development, and in its reluctance to speak plainly about the reduction of levels of consumption in the North, Brundtland reveals a Northern bias.

How such a bias affected UNCED — the Earth Summit — at Rio in 1992, is discussed in Chapter 9. In the meantime, in Part II, we re-examine the notion of sustainable development in the light of human need, ecological limits and the scope for extending the limitations represented by the state of technology and social organization, before discussing in Part III the deep-seated obstacles to sustainable development.

# Part II

## The Implications of Brundtland's Definition Examined

# Chapter 4 | MEETING the NEEDS of the PRESENT

In 1973, the year preceding the Cocoyoc Declaration (see p45–6), Ernst Friedrich Schumacher's *Small is Beautiful*, subtitled "a study of economics as if people mattered", was published. For Schumacher people did matter. For him, "the farmer is not merely 'a factor of production' but, before anything else, he (or she) is 'an end-in-itself', meta-economic, and in a certain sense 'sacred'" (Lutz, 1992, p102).

However, development, according to Schumacher, was more interested in factors of production than people. Although 85 per cent of the people in the South then lived in poverty in rural areas, most development funding went to projects that promoted the growth of the modern sector in the cities, thus creating a dual economy. A project such as an oil refinery was "a foreign body depending for most of its life on some other society" (Schumacher, 1973, p138), and was unrelated to the needs of the majority. Its associated economic activities would, if they depended on imported technologies and skill, hinder rather then help "healthy development", for they could not be integrated with the local society and would tend to destroy its cohesion. Development operated on the principle that "What is good for the rich must also be good for the poor", and was based on a materialist philosophy "which makes us liable to overlook the most important preconditions of success, which are generally invisible" (Schumacher, 1973, p138).

Instead, development must address the primary causes of poverty, which are "immaterial", not material: "Development does not start with goods; it starts with people and their education, organisation, and discipline. Without these three, all resources remain latent, untapped, potential" (Schumacher, 1973, p140).

Therefore, development is not primarily a problem for economists, "least of all for economists whose expertise is founded on a crudely materialist philosophy" (Schumacher, 1973, p141). Economists may well have a role to play, "but only if the general guidelines of a development policy to *involve the entire population* are already firmly established" (Schumacher, 1973, p141, original emphasis).

## WHAT NOW? ANOTHER DEVELOPMENT

Two years later, in 1975, there appeared a comprehensive analysis of the international development effort — *What Now? Another Development*, a report on "development and international co-operation". The report, which acknowledged its debt to the Founex and Cocoyoc conferences, was published by the Dag Hammarskjöld Institute in Uppsala in Sweden in time for the UN's Seventh Special Session, which was to discuss constraints on the implementation of the *International Development Strategy* formulated in 1970 (see p45).

*What Now? Another Development* argued that there was a crisis of development which affected both the North and the South. It could be seen not just in the failure to meet the basic needs of the masses in the South, but also in the "growing feelings of frustration that are disturbing the industrialized societies", and in "the alienation, whether in misery or affluence, of the masses, deprived of the means to understand and master their social and political environment" (Dag Hammarskjöld Institute, 1975, p5). These symptoms were not unrelated, so a holistic view was needed — one of the major themes of the report:

> The situation cannot be properly understood, much less transformed, unless it be seen as a whole: in the final analysis, the crises are the result of a system of exploitation which profits a power structure based largely in the industrialized world, although not without annexes in the Third World; ruling "élites" of most countries are both accomplices and rivals at the same time.

Meeting human needs in full, it was stressed, meant more than providing the wherewithal for basic subsistence. It required a form of development that respected people and the distinctiveness of their traditions and culture. Development — another development — was primarily about people:

- it meant the development of people — of the whole man and the whole woman, and not just an increase in the number of things;
- it should aim first to meet the basic needs of the poor, the majority of the world's population; and
- it should lead to the "humanization" of people by fulfilling their needs for "expression, creativity, conviviality" and control over their own affairs.

"Another development" must be viewed in a holistic conceptual framework containing three central elements, which, though they can be individually specified, must be taken together:

- development must be geared to the satisfaction of needs, beginning with the eradication of poverty,
- development must be endogenous and self-reliant, and
- development must be in harmony with the environment.

Two other points were also considered important, namely:

- "another development" requires structural transformations,
- immediate action is necessary and possible.

The report emphasized that development was about much more than economic growth, that it could not be imposed according to a single pattern, and that it must spring from people's own initiatives (Dag Hammarskjöld Institute, 1975, p7):

> *Development is a whole: it is an integral, value-loaded, cultural process; it encompasses the natural environment, social relations, education, production, consumption and well-being. The plurality of roads to development answers to the specificity of cultural or natural situations; no universal formula exists. Development is endogenous; it springs from the heart of each society, which relies first on its own strength and resources and defines in sovereignty the vision of its*

*future, co-operating with societies sharing its problems and aspirations.*

Between them, Schumacher and the Dag Hammarskjöld Institute outlined a model of development which challenged the conventional model. They led the way for a number of commentators who explored the themes of meeting the full range of human needs — self-reliance, endogenous development, diversity and living in harmony with the environment — and showed that these notions were incompatible with a development that placed so much emphasis on economic growth.

## SELF-RELIANCE

Soon after publication of *What Now? Another Development*, Johan Galtung, then professor of peace studies at Oslo University, produced the first formulation of his views on self-reliance, which he regarded as essential if the full range of human needs was to be met. Human needs could not be fulfilled, he felt, by a programme of economic development that attempted to integrate a national economy into an international economy dominated by more economically powerful nations and corporations. Such development created forms of dependence which thwarted the full development of human potential.

In looking at international economic relations, Galtung distinguishes between centre and periphery (terms used in *What Now? Another Development*), the centre dominant because of its economic (and often military) power, the periphery forced into the subservient roles of supplier of primary products and recipient, with little choice in the matter, of the technology on which its attempt to industrialize is to be based. (Such domination of the periphery by the centre also operates, according to Galtung, within a nation and within a region made up of several nations.) Economic integration means that "a division of labour takes place with the centre applying refined factors for the refined production of refined products and the periphery applying crude factors for the crude production of crude products, exchanging these with each other" (Galtung, 1986, p100).

Thus the South has become an "external sector" of the Northern economy — a source of materials, cheap labour and educated people (through the brain drain), a dump for waste and excess labour (as in colonial times), and a market where the terms of trade work to the advantage of the centre.

Galtung is particularly concerned about the impact of industrialization on peripheral countries attempting to achieve economic growth. He is not opposed to economic development as such, if it is appropriate — that is if it first meets the needs of the poorest and ultimately fulfils the larger, especially non-material, needs of all. In his view, however, industrial development fails the countries of the South on both counts. We are already familiar with the first charge (see Chapter 1). The second needs some discussion here.

Given the economic order, growth-led development necessitates the adoption of a production system, a programme of industrialization, which for a number of reasons does not directly address the needs of people. For Galtung, the most significant of these reasons is that the technological innovation which accompanies development is not just a matter of technical advance — the importation of superior but culturally neutral knowledge, skills and equipment — but also imposes alien cognitive and behavioural patterns. It therefore leads not just to changes in material standards of living, but to a cultural and even psychological dependency in the people of the peripheral nation. At both individual and community levels, people respond to economic pressure by buying the products, adopting the lifestyle, assimilating the values, and eventually sharing the preferences and assumptions of the dominant power. There takes place what Galtung (1980, p30) calls "the silent subversion of local culture through the culture and structures that always accompany the import of foreign techniques and material things in general".

In contrast, self-reliance protects a community's right — and asserts its ability — to make its own decisions about how best to satisfy the needs of its members. It emphasizes the need to respect the distinctiveness of the culture of a community, build on its traditions, and either maintain its autonomy or work for a larger degree of independence from more powerful and potentially oppressive communities. Although development agencies have not encouraged self-reliant communities, they could initiate moves that would lead to their birth, or rather rebirth, for, as

Galtung points out, small communities relying on their own resources are as old as history. (External agencies cannot, of course, lead such initiatives because communities must do this for themselves, if they are to be self-reliant.)

For Galtung, self-reliance has five basic principles:

- First, the satisfaction of basic human needs, which is a *sine qua non* of development, must not depend solely on the market, nor should economic activity be limited to this one goal.
- Second, a society seeking to become self-reliant must try to produce what it needs by relying on its own resources. This may be very challenging, but the effort of meeting such a challenge brings rewards. Galtung encourages communities contemplating self-reliance with these words: "produce what you need using your own resources, internalizing the challenges this involves, growing with the challenges, neither giving the most challenging tasks (positive externalities) to somebody else on whom you become dependent, nor exporting negative externalities to somebody else to whom you do damage and who may become dependent on you" (Galtung, 1986, p101). Thus the self-reliant society both enjoys the benefits of development and accepts responsibility for the costs, which orthodox development, operating on a larger scale, can ignore. (As examples of these costs Galtung instances "pollution, depletion, dirty, degrading, boring work, highly inegalitarian income distributions, top-heavy social formations".)
- Third, even a self-reliant society will need to trade when it finds it cannot produce all it needs from its own resources. Trade is not incompatible with self-reliance provided it takes place according to two rules: "1. The exchange should be carried out so that the net balance of costs and benefits, including externalities, for the parties to the exchange is as equal as possible. . . . 2. One field of production — production for basic needs — should be carried out in such a way that the country is at least potentially self-sufficient, not only self-reliant" (Galtung, 1986, p102). For the first rule to be met it is important for trade to be "intrasectorial rather than intersectorial; in other words exchange of primary products

(raw materials, commodities, agricultural products); or exchange of secondary products (manufactures, industrial goods including high technology); or tertiary products (services)" (Galtung, 1986, p102). Galtung sees a readiness to engage in "intersectorial" trade as ill-advised: the countries involved should pay less attention to the question of price, and give more thought to the impacts of the bargain, such as loss of positive externalities and an erosion of autonomy. Trade, especially for small communities, is also a means of exchanging non-material benefits: for Galtung (1986, p105), exchange is "one of the most powerful means of communicating, learning the habits and thoughts of others and expressing one's own".

- Fourth, self-reliance allows a community to consider moral criteria as well as purely economic ones in deciding whether to enter into transactions. Galtung (1986, p103) asserts, "Self-reliance is psycho-politics as much as economics; it presupposes, and builds, self-respect."
- Fifth, self-reliance applies not just to nations, but also to local communities and to regional groupings of nations. It is thus the basis for a form of global interdependence that does not make any one nation dependent on a more powerful one.

Self-reliance does not mean isolation. The need to trade means the interdependence of communities, each of which respects the other's aspirations to self-reliance because one community cannot achieve self-reliance by exploiting another.

A community, whether local, national or regional, maintains its self-reliance by ensuring that it trades "horizontally", that is with other communities of similar size. Galtung uses the analogy of Chinese boxes: local communities nestle inside nations, which fit into larger regions. Thus it is possible to have a system of genuine global interdependence in contrast to the inter-dependence of the prevailing economic order, *if* — a crucial proviso — the principles of self-reliance are followed (Galtung, 1986, p103).

If such a system of interdependence were established, it might result in a two-tier world in which large economic powers, or TNCs, traded with each other on one level, and countries with less economic power traded with each other on another level. Some might object to such a system, but Galtung defends it. First, it would be preferable to the existing order, which is in effect an exploitative two-tier system. Second, such an arrangement would give peripheral nations the best chance of freedom, without interference from more powerful nations or TNCs, to develop their own social and economic potential, benefiting from the challenges and accepting the responsibilities. Nations and other communities should do as much as they can for themselves. Basic human needs will only be met if communities take direct responsibility for removing obstacles and deprivations. The full range of human needs cannot be met if, by relying on others, we fail to develop our own capacities. There is no reason, Galtung suggests, "why the rest of the world should be dependent on Japan for electronics of all kinds, cameras, watches, cars and motorcycles" (Galtung, 1986, p106).

No reason why, except that the existing economic system has made it possible and is controlled (to the extent that it is possible to control such a system) by leaders who accept its momentum, if not its logic. Even people in high positions in the exploitative centre–periphery system may have something to gain from a system founded on the principle of self-reliance, for their independence too is severely constrained by the system. Their chances of meeting their own needs in full are threatened by their dependence on powerful systems which undermine their autonomy: "And even those at the very top may contemplate whether it is not also in their interests to seek arrangements with some built-in stability, being neither dependent on somebody, nor threatened by somebody dependent on them in a situation from which, sooner or later, they may want to withdraw, possibly in a very violent manner. Ultimately dependency is very unpleasant to everyone involved. Yet it is the consequence of conventional economic theory and practice" (Galtung, 1986, p106).

Thus Galtung argues that both the cultural autonomy of communities and ultimately the empowerment of individuals is essential for the fufilment of our needs. Self-reliance means not just meeting basic human needs, but also fulfilling our needs for identity, creativity, self-expression and action. In the absence of self-reliance, development, which is an agent of exploitative economic power, creates a psychological dependence. The citizen of a periphery, becomes "a pupil learning how to produce and consume" (Galtung, 1980, p29). He or she abandons traditional values and may come to despise indigenous products and practices. Such effects are in Galtung's opinion "possibly the most devastating consequence of the present world order and the most difficult to remedy" (Galtung, 1980, p29). The role of the passive "pupil" of alien ways is very difficult to unlearn. Dependence once established is very difficult to undo. All the prestige of the refined factors emanating from the centre work against efforts to end it, even supposing that the dependent see the need to do so. Successful efforts to achieve self-reliance have other and larger benefits than material gains. As Galtung points out, a community that devises its own way of meeting a need does less damage to its autonomy and self-respect than one that adopts a ready-made product or technique, even if its solution is technologically less advanced. Ultimately, the community that seeks its own solutions with some support from other communities with no interest in domination will gain — in initiative, creativity and problem-solving capacity — over the community that cannot prevent others taking over, or allows them to do so.

In considering the plight of peripheral communities Galtung is thinking primarily of the countries of the South. However, his centre–periphery analysis is equally valid when applied to the nations in the North. It is also of fundamental importance for local and community development in the North, for it challenges deeply entrenched assumptions about development which have destroyed diversity in both rural and urban peripheries and removed a range of skilled workers who could once provide goods and services for which we are now dependent on larger centres or distant conglomerates.

## LOCAL SOLUTIONS: CENTRE AND PERIPHERY REVISITED

Robert Chambers of the Institute of Development Studies at the University of Sussex also makes a distinction between centre and periphery. Where Galtung examines how the fulfilment of needs is affected by the economic power of the centre, Chambers focuses on how those most in need fail to benefit even from "well-intentioned" aid and development programmes unless they have an opportunity to participate in and contribute to the planning process. Chambers first formulated his critique in his *Rural Development: Putting the Last First* (1983) and developed it in later work. Although Chambers confines himself to rural poverty in the South, much of what he says applies to urban poverty there too. Moreover, a great deal of what he says can be applied to poverty in the North as well.

Centres, or "cores", which exist in even the poorest countries, concentrate wealth and power, as Chambers (1986, p305) notes:

> *The wealth and power of the cores attract and sustain concentrations of professionals, resources and capacity to generate and spread knowledge. The knowledge of the cores is prestigious, and described as modern, scientific, advanced, sophisticated and high technology. It is also powerful, being supported by and supporting the machinery of the state and of commerce. As a colonizing, unifying and standardizing force, it pushes out into the peripheries, propagated through communications, commercialization and education.*

In contrast, peripheries are inhabited by an "unconnected scatter" of "powerless, low status and poor" people, whose skills and knowledge are undervalued, even when recognized, by the "bearers of modernity". In a sardonic allusion to core priorities, Chambers refers to the attitudes and values of "core people" as "first thinking", and the outlook of "periphery people" as "last thinking". However, it is astonishing, says Chambers, how often the professionals (and he has the grace to include himself), with all the power of science and other resources behind them, have been wrong — about the poor, about their methods of subsistence, about the nature of deprivation, about malnutrition: "It is alarming how wrong we were, and how sure we were we were right. And it is humbling and sobering to speculate on how many of the 'first' beliefs of today may in their turn prove to be wrong" (Chambers, 1986, p306).

Such errors may be due to a number of factors such as arrogance, bias, prejudice and stereotypes. However, in Chambers's opinion, two explanations stand out. First, core values dominate development planning. However, the solutions that commend themselves to core thinking (for example, exotic breeds, cash crops and "high-tech" inputs) are not necessarily appropriate to the conditions with which the poor have to contend. The net result is that "first" solutions are most appealing and beneficial to the "least poor", while the needs of the poor for a greater number of basic inputs and fewer sophisticated ones are neglected.

The second centres on what Chambers calls "the structure of first thinking", which is based on three assumptions: the growth and spread of economic activity is essential for development; analyses or solutions based on science and quantification are better than those that are not; and "first people" teach "last" people and not vice versa: "thus, instead of open-ended empirical investigation of the last being allowed to generate last theory, first theory is imposed on it" (Chambers, 1986, p311).

The emphasis on creating employment is an illustration of how elitist preconceptions shape development patterns. The notion of formal work carried out at a workplace during set, fixed hours for a wage paid in cash may be alien to the rural poor, whose priority is to sustain and improve "a repertoire of activities which will provide them with an adequate and secure level of living around the year" (Chambers, 1986, p313). Such livelihoods are threatened both by the preconceptions of development professionals and by the encroachment of progress generally. Where core people see progress, "last people" feel their survival threatened. As Chambers (1992, p215) puts it:

> In that view [the view from the periphery], the rich are seen as engaged on a massive scale in destroying and rendering less secure the livelihoods of the poor. The rich compete for and appropriate resources. Common land is enclosed and encroached by the wealthy. Forests, fisheries and ranching lands are appropriated by government and commercial interests. A common pattern is that logging and ranching interests, sometimes with corrupt forestry officials, contractors and politicians, come first and cut out the timber, and then poor cultivators come in their wake. ... There are many patterns and variations, but on a very wide scale, the core invasions of the rich North and of the rich in the South are appropriating and degrading resources on which the rural poor depend.

Chambers points out that although people working in development have begun to study more closely the question of who gains and who loses by development, the poor are rarely given priority in development planning. When they are consulted about their needs, their priorities vary but, Chambers (1992, pp216–17) argues, certain themes predominate:

> In addition [to health], a common and almost universal priority expressed is the desire for an adequate, secure and decent livelihood which provides for physical and social well-being. This includes security against sickness, against early death, and against becoming poorer, and thus secure command over assets as well as income, and good chances of survival. Again and again, when they are asked, poor people give replies which fit these points. A phrase to summarize all this is livelihood security.

In place of such obviously unsustainable development, Chambers (1992, p217)) proposes sustainable livelihood security, an "integrating concept" developed by the Brundtland Commission's advisory panel on food, agriculture, forestry and the environment: "Livelihood is defined as adequate stocks and flows of food and cash to meet basic needs. Security refers to secure ownership of, or access to, resources and income-earning activities, including reserves and assets to offset risk, ease shocks and meet contingencies. Sustainable refers to the maintenance or enhancement of resource productivity on a long-term basis."

Programmes designed to enhance sustainable livelihood security will have a beneficial impact on the interconnected problems of population, resources, development and the environment. Their effect will be fourfold. Security of land tenure, for example, should

- help slow the rate of population growth;
- reduce migration into areas vulnerable to human pressures, for the poor will have an incentive to manage the resources to which they have access;
- help the poor survive bad times and so be better able to ward off encroaching "core" appropriation, ever ready to snap up the assets impoverished people are forced to sell: "it is where people are legally, politically and physically weak, and lack secure rights to resources, that they are most vulnerable" (Chambers, 1992, p218);

- encourage the poor to have confidence that, with secure ownership of resources, they have reason to farm wisely and develop assets to pass on to their children: "poor people ... can be, and often are, tenacious in their retention of assets and far-sighted in their investments. It is misleading to confuse the behaviour of those who are very poor and desperate with that of those who are poor but not desperate" (Chambers, 1992, p218).

Such behaviour differs considerably from that of many representatives of "core" interests who often take a short-term view, looking no further than the next election, or the quick profits to be made out of community resources. In contrast, the poor, without the supposed benefit of "core" economic concepts, have the wisdom to resist the temptations of the high internal rate of return and instead apply negligible discount rates to their assessment of future benefits.

In a paper for the Only One Earth Conference in 1987, Chambers (1989) reported how case studies confirmed that "the ability of poor people to take a long-term view depends on how secure they judge their rights and gains to be". The studies also showed that the sustainability of the projects owed more to "last" than to "first" thinking, for the promoters of projects put the livelihoods of local people first, allowing them to gain secure and decent livings for themselves and their children. The five major lessons of such work are:

- "development" is a learning process, not just the application of a predetermined blueprint;
- the priorities of the people must be put first;
- the rights and gains of local people must be made secure;
- sustainable livelihood is achieved through self-help ("all forms of paternalism should be avoided completely" — except in cases of extreme hardship); and
- the "calibre, commitment and continuity of staff" is crucial.

Chambers (1992, p219) concludes his critique of "core"-initiated development in unequivocal terms:

*The implication . . . is that poor people are not the problem but the solution. . . . If conditions are right they can be predisposed to want smaller families, to stay where they are, to resist and repulse short-term exploitation from the cores, and to take a long view in their husbandry of resources. The predisposing conditions for this are that they command resources, rights and livelihoods which are adequate, sustainable and above all secure.*

## HUMAN SCALE DEVELOPMENT

The idea that poor people are the solution rather than the problem is one of the major themes of *Human Scale Development* by Manfred Max-Neef, who is rector of Valdivia University and has directed the work of the Alternative Development Centre in Chile, which attempts to plan the basis for action programmes in various parts of South America. Max-Neef criticizes conventional economic development in South America, but also argues that the fulfilment of human needs is not just a long-term objective, but also the essential means by which people-centred development comes about: "fundamental human needs must and can be realized from the outset and throughout the entire process of development. In this manner, the realization of needs becomes instead of a goal, the motor of development itself" (Max-Neef, 1991, p53).

Max-Neef formulates a theory of human need which is partly a response to the emphasis on basic needs in the UN and elsewhere, and partly a reaction to the economic development in South America, where the neo-liberal monetarism of the 1980s had "social costs" which, he claims, were kept under control only by repression. His model of development has therefore a special application in South America, with its particular problems of hyperinflation, social inequalities and fragile democracy, but also has a much wider relevance.

Max-Neef argues that if development is to serve people it must aim not simply to raise material standards but also to improve the quality of their lives. This depends ultimately on satisfying their non-material needs, for example developing their creative potential as individuals so that they can contribute to and benefit from the communities to which they belong.

Development must aim to fulfil *fundamental* rather than *basic* human needs. Max-Neef sees the basic needs approach as an extension of conventional development with its assumption that there is a simple relationship between the production of material goods and the fulfilling of human need. Development has encouraged people to think of both wealth — and poverty — in material or monetary terms. There are several "poverties", for example of protection, understanding and participation as well as of subsistence. Each of these can be disabling, preventing people from fulfilling their individual potential and barring society from developing the institutions and civil processes on which a civilized way of life depends. As a result "collective pathologies" develop, with huge social costs and these have increased dramatically (and will continue to increase), for attempts to treat the social symptoms have proved ineffectual.

Max-Neef asserts that human needs, unlike wants, are few and finite in number, are the same in all cultures and have been virtually the same throughout history, changing only at the pace of the evolution of the human species. In fact, including subsistence, there are just nine fundamental needs, the other eight being protection, affection, understanding, participation, idleness, creation, identity and freedom.[1] These must be seen as interacting in a systematic way rather than being related hierarchically, with the exception of the need for subsistence which he accepts has priority over the others.[2]

Needs may be few and unchanging, but the ways in which we satisfy these needs — "the satisfiers" — vary both from time to time and from place to place. A culture is partly defined by the satisfiers it has chosen or developed, and part of what is happening during the process of cultural change in a society is that some satisfiers are being abandoned in favour of others. Maintaining his objection to the materialist conception of need referred to above, Max-Neef insists on a distinction between satisfiers, "a whole range of forms of social organization and the cultural 'products' available, and goods, which are in a *strict sense*

1. Max-Neef has recently identified a tenth fundamental need — transcendence (Ulrich Loening, personal communication).
2. Here Max-Neef seems to be reacting against Maslow's (1970) hierarchy of needs, which is probably still the best starting point for those who would like to explore this topic in more depth.

the means by which individuals will empower the satisfiers to meet their needs" (Max-Neef, 1991, p25). For example, one of the satisfiers of the need for protection is some form of health care. Whether it be traditional medicine, or a health service, it will make use of whatever physical means are available: drugs, equipment, buildings will vary from society to society. However, when the forces controlling economic activity "make goods ends in themselves, then the alleged satisfaction of a need impairs its capacity to create [human] potential" (Max-Neef, 1991, p25).

Max-Neef goes on to introduce two very important ideas. First, despite their name, not all satisfiers satisfy. Some fail to do so and so help generate the pathologies referred to above: for example, participation in the nuclear arms race is a non-satisfier, a "destroyer", of the need for protection and generates an additional need for protection from an additional fear. Max-Neef distinguishes five types of satisfiers, four of which are unsatisfactory. These four — destroyers, pseudo-satisfiers, inhibiting satisfiers, singular satisfiers — are imposed from above or from outside. Thus formal democracy is a pseudo-satisfier, seemingly satisfying the need for participation; authoritarian teaching is an inhibiting satisfier, seemingly satisfying the need for understanding, but inhibiting needs for participation, creation, identity and freedom; "food aid" is an example of a singular satisfier that may satisfy one need but contributes nothing to the satisfaction of other needs. The fifth type of satisfier is the "synergic satisfier", which can both satisfy a given need and also contribute to the fulfilment of other needs. For example, a mother feeding her baby not only meets its need for subsistence, but both awakens and provides for its need for protection, affection and identity. Synergic satisfiers are non- or even anti-authoritarian and challenge conventional values of coercion and competitiveness. They frequently originate in voluntary action, which usually involves co-operation at grass-roots level.

Second, discussion of needs tends to concentrate on the idea of need as deprivation. Max-Neef reminds us that need has a positive aspect, which should be viewed as a potential rather than as a lack or deprivation. Our need for subsistence impels us to develop ways of making food available for ourselves, our families and our communities; our need to be creative members of society is not simply experienced as an unfulfilled yearning or a dissatisfaction at the lack of various opportunities for social interaction, but also as a positive urge to interact with people and make something happen — just as our need for affection leads us to "give" in ways that enrich the lives of others as well as to feel deprived when excluded from or bereft of loving attention.

These two ideas, the endogenous source of synergic satisfiers (springing from the hearts and imaginations of people themselves, even, paradoxically, in a people dominated by economic power and at risk of being disabled by a variety of "false" satisfiers) and, second, the potential for human achievement that fundamental needs represent are at the centre of Max-Neef's (1991, p38) conception of human scale development. They are both the aim of development and the means by which that aim is fulfilled:

> *Development geared to the satisfaction of fundamental human needs cannot, by definition, be structured from the top downwards. It cannot be imposed either by law or decree. It can only emanate directly from the actions, expectations, and creative and critical awareness of the protagonists themselves. Instead of being the traditional objects of development, people must take a leading role in development.*

Human scale development means moving from dependence on a complex of closely allied political and economic interests to autonomy or self-reliance. Max-Neef's self-reliance has much in common with Galtung's. It involves small-scale development at the community level where personal and social development can support one another, working first with those most in need (for the synergic satisfiers work most effectively "bottom up"). This micro-development must be complemented at the macro level by the "horizontal" interdependence of nations, which will not only pursue the objectives of economic development, social justice, personal development and freedom, but will also respect diversity and refuse to make progress at the expense of others' self-reliance. Any move from dependence to autonomy will require "deep structural changes" in relations between the state and civil society. The state will have to be willing both to surrender power and play an enabling role, for it will not be enough simply to end domination: "we cannot do away with dependence till we rediscover and then nurture the initiatives of social organizations at grass-roots level" (Max-Neef, 1991, p62).

Max-Neef regards "the invisible world" of the informal sector of the economy, which is extremely large in South America, as very important for human scale development. Here people struggle to improve livelihoods on the margins of formal economic activity in inauspicious circumstances. These both indicate the extent of the sociopolitico-economic crisis in South America and point to the future, for Max-Neef sees a network of embryonic self-reliant communities, which has evolved "an ethics of solidarity" and represents "a wealth of social creativity".

The "invisible world" maximizes the resources economics disregards. Within it, work is not just a factor of production but a form of social interaction through which, in a variety of settings — individual self-employment, family workshops, associations, small community organizations and micro-enterprises — individuals refine skills and develop their abilities in ways that help them improve their living conditions. Work is thus not just a factor of production but a varied resource which "fosters creativity, mobilizes social energy, preserves community identity, deploys solidarity and utilizes organizational experience and popular knowledge for the satisfaction of individual and collective needs" (Max-Neef, 1991, p77).

However, work — "more than just a resource, . . . a generator of resources" (Max-Neef, 1991, p78) — is only one synergic satisfier. Others include "nonconventional resources" (that is, resources other than those normally thought of as "economic resources") — "social awareness, organizational know-how and managerial ability, popular creativity, solidarity and ability to provide mutual aid, the expertise and training provided by training agencies, and dedication and commitment from internal and external agents" (Max-Neef, 1991, p79).

Max-Neef points to the great potential and special nature of these resources: "It is necessary to stress a very special peculiarity that distinguishes conventional from nonconventional resources. While the former are depleted when used, the latter are lost only to the extent to which they are not used". In contrast to power and money, solidarity grows when shared; knowledge is enlarged as it is communicated (Max-Neef, 1991, p79). Human resources are abundant, and their potential huge: "unlike conventional economic resources, which are characterized by scarcity, nonconventional resources are plentiful. They also have a tremendous capacity to preserve and transform social energy for processes of deep change" (Max-Neef, 1991, p79).

Nonconventional resources have one other important quality — they complement conventional resources. Empowered local people get the best out of local resources. Max-Neef contrasts their efforts with the frequent lack of success of prestigious and often lavishly resourced projects. Such failures can be ascribed to "their inability to motivate people and arouse the endogenous potential of the groups that they intend to benefit" (MaxNeef, 1991, p80). They underline the fact that it is "the capacity of the human being to activate his or her sensitivity, imagination, volition, and intellectual talent" that is the most valuable resource in furthering the true aims of development, for "the strengthening of these nonconventional resources also involves the strengthening of community participation and of self-reliance (Max-Neef, 1991, p80).

## CONCLUSION

Needs cannot be fully met either through economic development, which serves alien economic interests and therefore oppresses rather than liberates people, or by "help" from external agencies, which assume that local people have nothing to contribute to the development process and attempt to impose "top-down" or "centre-outward" approaches.

Instead, to meet needs in full we need to support people so that they can liberate and then harness the potential their own innate abilities represent. Needs begin to be met from the moment true (that is liberating or enabling as opposed to alien, imposed or excessively materialistic) development starts. At this point the distinction between ends and means, the "end-product" of fulfilled needs and the process of development, begins to disappear. Once the basic material needs of subsistence are met, people do not benefit from aid projects unless they have some involvement in the process. Needs are met as potential is fulfilled — as people respond to the enabling actions of others on their behalf and find challenges and discover opportunities to which they are drawn or feel impelled to respond. In so doing they find themselves fulfilled and their lives enlarged as they are enabled to participate, to enlarge their understanding and awareness, to interact with others, to use their creativity, to discover their identity and to enjoy liberation.

# Chapter 5

# THE SUSTAINABLE USE of RESOURCES

Given unlimited resources, we would be able to meet the fundamental human needs of the present generation without having to consider whether our activities might deny similar opportunities to succeeding generations, whose fundamental human needs will, if Max-Neef is correct, be similar to our own. In a finite world, however, in which the human population is set to double and natural capital is depleted and degraded in increasing quantities, we cannot assume that resources exist in sufficient quantity to continue to meet fundamental needs.

It is therefore important to try to formulate principles for the sustainable use of natural resources, now and in the future, and in particular for the use of nonrenewable resources, for any consumption of these reduces the quantity available for future generations. Can we devise a set of principles for the sustainable use of resources that will lead to practical guidelines for sustainable development?[1]

## THE BIOSPHERE

Any form of social or economic development is, like life itself, ultimately dependent on the biosphere, a complex "whole" which sustains a multitude of living species in a variety of media. It is held in balance by interwoven and often interdependent

---

1. This chapter is much indebted to Michael Jacobs's treatment of these issues in *The Green Economy*.

ecosystems whose stability is maintained by flows of energy (derived from the sun), the recycling of nutrients and the inter-actions of animate organisms and inanimate matter. These eco-systems are of different scales, larger systems being composed of smaller ones and ascending hierarchically to the biosphere itself.

This complex provides us with a vast range of "resources" or "goods", which are commonly grouped in three categories:

- material resources, the "primary products" which we mine, extract or harvest;
- assimilative capacities, which allow us to dispose of wastes;
- "services", which can be subdivided into "life-support" ser-vices such as the maintenance of the gaseous composition of the atmosphere, the regulation of the earth's temperature and the maintenance of weather patterns (on which the stability and diversity of ecosystems depend); and amenity services, the satisfactions (such as aesthetic pleasure, recreation, com-munion with nature and the satisfaction of intellectual curiosity) which we gain from the diversity of landscapes, flora and fauna.

In practice it can be quite hard to separate these categories. For example, renewable resources contribute to systems that have the capacity to absorb and assimilate waste; the atmosphere has an assimilative capacity and also plays a major role in the maintenance of life-support services.

## NATURAL CAPITAL

The word "resources" is commonly used to refer to material resources. The full range of resources or goods with which the biosphere supplies us — material resources, capacities and ser-vices — is frequently referred to collectively as "natural capital". Despite its overtones of economic valuation, this seems a useful and appropriate term for several reasons. It suggests that these "goods" are analogous to a stock of wealth which can provide an income. Moreover, such an income can be maintained over time if capital is conserved. We can deplete such capital for short-term gain, but this reduces the level of future income. It may be very difficult to make good any depletion of capital and in extreme cases, of course, squandering capital leads to permanent impoverishment.[2]

## Material Resources

Material resources are "products" of the natural world with an economic value for humankind. The Indians of the American plains valued every part of the buffalo as a resource. Present day perceptions of what constitutes a resource vary from place to place. The poorest people in Delhi scavenge so thoroughly that a waste incinerator supplied under foreign aid has nothing to burn. People in several African countries regard a species of flying ant as a food resource, although most people in the North are probably uncomfortable with the thought of eating insects. Our perception of resources also changes over time. Whalebone, which was considered an important resource in this country 100 years ago, no longer seems of any particular value. Derelict machinery indicates where the extraction of small local deposits of minerals was abandoned long before the resource was exhausted.

The identification of features of the natural world as resources reflects human priorities among the many options for satisfying needs (and indulging desires) as well as the range and sophistication of available technologies. Resources are social constructs rather than entities in the natural world. Our assessment of the economic value of the resources we identify as important to us leads to statements about reserves, the known quantities of specific resources that can be exploited economically. It is for instance in this functional, utilitarian mode that we talk of people as a "reserve of labour".[3]

These considerations lead many writers to the view that the most important resources are not natural but human, and that the most important of these are humankind's ingenuity, resourcefulness and adaptability. It is these qualities — the creative potential in our fundamental needs, in Max-Neef's terms — that have made possible human settlements in environments as

2. For an account of one community afflicted by permanent impoverishment, see Clive Ponting's chapter, "The Lessons of Easter Island" (Ponting, 1991).
3. I am grateful to John Kirkby for suggestions in this section.

diverse and "inhospitable" as the Arctic fringe of northern America, the high dry plateaux of the Andes and Himalayas, and the equatorial rainforests. These qualities have also made possible the accumulation over generations of social and human-made capital, which has allowed us to develop technological expertise, financial institutions and educational systems. These in turn have led to the identification and exploitation of other resources in the natural world and have, in so doing or even by their very existence, created a demand for an even greater range of resources. Technological advance and entrepreneurial expertise function as positive feedback, continually spurring on human inventiveness and stimulating the "discovery" and exploitation of more and more resources.

In discussing material resources it is customary to distinguish between renewable and nonrenewable ones. Renewable resources are mostly derived from living organisms, such as animals and plants. They regenerate by natural processes and are not necessarily depleted when a "crop" is taken. They regenerate naturally more or less continuously, or can be managed in order to replace depletion of their stocks over relatively short time scales (in Britain up to say 200 or 300 years in the case of hardwoods). Their ability to renew themselves is of course dependent on the systems that supply moisture and nutrients, and that maintain the media of air and soil in which they grow. Air and water are also regarded as renewable resources. They too are dependent on the health of the ecosystems in which other renewable resources, particularly plant life, play an important role.

Nonrenewable resources do not reproduce themselves in nature. They are mostly minerals, for example metals and fossil fuels. Soils are generally included, although they contain living organisms. Nonrenewable resources are replenished, if they regenerate at all, only over geological time, for example through the formation of soil and fossil fuels. Many minerals exist in vast quantities in the earth's crust, but usually in very low concentrations: geological formations containing high concentrations of minerals are comparatively rare. There is a large quantitative difference between, say, a mineral resource — the total estimated amount of that mineral dispersed throughout the earth's crust — and the reserves of that mineral, namely the quantities known to exist (as a result of prospecting or exploration) and which it is technically possible to extract. There may be economic reasons why some reserves are not worth extracting, so we need another distinction between reserves and usable or recoverable reserves (see Figure 5.1). Changes in economic conditions may increase the quantity of usable reserves. The limits to the proportion of reserves that can be extracted are, however, set by the amount of energy required for their extraction and not by price. Reserves of nonrenewable resources may increase as further exploration is carried out. This can happen even during rapid industrial growth, which may stimulate exploration. Advances in technology, such as new deep-sea drilling techniques, can also mean that reserves in accessible places become recoverable. Advances in technology that reduce the amount of a resource used in a production process also lengthen the life of a reserve.

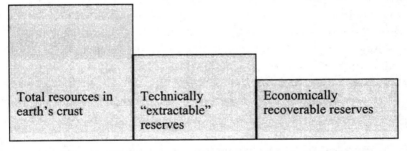

*Figure 5.1 Resources and reserves (not to scale)*

The distinction between renewable and nonrenewable resources only takes us so far, however. First, nonrenewable resources are depletable (or exhaustible), but so are flora and fauna, which are renewable. The other renewables — air and water — are nondepletable (or inexhaustible), and are more accurately described as "self-renewing", or better still, "continuing". Second, the distinction between renewables and nonrenewables is less useful when we turn from material resources to look at assimilative capacities and services. Though these depend largely on the continuing rather than the renewable resources of the planet, they also partly rely on cycles (for example the oxygen, carbon and hydrological cycles) that are themselves dependent on depletable living organisms (such as trees and other flora). To complicate matters even further, though these cycles operate on a global scale, they may be dependent on small but significant inputs from nonrenewables (such as chemicals released from minerals in rocks and soils) and may contribute over aeons of geological time to the renewal of "nonrenewable" resources. This complexity means that it is necessary to look at resources very carefully when considering implications for sustainable development.

The principle underlying the sustainable use of renewable resources is clear. To ensure that succeeding generations have as much access to these as we have, we must utilize them at rates lower than, or at most equal to, the rates at which they regenerate. This principle applies equally to depletable renewables (flora and fauna) and to other renewable resources (fresh air and clean water) the quality of which can be maintained only if wastes are kept below critical rates of emission. Renewable resources can also be increased in certain circumstances, given appropriate management. For example, forest cover in Denmark has more than doubled over the last 100 years. As Michael Jacobs points out in *The Green Economy* (1991), we can think of renewable resources as being like a savings account: it is possible not only to live off the "interest" but also to increase the holding.

In calculating a sustainable rate of "harvest" we must, however, bear in mind that the renewability of these resources depends on the health of the ecosystems in which they regenerate. Neither forests nor fish stocks renew themselves unaided. Continuing yields of timber will depend on the maintenance of vegetative cover and soil fertility, the survival of micro-organisms and the preservation of suitable hydrological conditions, just as future catches of individual species of fish depend on maintaining the integrity of marine ecosystems.

It is possible to exceed sustainable rates of use or extraction for relatively short periods over comparatively small areas without completely destroying the chances of a return to sustainable production, provided human communities manage the recovery of an unsustainably depleted stock before it declines to a critical minimum below which survival or regeneration is impossible. While the recovery is taking place people must either make do

with less or turn to some other natural or manu.
To fulfil the criterion of sustainable use, the rate
of any alternative resource would also have to b₁
recovery rate.

Therefore the recovery must restore the full di
ecosystem. All too often, unfortunately, this does n₁ ...appen, as
in attempts at re-afforestation after the clear-felling of old-growth
forests. Even when regeneration or replanting is successful in the
sense that biomass production is resumed, sustainability is not
met if biodiversity — the full range of species belonging to the
forest ecosystem — is permanently reduced, or if the livelihoods
of forest peoples are irreversibly impaired.

Full ecological restoration after a period of unsustainable
extraction or depletion is only possible if the crucial systems —
the cycles supplying vital chemicals and rainfall, and ensuring
temperature, humidity and atmospheric composition — are
unimpaired. Since forests contribute to the maintenance of these
systems by protecting soils, modifying climate and absorbing
carbon dioxide, unchecked deforestation will eventually reach a
point at which the reduction of living biomass means a
disruption of these cycles, with local and possibly global impacts.

Our current dependence on fossil fuels and extracted minerals
is an immediate and obvious challenge to any attempt to
formulate a principle for their sustainable use. Any consumption
of nonrenewable natural resources, for example, soils, metals and
fossil fuels, means a reduction of the future stock. However, it is
equally clear that the industrialized world would come to a
complete halt within a matter of days if a total ban on the further
use of nonrenewables were suddenly imposed.

Many nonrenewable natural resources (for example mineral
deposits) can be thought of as "inert" in that they do not
contribute, except possibly over geological time, to flows through
ecosystems and to the cycles of essential chemical elements. They
therefore make little contribution to capacities and services and
their value to humankind depends largely on the size of the
demand for them. This in turn will be affected not only by our
estimates of their importance in meeting human needs but also
by such questions as the availability of substitutes, the perceptions of the ecological and human costs of extracting them

which include, for example, spoil tips on good land, tailings and effects on miners' health). The scarcity of, say, a mineral may not be important if there is no demand for it. However, a strict application of the Brundtland definition would mean that we should take deliberate steps to conserve even a relatively small stock so that each generation has the chance to decide for itself that there is indeed no demand.

A number of attempts have been made to formulate principles for the sustainable use of nonrenewable resources for which there is a demand. These are based on two ideas: relative rather than absolute scarcity (a mineral may be in short supply, but this will not matter if there is little demand for it); and some form of management of demand as well as supply. One suggestion is that the rate of depletion of nonrenewables should be adjusted to ensure that known reserves do not fall below a certain minimum level of "stock" equivalent to consumption for a specified number of years at current rates. However, this could only be regarded as the basis of a policy for sustainable use if new recoverable reserves continue to be found. If they are not, the choice is between depleting the minimum reserve and a collapse of production systems dependent on the resource. Moreover, because discoveries of new reserves are not made at an even pace, the permitted rate of depletion would presumably fluctuate, depending on how near the minimum level consumption had brought known reserves. Furthermore, the idea of a minimum reserve raises problems. How large or small should this reserve be? Have we a right to specify for future generations an "adequate" minimum that would almost certainly be less than the amount we have consumed?

Another suggestion is that demand for a renewable resource should be managed so that the rate of depletion falls as the demand declines. Any policies based on such a principle would rest on three assumptions: first, that a substitute is readily available; second, that the transition can be made in time; and third, that the exhausted stock is not only regarded as non-essential by the present generation, but will also prove to be regarded as such by succeeding ones (if they have any knowledge of it). An amendment of this policy would better safeguard the interests of future generations, namely that the present generation be required to begin to manage demand early enough to ensure that declining demand and declining rates of depletion both reach zero before the stock is exhausted. This is one example of a precautionary approach which, as we shall see in Chapter 6, is an important element of a sustainable strategy.

However, unless substitutes are available, neither suggestion guarantees a long-term sustainable solution to the problems posed by the exhaustion of a nonrenewable resource on which we depend for life as we know it. A more satisfactory approach is based on two principles:

- minimizing our consumption of nonrenewable resources — the various ways in which this can be done are discussed in Chapter 6 — and
- using at least some nonrenewable resources for developing "renewable" replacements.

The key element in any policy based on the second principle would be to use nonrenewable resources to build renewable energy-generating capacity, which would free us from our dependence on nonrenewable fossil fuels. Renewable energy would then be used to implement policies for reducing our consumption of other nonrenewable resources.[4]

The ideas of a minimum stock and reduction in demand being matched by reduction in depletion have a part to play in such a policy; they help to focus the debate on such matters as the speed with which renewable replacements can be made available and the rate at which demand should be reduced. This in turn would affect decisions about what proportion of fossil fuels and other nonrenewable resources should be earmarked for creating the substitutes to replace them.

The limited reserves and the ecological impact (such as acidification and $CO_2$ emissions) of the fossil fuels on which we currently depend mean that we should give a high priority to

4.  Salah El Serafy, an Egyptian economist working in the USA, has devised a formula for dividing income from a nonrenewable resource, North Sea oil, into 'capital' (to be used to fund replacement renewable generating capacity) and income. For a brief account, see Ekins and Max-Neef (1992, pp413–416).

finding replacements. However, the importance of minimizing our consumption of other nonrenewable resources, such as aluminium or copper, may need more explanation. Why should their depletion be reduced to zero when there are large reserves of many nonrenewable resources? And what sense does it make for generation after generation to hand on constant stocks of resources that are never exploited?

There are several answers to the first question. For a start, even if we can "afford" to deplete reserves, their extraction, consumption and eventual "fate" as one form of waste or another will have serious costs — which will be measured in terms of impacts on human welfare (for example the health of miners) and the degradation of both human-made capital and other forms of natural capital. Also, continued wasteful, inefficient or profligate use of nonrenewable minerals hastens the day when the energy problem becomes a major crisis and increases the urgency of the need to find renewable substitutes for fossil fuels. Such use also increases the human and environmental costs. The latter argument is reinforced by the fact that new reserves tend either to have lower grade ores or be in inaccessible places, thus requiring more energy to extract them.

However, the second question remains. What, it might be argued, is the point of handing on indefinitely into the future a stock of resources if it is never to be used? There are at least two answers. First, passing on such a legacy is the consequence of imposing rigorous limits on the scale of pollution and other impacts of the consumption of nonrenewable resources: an undiminished legacy demonstrates that we have prevented an increase in the unsustainable costs of further depletion. The second is based on our inability to guarantee that such assets will never be used. Just as for this generation one of the most important contributions to the development of a more sustainable use of resources — the creation of a renewable energy-generating capacity — requires the consumption of more nonrenewables, so for future generations there may arise similar situations in which the availability of a nonrenewable resource may be crucial in helping avoid massive social, economic or technological break-downs. Thus the principle of intergenerational equity requires us to manage our transitions to more sustainable systems without denying future generations the same ability to meet contingencies. This we may do if we fail to conserve natural assets that may prove valuable to future generations in their attempt to maintain the transition to sustainable development. The wider the range of nonrenewable resources we conserve, the fewer the constraints we impose on future generations.

For sustainability, the optimal rate of depletion of "resource" natural capital is not that of conventional economics (see for example Pearce and Turner, 1990), but is determined by three factors:

- estimates of the amount of resources required to build replacement human-made capital;
- the speed at which such replacement can be carried out; and
- assessments of how much other natural capital we feel entitled to consume.

A sustainable policy on nonrenewables does not require a complete ban on their consumption, but involves wise, economical use so we leave as large stocks as possible for future generations. Most importantly, a proportion of nonrenewables should be set aside for producing replacements. The use of fossil fuels (a form of natural capital) to help manufacture renewable energy-generating capacity (replacement human-made capital) is considered a sustainable use of nonrenewable capital. If such a policy is followed, "no future society should find itself built around the use of a resource that is suddenly no longer available or affordable" (Meadows, 1992, p209).

### Capacities

So far the discussion has focused on the material resources we mine, extract or harvest in some way. The earth's assimilative capacities — the atmosphere, rivers, oceans and terrestrial ecosystems we use as "sinks" for wastes — are best thought of as renewable resources.[5] They are valuable as resources not only because of their capacity to assimilate wastes, but also because

---

5. Landfill sites would seem to be an exception here. They are most appropriately thought of as an exhaustible stock of nonrenewable resources.

they play a role in supporting depletable renewable resources (flora and fauna) and in contributing to the recycling of continuing resources such as fresh air and clean water. Rates of emission must therefore take into account the full ecological value of these capacities. Once the quality of the media on which we rely for the dispersal of wastes is impaired, the ecosystems they support may no longer produce yields that can be harvested usefully or even safely, and may even collapse. The Great Lakes fisheries are a salutary example. Toxic substances may prevent the full recovery of ecosystems for many years, or effectively in perpetuity, as in the contamination of soils and ground water by heavy metals, dioxins or radionuclides leaching from a nuclear waste repository.

Therefore, only wastes that can be broken down by natural processes should be discharged into ecosystems where they are dispersed and assimilated. The principle for sustainability is that the rate of discharge of wastes must not exceed the rate at which these flows can be assimilated without the ecosystem suffering negative impacts. The ability of air and water to disperse wastes over wide areas or through large volumes is an important factor in determining the rate at which systems can assimilate wastes and hence the rate at which quantities of wastes can be emitted. This is not, however, an argument for dispersing "non-bio-degradable" or toxic substances at low concentrations over wide areas, although this has been a common practice. Emissions of radioactive material from the Sellafield nuclear complex in northwest England are just one example. Recent evidence of the effects of waste oestrogen compounds on male fertility in certain aquatic species in Florida and in the UK also indicate the possible dangers. The evidence of DDT in the milk of Inuit mothers and of the dispersal of radioactive material after Chernobyl illustrates both how widely wind and water may disperse substances and also how the value of dispersal becomes a liability once eco-systems are contaminated.

It follows that "stocks" of toxic wastes should not be stored in the environment if there is a risk of their accidental dispersal. As the production of such wastes cannot cease overnight, the principle for sustainable use of resources must be that their production should cease as soon as possible, and certainly before so-called "safe" — often, more accurately remote — storage sites are used up. Technologies that depend on storage in the biosphere, or indeed in the geosphere (as in the case of proposed nuclear waste repositories), should be foregone.

## Life-Support Services

Life-support services depend on global ecological systems, which maintain a dynamic balance of stocks and flows in the biosphere and so help regulate the composition of the atmosphere, global temperature, climatic zones and weather patterns. The processes on which these large systems depend are partly driven by resources that are unaffected by human activity, such as sunlight and gravity. However, though global in scale and impact, they do not exist as discrete super-systems at a meta-level, but work through ecosystems on smaller scales, including bioregional and local, and in so doing help to maintain their stability and genetic diversity. Many of the systems we raid for resources and use as sinks for discharges and emissions (such as the oceans, forests and the atmosphere) thus play a part in maintaining systems such as those that underlie weather patterns and climatic zones, and therefore have a critical role in supporting life on earth.

These global ecosystems should be regarded as a special category of critical natural capital (Pearce et al, 1989). Their impairment or degradation could lead to catastrophe for the human race, and probably for many other forms of life on earth as well. They are a complex area about which we are still probably largely ignorant, for they almost certainly depend on still undetected cycles. For example, James Lovelock's hypothesis (1979) about the role of dimethyl sulphide in the sulphur cycle suggests that the balance on which life-support systems depend is maintained though a complex web of intricate mechanisms which weave in and out of ecosystems. It is therefore a moot point how much natural capital can be regarded as non-critical and thus exempt from special conservation or the application of sustainability constraints, or absolute limits, to its depletion. Although peat and timber may be classed as renewable resources, blanket peat deposits and forests — whether tropical or boreal — almost certainly play major roles in maintaining weather patterns and the balance of gases in the atmosphere. Thus peat and forest cover are forms of critical natural capital. So too are individual trees: their removal in vast numbers, through continuing timber extraction, may eventually lead to the disturbance of larger systems and even possibly of the balance of stocks and flows on which life-support systems depend. On another level in forest ecosystems, inconspicuous organisms, on the existence of which several other interrelated species depend, may also be a key component in maintaining critical natural capital.

For sustainability, then, critical natural capital must be conserved in sufficient abundance. This will require not just simple quantitative measures ("how much of x or y do we have?"), but qualitative assessments ("do we judge an ecosystem is in good enough 'health', given the information available from quantitative indicators?").

## SUBSTITUTABILITY

Another approach to the question of the sustainable use of nonrenewable resources is via the notion of substitutability between natural resources and the goods and services we create from them, in other words between natural and human-made capital. Mainstream economics assumes that human-made capital is a near-perfect substitute for natural capital and that this substitutability is reversible: an economy that creates human-made capital, which fully compensates for the decline in natural capital, may be said to be using natural resources sustainably. David Pearce, professor of economics at University College, London, calls such substitution "broad sustainability" or constant wealth, as opposed to "narrow sustainability", where the approach "is to focus on natural capital assets and suggest that they should not decline through time. *Every generation should inherit a similar natural environment*" (Pearce et al, 1989, p37). Pearce points out that his narrow sustainability "seems consistent with many of the contributions made to the literature on sustainable development" (Pearce et al, 1989, p37) and seems closer on the whole to what Brundtland had in mind. He gives several reasons why narrow sustainability deserves consideration:

• non-substitutability,

- uncertainty (substitutability may be possible one day, but we cannot assume this will definitely be the case),
- irreversibility (once a resource or species is extinct it is gone forever), and
- equity (the poor need all the natural capital they can get if they are to build sustainable livelihoods).

Herman Daly (1992a, p254) makes a similar distinction but uses different terms:

> Maintaining total capital [natural and human-made capital] intact might be referred to as "weak sustainability", in that it is based on generous assumptions about the substitutability of capital for natural resources in production. By contrast, "strong sustainability" would require maintaining both man-made and natural capital intact separately, on the assumption that they are really not substitutes but complements in most productive functions.

Just how generous is the assumption that human capital can be substituted for natural capital is illustrated by Daly's analogy with house building: no number of extra chain saws will ensure completion of a house once the supply of timber has been used up. As Daly goes on to point out, if there were substitutability between the two types of natural capital, the one could be changed into the other and back again, but this is clearly not possible. He observes (Daly, 1991a, p32): "It is quite amazing that the substitutability dogma should be held with such tenacity in the face of such an easy *reductio ad absurdum*." Thus the fallacy of the substitutability assumption supports the principle that the stock of natural capital must be conserved and that absolute constraints may be necessary.

There is another reason why "strong" or "narrow" sustainability ("strong" seems to have better associations) is a more adequate guide for sustainable development — the dynamic relationship between the two types of capital. Human-made capital, which is created out of natural capital (and human ingenuity), may well, unless controlled, develop amazing capacities to consume natural capital, for example the latest machines used in clear felling or the most sophisticated echo-sounding equipment for detecting shoals of fish. Unless we make a deliberate effort to apply some form of artificial negative feedback, it is all too easy to fall in with the thinking that regards the serving of the "needs" of human-made capital and its continually improved extensions of itself as the function or *raison d'être* of natural capital.

The basic principle governing the use of environmental goods (resources, capacities and services) should be that the stock of natural capital should not diminish. From this general principle we can derive more specific principles for each of the main categories of environmental goods (see box opposite).

## SCALE

Because the resources of ecosystems are finite, the key concept for their sustainable use is scale. The impacts of the economy, its consumption of natural capital, must not exceed the limits that must be observed if ecological sustainability is to be achieved. These limits will be determined by the rates of recovery — both the regenerative rate of renewable resources and the recovery rate of the assimilative capacities of sinks — in ecosystems of different scales up to and including the global. Together, these limits can be thought of as an "ecological boundary" within which the economy must operate (see Figure 2.1, p34 where the line of the rectangle with the rounded corners marks the ecological boundary). Solar energy flows into the ecosystem, and low-grade heat flows out, but all the other flows generated by economic activity must be restricted to a scale that allows them to be retained, and, ideally, recycled or reabsorbed, within the boundary.

## LOCAL, NATIONAL OR GLOBAL SUSTAINABILITY?

Up to this point we have tended to discuss sustainability on a global basis without making explicit references to sustainability at the local or national level. In a way this has not been necessary, because the principles apply at all levels.

Obviously sustainability must operate at the global level: the total global impacts of economic activity must not exhaust the resources or upset irretrievably the balance on which we depend. Sustainability must also operate at the national level. A nation that consumes its own natural capital faster than it can regenerate

## PRINCIPLES FOR THE SUSTAINABLE USE AND MANAGEMENT OF ECOLOGICAL GOODS

### Resources

#### Renewables

- The rate of extraction of a renewable resource should not exceed the rate at which the resource is renewed. (This may be exceedingly low.)
- The extraction of a renewable resource must not jeopardize the biodiversity of the ecosystem. (For example, replacing native woodlands comprising a variety of species with plantations of a single species is not sustainable forestry.).

#### Nonrenewables

- The depletion of nonrenewable resources should be minimized.
- A proportion of nonrenewable resources should be set aside for the physical manufacture of renewable substitutes and the development of such substitutes should be given priority in resource consumption.
- The depletion of nonrenewable resources should not fall below agreed minimum strategic levels.

### Capacities

- The assimilative and regenerative capacities of soils, air and water should receive waste emissions at rates which do not exceed the rates at which these media can absorb, assimilate, reconstitute and recycle the emissions.
- The assimilative and regenerative capacities of soils, air, and water should not be used for the dispersal of substances which cannot be decomposed and recycled, that is those compounds not occurring naturally in the environment. Such compounds may be stored as opposed to dispersed if they are considered non-toxic. Toxic compounds must be phased out as soon as possible, as long-term storage presents problems.

### Services

- The global life-support systems which maintain the biogeochemical cycles, the composition of the atmosphere, the ozone layer, the earth's temperature and climatic zones and patterns must not be destabilized.
- The quality, that is the full natural functioning, of the resources (for example, soils), cycles (for example, the hydrological cycle) and ecosystems which are necessary for the renewing of renewable resources must not be degraded.

it is obviously not acting sustainably. Nor is a nation that maintains its development or protects its own natural resources by drawing on the natural capital of other nations. It can do this, for example, by importing resources, by exporting toxic wastes, or by consuming more than its share of the life-support services that depend on global systems. Such a nation is said to be "importing sustainability" from others that are "exporting" theirs. This of course is what is happening on a large scale in many parts of the world. Two examples are the rates of extraction and sale of tropical hardwood (and the purchase of virtually all of it by Japan and the European Union), and the appropriation of more than their share of the world's carbon sinks by the countries of the North, which, with approximately 20 per cent of global population, produce almost 60 per cent of global $CO_2$ emissions (World Bank, 1991, p204, Table A9). Thus, as Michael Jacobs (1991, p79) points out: "A national economy can only be described as "sustainable" if its activities not only do not reduce environmental capacities within its own borders, but do not cause their reduction elsewhere." The same principle can also be applied at the local level within a nation. Arguments based on it are most likely to be advanced where an area with resources does not receive its full share of the benefits resulting from their exploitation by other dominant areas.

It may be possible to achieve a state of global ecological sustainability in which global resources are conserved but inequitably distributed between nations. Such an arrangement could perpetuate current inequities, a matter of great concern to the South, as we shall see in Chapter 9. It might resolve some aspects of the global crisis, but would not be consistent with the sustainable development of Brundtland's definition.

The formulation of principles for the sustainable use of resources falls far short of a blueprint for sustainable development. For instance, we still have to examine how we can devise and implement practical policies for a sustainable society based on these principles. Chapter 6 examines both the technical and social possibilities on which such policies will depend (Brundtland's "social organization"), as well as other issues which affect the implementation of any proposals for meeting the needs of both this generation and its successors.

# Chapter 6 | PRINCIPLES, POLICIES and PROCESS

The principles formulated in the previous chapter will have little effect on prospects for sustainable development unless it is possible to put them into practice. To do this we need some means of measuring both the consumption of natural capital and progress in our attempts to reduce it. We need measurable targets at which to aim and other statistical measures to allow us to tell whether or not we are meeting these targets.

Fortunately, there are indicators that allow us to monitor our use of each type of resource. In the case of renewable and continuing resources we can assess the rates at which resources are extracted or wastes released to the environment. Yields from fisheries, forests and farmland tell us whether or not these resources are being depleted in an unsustainable fashion. Ultimately, with terrestrial ecosystems, the fertility and conservation of the soil are the key indicators, and declining yields may well be a sign that fertility is being lost. We can define the health of marine and aquatic ecosystems, measure the quantity and "quality" of water stocks and select indicators that will alert us to unsustainable depletion. In the case of nonrenewables we can estimate recoverable reserves and measure rates of extraction. On the basis of such information we can set targets for reductions in demand, and for reuse, which may vary with the discovery of new economic reserves. Similarly, it is now possible to measure and monitor not only the state of the planet's capacity to absorb waste but also its life-support services, using such indicators as average global temperature, incidence of ultraviolet radiation, the balance of gases in the atmosphere and the rate of loss of biodiversity.

## UNCERTAINTIES

Our ability to make such quantitative measures and (interpret them appropriately) means it is possible to devise practicable policies based on the principles for the sustainable use of natural capital outlined in the previous chapter. However, no one knows with certainty how many fish we can catch or how many trees we can cut down or how much we will have to reduce emissions of $CO_2$ and other greenhouse gases if we are to meet sustainability criteria.

The problem is not confined to questions of fish stocks, forests and climatic change. In many cases the sustainable rates of resource use are unknown. Many can probably only be established by trial and error over fairly lengthy time scales of more than a generation, possibly more than a human lifetime. In surveying the degraded and polluted ecosystems of modern industrial societies, we cannot know for certain which regional and global ecosystems are ecologically sustainable, what exactly may be needed to restore them to sustainability, or indeed even if that is possible. All we know for certain is that natural systems remained in balance for thousands of years before being affected by human impacts, although this balance was dynamic rather than static.

For these reasons attempts to move towards sustainable resource use and management will be haunted by uncertainty. Some of the impacts of human activity on biophysical systems may have passed a threshold, which may mean unpredictable and possibly catastrophic change before the global system finds a new balance (Ehrlich, 1989). Even if such a threshold has not been passed, we do not know how long we have before we reach it if resource use and population growth increase as currently projected. Nor do we know whether societies will be able to accept the constraints required to curb unsustainable practices, let alone to maintain sustainable development over the longer term. As resource depletion continues and global pollution levels rise, the goal of sustainability recedes, for as Garret Hardin (1991, p55) points out, "carrying capacity transgressed is carrying capacity reduced".

Unless action is taken soon, there is a real prospect that the sustainable system eventually achieved will represent a much reduced biotic system and an impoverished lifestyle for the human population dependent on it, with ecological degradation proving irreversible under, say, population pressure. The seriousness of the problem is compounded by the fact that, although we have talked of the ecological boundary for simplicity's sake, there is not just one ecological boundary but many, some of which may be close, as Boulding (1991, p26) points out, reminding us of Liebeg's law: "We have paid far too little attention to what the limiting factors are. It is the *most* limiting factor which is important. It is the first fence that we come to that stops us." The breakdown or degradation of ecosystems to the point where they no longer provide us with essential services is not necessarily an even, gradual, plainly visible, erosive process, but may possibly be triggered by some slight modification in conditions, or by the loss of some inconspicuous species.

## THE PRECAUTIONARY PRINCIPLE

The precautionary principle offers a way of living with uncertainties about limits and about the impacts of economic activity or new technologies on ecosystems. It states simply that we should avoid risk and abandon or reject policies and practices that could have unsustainable outcomes or negative impacts on ecosystems. As Robert Costanza of the International Institute for Ecological Economics at the University of Maryland (1989, p5) explains: "If we are unsure about future limits the prudent course is to assume they exist. One does not run blindly through a dark landscape that may contain crevasses." Costanza demonstrates the operation of the principle with a "payoff" matrix from Maximin game theory. If we really are uncertain about global ecological health, we should choose policies that result in the "largest minimum" alternative. If we are facing serious damage to global ecosystems, then a precautionary policy founded on "technological pessimism" (the assumption that "technological" solutions will not prevent ecological catastrophe) will lead to a more satisfactory outcome than one founded on "technological optimism" (see Figure 6.1). If such caution proves to have been unnecessary, the consequences of the "wrong" choice (technological pessimism), are far less serious than those of technological optimism, which may lead to disastrous outcomes.[1]

| | | Real state of world | |
|---|---|---|---|
| | | optimists right | pessimists right |
| Current policy | technological optimism | high benefits | disaster |
| | technological pessimism | moderate benefits | tolerable disbenefits |

*Source*: Costanza (1989)

**Figure 6.1 Maximin matrix**

## PRIORITIES FOR THE SUSTAINABLE ECONOMY

The existence of uncertainties should not become an excuse for inaction.[2] Many rates of consumption or depletion of natural resources are all too plainly unsustainable. Such a view is borne out by a significant consensus on emissions to the atmosphere. For example, the 1988 Dutch *National Environmental Policy Plan* called for reductions of between 60 and 80 per cent in a range of gases, and of 100 per cent in the case of CFCs. Two years later the Intergovernmental Panel on Global Change recommended that greenhouse gases should be reduced by similar amounts — by more than 60 per cent in the case of $CO_2$, by between 70 and 80 per cent for $N_2O$ and over 70 per cent for CFCs.

Such data suggest that the problem of unsustainability is of such a scale and urgency that the fact that we may not precisely know the "sustainable" rate of $CO_2$ emissions becomes unimportant: questions of the extent of uncertainties or the percentage error in estimates of what is needed to restore or achieve sustainability become academic. For a long time to come the answer to such questions as "How much natural capital is being consumed? How much pollution are we producing?" will be, very plainly, "Too much".

---

1. See Costanza (1989). Orr (1992b) makes a similar point, applying the principle of Pascal's wager, as a rational response to uncertainty about the existence of God, to the global crisis.
2. It all too frequently has.

Thus the first priority in an unsustainable society is to reduce the ecological impacts of economic activity to the level at which they can be contained within the ecological boundary. No matter how efficient the economy by the standards of conventional economics, it is not sustainable unless it observes the constraints which follow from the fact that resources are finite.[3]

Another way of looking at the problem is to say that humankind must live within carrying capacity. Applied to animal populations, carrying capacity expresses a very direct relationship between population and food supply: if disease, drought or even species loss reduces the food supply, population drops to a level the ecosystem can support. However, carrying capacity is a relative concept when applied to human populations, because societies differ in their levels of consumption. Therefore the impact of an economy is the product of two variables — population and the average level of consumption of resources, as Garret Hardin (1991, p54) succinctly points out: "Cultural carrying capacity and the standard of living are inversely related. The higher the standard of living, the fewer the number of people who can enjoy it."

## OPERATING WITHIN THE SUSTAINABILITY BOUNDARY

There are two ways of bringing the total ecological impacts of economic activity within the sustainability boundary: extending the ecological boundary, or reducing the economy's consumption of natural capital.

### Extending the Ecological Boundary

Extending the ecological boundary involves increasing natural capital and so enlarging the ability of the ecosystem to absorb the impacts of the economy, thus providing more environmental or ecological "space". There are several ways of doing this, though their potential is limited:

---

3. On this point see Daly's analogy (1991b; 1992a, p222) of the loading of cargo onto a boat, in which the Plimsoll line is compared to sustainability constraints.

- restoring the full production of ecosystems,
- increasing the level of sustainable yields without ecological costs, for example by building up the quality of soil in organic farming,
- increasing total production by using better adapted varieties or more productive species,
- improving agricultural, silvicultural and fishery practices and, for nonrenewables,
- increasing through exploration the size of economically recoverable reserves

Thus it is possible to contribute in various ways to what has been called the "building of nature".[4] In theory, biotechnology has much to contribute to the enlargement of natural capital if it operates from a sustainable base, although some initiatives, for example in the Green Revolution, suggest that the gains are dependent on possibly scarce inputs and are offset by both ecological and human costs. The high profile of current "advances" in biotechnology should not blind us to the laborious and heroic work of local people using their local knowledge and skills to extend ecological boundaries, as for example in Bangladesh where people reconstruct and improve flood defences using only their own labour and their knowledge of the river system.

## Reducing the Economy's Consumption of Natural Capital

There are two ways in which it is possible to reduce the economy's consumption of natural capital. The first is to contract the economy and so reduce the scale of its impacts and the per capita level of consumption; for example we can build fewer houses, or smaller houses, or both. The per capita level of consumption, however, also depends on how efficiently the economy uses natural capital. For example, a society that develops a technique for constructing houses that reduces by 50 per cent the amount of timber required can reduce significantly its consumption of a renewable resource (without its houses becoming either

---

4. I am indebted to John Kirkby and Phil O'Keefe of the University of Northumbria for drawing my attention to this concept.

fewer in number or smaller) and so maintain its material standard of living. (If it can then improve the thermal insulation without increasing its use of resources, it makes another important reduction in consumption of natural capital — this time of the capacity of the atmosphere to absorb $CO_2$ emissions.) Therefore, in assessing an economy's consumption of natural capital we need to consider not only the average material standard of living but also ecological efficiency, the degree of efficiency in the use of natural capital.

Thus there are three factors that go to make up the total ecological impact of economic activity: the size of the population, the material standard of living, and the ecological efficiency of the economy, which is determined by the level of technology. Paul and Ann Ehrlich (Ehrlich and Ehrlich, 1990) express these relationships by the formula $I = PCT$, where

$I =$   the total ecological or environmental impact of the economy,
$P =$   the size of the population,
$C =$   the average material standard of living, or per capita consumption of resources, and
$T =$   the state of technology, or the ecological efficiency of the economy.

If, for example, motorists reduce the number and length of their journeys so that they need buy only 250 gallons of petrol a year instead of 500, they have halved $C$ in the above equation. If they then switch to cars with engines that burn petrol or diesel twice as efficiently and remain content with the reduced mileage, they reduce $T$ and drive down $I$ even further — to a quarter of the original figure. Let us look at each of these factors in turn.

## Population

Even if $C$ and $T$ remain constant, any increase in $P$ will make it more difficult to observe sustainability constraints. The exponential growth in world population this century has led to much concern in the North about population growth rates in countries in the South. However, an increase in population in a country in which $C$ is very low will have a much smaller environmental impact than a similar increase in one with a higher $C$. Even a large rise in population in a "poor" country may have a smaller effect on *I* than a lower rise in a "rich" one, if the difference in levels of consumption is large. In the opinion of the Ehrlichs, we live in "a world where US consumption is so profligate that the birth of an average American baby is hundreds of times more of a disaster for the earth's life-support systems than the birth of a baby in a desperately poor nation" (Ehrlich and Ehrlich, 1990, p10).[5]

Thus population growth is not just a problem in the South. Small increments of population in the North add to North–South inequities because many resources are in greater supply in the South. Furthermore, the populations of most countries in the North far exceed carrying capacity at their current levels of consumption, and depend, as we have seen, on imported sustainability or "appropriated carrying capacity" to maintain these levels.[6] Lastly, these levels mean the export from the South of the resources which, properly applied, could help to reduce population growth by providing the "five critical prerequisites to reduced fertility: ... adequate nutrition, proper sanitation, basic health care, education of women, and equal rights for women" (Ehrlich and Ehrlich, 1990, p216).

There is little awareness of these issues in the USA (and indeed in other Northern countries), which Ehrlich regards as "a demographic dream world, failing to recognize the impact of our gross overpopulation on our own nation's environments and resources, and on the planet as a whole" (Ehrlich and Enrlich, 1990, p217).

### Average per Capita Material Standard of Living

There are two reasons why it is difficult to reduce the per

---

5. More precise details are equally impressive. For example, according to the index of per capita use of commercial energy (Ehrlich and Enrlich, 1990, p134): "A baby born in the United States represents twice the destructive impact on earth's ecosystems and the services they provide as one born in Sweden, 3 times one born in Italy, 13 times one born in Brazil, 35 times one born in India, 140 times one born in Bangladesh or Kenya, and 280 times one born in Chad, Rwanda, Haiti or Nepal."

6. This term has been coined by William Rees and Matthis Wackernagel of the University of British Columbia, who use "carrying capacity" to mean not the population that can be supported by the ecosystem, but the capacity of the ecosystem to support a population.

capita material standard of living. First, any improvement in the welfare of the poorest in both North and South will mean rises in their material standard of living and hence in the average material standard of living. Second, the spread of "consumerism" across the globe means a larger per capita consumption of natural resources. Thus welfare and quality of life are increasingly closely associated with the consumption of natural capital.

### Ecological Efficiency

If we can reverse consumerist preferences and weaken the association between welfare and material standard of living, or decouple the link between them, we can reduce $C$, average per capita consumption of natural capital, without lowering welfare. Similarly, decoupling the other links in the chain between material standard of living and resources (see Figure 6.2) will lead to a reduction in linear entropic throughput and therefore to gains in ecological efficiency, and a reduction in $I$.

WELFARE
*is related to*
MATERIAL STANDARD OF LIVING
*which depends on*
PROVISION OF MANUFACTURED GOODS &
SERVICES BASED ON MANUFACTURED GOODS
*which in turn requires*
CONSUMPTION OF NATURAL CAPITAL
*which means*
EXTRACTION OF NATURAL RESOURCES
*which involves*
*(as does every other link in the chain)*
DISCHARGES OF WASTES

*Figure 6.2 Links between welfare and natural capital*

We can decouple the links that exist between material standards of living and consumption of natural capital in a number of ways. Often technical changes and technological advances provide the key. For example, we can

- switch to products and services that use less materials,
- choose local products (thereby saving both the energy con-

sumed in transport and the embodied resource and energy costs of the means of transport),

- change to more energy- and resource-efficient manufacturing processes at each stage in converting resources into material goods,
- change to processes that produce less damaging and smaller quantities of waste, and
- change to technologies that process or recycle wastes in ways that consume less natural capital.

In these ways we can reduce consumption of natural capital without lowering our material standard of living.

If we can improve ecological efficiency sufficiently, it may be possible not only to reduce the impacts of the economy to sustainable levels but also to remain within ecological limits even as population rises. It is also theoretically possible, if the reductions in $T$ are large enough, to maintain our material standard of living without any overall increase in material consumption, $C$.

## Growth

It is even theoretically possible to improve economic efficiency to such an extent that economic growth, which has always meant increased consumption of natural capital, is compatible with a reduction in environmental impact. It is unclear whether this can be achieved in practice, given the extent and seriousness of current unsustainable practices and the time required to develop the very large improvements in ecological efficiency which would be required.

However, there are obstacles to introducing more ecologically efficent practices and technologies. One of these is financial — they may not be economic at current prices. Second, practices such as recycling may have higher ecological costs than the intended gain in ecological efficiency. For example, the ecological costs of the dioxins used to bleach recycled paper (white recycled paper requires the use of many times more bleach than "new" white paper) may exceed the "ecological savings" of using recycled paper.

Recycling can consume more energy than it saves, particularly when materials have been widely dispersed or intricately combined with others.[7] Systems for reuse, such as returnable containers with a refundable deposit or the traditional British milk bottle, are generally more ecologically efficient than recycling schemes, which should therefore focus on resources offering the biggest savings in energy and resources. For example, producing aluminium goods from recycled aluminium requires only a fifteenth of the energy needed to produce them from bauxite. The ecological efficiency of recycling can also be improved in a number of ways such as designing goods to facilitate the recovery of materials at a later stage.

Energy efficiency alone can make a substantial contribution to the ecological efficiency of the economy. Ernst Ulrich von Weizsäcker (1994, p58), president of the Wuppertal Institute in Germany, estimates that with "political determination" over a period of 30 years "a doubling of energy efficiency at no loss of convenience, ie with no change in lifestyles seem[s] like a *very* conservative estimate for what can be achieved."

However, Weizsäcker suggests that we ought to think more in terms of energy productivity (devising more energy efficient processes) than energy efficiency (improving the efficiency of existing uses of energy), and encourages us to think of ourselves as "living through the early days of a new industrial revolution, a revolution in energy productivity", which would be "the essence of the new progress, the progress towards a sustainable economy" (Weizsäcker, 1994, p59).

It may well be possible to make gains in ecological productivity (as opposed to efficiency) in other activities within the economy, such as extracting nonrenewable resources, agriculture, industrial processes and dealing with wastes (for example not producing waste is better than having to devise a means of recycling it).

There are already many examples of products and processes which, if widely adopted, would improve ecological efficiency. The most important reduce the flow of matter and energy through the economy — the entropic throughput — and are not dependent on inputs of, say, energy, as recycling inevitably is: for

---

7. Extreme examples are lead in petrol, rubber in car tyres and mercury fillings in teeth.

example, solar-powered appliances for cooking, water heating, refrigeration and desalination. For this reason, the single most important step towards improving the ecological efficiency of the economy is almost certainly the development of renewable energy-generating capacity. Not only will it provide a continuing supply of an essential commodity after nonrenewable fuels are exhausted, but it also generates electricity without producing the vast quantities of wastes produced in the conversion of fossil (and nuclear) fuels into energy.

## IMPLEMENTING ECOLOGICAL EFFICIENCY

Many means of reducing various environmental impacts and improving the overall environmental efficiency of economic activity have aready been developed and shown to be feasible. However, we are very far from a world where these have advanced from a marginal position to play a major role in our still profoundly unsustainable economic life. Thus, as Jacobs (1991, p106) points out we need:

> *financial, regulatory and institutional policies by which we can ensure that the technical possibilities are actually introduced in practice. It is after all the fact that existing technical advances are not widely in use which is in many ways the key problem. We have the ability to tackle the environmental crisis, but the economic system is still not allowing these solutions to be implemented.*

There are four main instruments governments can use to improve ecological efficiency. First, they can encourage individuals and organizations to adopt practices that reduce the throughput of matter and energy in the economy. For example, they can inform householders of the benefits of condensing boilers, distribute posters to remind people to switch off unnecessary lights and publicize telephone numbers that members of the public can ring to report vehicles emitting excessive exhaust fumes. However, in isolation such actions tend to be palliatives. To be effective they need to be part of a comprehensive, coordinated campaign.

Second, governments can introduce legislation to improve ecological efficiency. Regulations have cleaned up rivers such as the Thames and Tees, and set minimum standards of house insulation. There is considerable scope for higher standards cf ecological efficiency to be set in many sectors of the economy, such as transport, packaging and food distribution.

Third, governments can invest in ecological efficiency in publi: utilities such as electricity generation and rail transport. They can also give financial support to the development of new cleaner technologies in the private sector, as Denmark has done with its wind turbine industry. The European Union could, for example, reallocate funds within the CAP in favour of organic agriculture.

Fourth, governments can use a number of financial incentives. They can give subsidies to reduce the price of low-energy ligh: bulbs, or to persuade farmers and other landowners to plant woods and conserve habitats. They can set up refundable deposit schemes of the kind drinks manufacturers used to operate. They can issue or sell tradeable permits to control the rate of depletion of resources. These can be issued to existing users of the resource who may opt to sell their quota. Taxes are probably the single most powerful instrument for influencing practices that consume natural capital. They represent ways in which the externalities of production can be internalized, and can be used to make prices "tell the ecological truth", in Weizsäcker's phrase. Weizsäcker suggests a programme of gradual ecological tax reform over 40 years, which would overcome the problems of "hypothecated" or "earmarked" taxes and political acceptability. He also argues that business and industry's suspicion of taxes on energy and other resources is unwarranted, pointing to evidence suggesting that the countries that did least to soften the impact of oil price rises in the 1970s have become most efficient in their use of energy and generally most successful economically (Weizsäcker, 1994, pp61–2).

## ASSESSING PROGRESS WITH $I = PCT$

Despite the lag in putting ideas into practice, we might appear to be poised to make progress towards sustainable development. We have a set of operational principles with which to manage resources in a "sustainable" manner; indicators to tell whether unsustainable practices are declining and, in time, whether sustainability criteria are being met; economic instruments to persuade organizations and individuals to adopt ecologically less damaging ways of using resources; and an awareness of what is required to fulfil human needs.

However, achieving a sustainable economy will not be straight-forward, even in the advantaged North. $I$ has to be reduced substantially, probably by well over 50 per cent, if the figures from the Dutch *National Environmental Policy Plan* and the Intergovernmental Panel on Global Change are an accurate guide (see p110). Even if $I$ has to be reduced by "only" 50 per cent, and even if we assume zero population growth, which many countries in the North have still not achieved, then $T$ has to drop to half its present value if the present average level of the material standard of living is not to fall as a result of sustainability constraints. If $I$ has to be reduced by an even greater amount, then ecological efficiency will of course have to improve even more, and thus $T$ will have to fall further.

If we think in terms of global sustainability, there is an even greater need for improvements in ecological efficiency. If we accept that $P$ will double over the next 50 years, then $T$ will have to drop to a quarter of its present value,

$$\frac{I}{2} = 2\,P \times C \times \frac{T}{4}$$

These reductions may be possible if Weizsäcker's optimism about gains in productivity are not misplaced and similar progress can be made in the efficient use of other resources. However, these calculations do not reveal the full seriousness of the situation. Not only are we making rather generous assumptions about the size of the reduction needed in $I$, but all that would be achieved by carrying out these reductions in $T$ would be a "greening" of business as usual, both nationally and globally: averages would conceal the inequities in levels of consumption on both national and global scales. Greening of the status quo hardly amounts to sustainable development.

These calculations fail to take into account that the material standard of living of a proportion of the population — both nationally (even in the rich North) and globally — does need to improve. However, existing economic arrangements do not distribute wealth very equitably as recent evidence demonstrates.[8] The poor have to rely on the "trickle-down effect" for any material gains, but wealth only trickles down to the poor when it first cascades on the rich. Under existing economic arrangements we can only meet the needs of the poor by increasing the standard of living of all — even though much material consumption in the North is already related to gratifying consumer wants rather than meeting human needs. It is plain that any approach to the problem of meeting needs which involves an increase in material consumption will require even greater gains in ecological efficiency.

Just how great a further gain in ecological efficiency is required to compensate for any increase in average per capita material consumption is illustrated by the results of some calculations made by Paul Ekins. Even if material growth continues at a moderate rate of 2–3 per cent per annum, $C$ will quadruple in 50 years, and "then $T$ must fall by 93 per cent, a factor of 16" (Ekins, 1992, p418).[9] Even if increases in material production were confined to the South where they are most needed, there would still have to be substantial improvements in ecological efficiency: "if $C$ is to grow by 2–3 per cent only in low- and middle-income countries, and if all population growth is taken to be in the former, then ... $T$ would have to be reduced by 79 per cent" (Ekins 1992b, p418). Acceptance of a continuing rise in $C$ on either the national or global scale implies dependence on improvements in ecological efficiency to achieve sustainability There must be some doubt as to whether such gains are possible, as Ekins suggests: "Any of these figures of reduction of environmental intensity represent an ambitious target. That of 93 per cent would only be considered feasible by technological optimists verging on the fanatic."

We are not, however, solely dependent on trade-offs between $C$ and $T$ for ecological sustainability. Decoupling the link between welfare and material standard of living discussed earlier (see

---

8.  It is not just recent evidence that demonstrates the widening gap betwen rich and poor, although it illustrates growing inequities very clearly. The gap has been widening for at least several decades and possibly many generations.

9.  The calculation is: $I = PCT$, therefore $\dfrac{I}{2} = \dfrac{PCT}{2}$, or $\dfrac{I}{2} = 2\,P \times 4\,C \times \dfrac{T}{2 \times 2 \times 4}$.

p115) has the potential to enlarge the "space" within the ecological boundary. This would require a general acceptance that quality of life does not depend on current Northern levels of consumption of both material possessions and services which are dependent on substantial inputs of natural capital (such as holidays on the other side of the world). A readiness to accept such decoupling would also presumably mean more support for a redistribution of wealth. That this would be both equitable and effective is illustrated by Ekins's calculation (1992, p419) that even if the South (with 75 per cent of the world's population) doubled its population and quadrupled its consumption over the next 50 years, "its average per capita consumption would still be less than 20 per cent of that currently in rich countries".

It thus seems that sustainability requires equity not only on moral grounds but also as a practical necessity. This conclusion is supported by evidence of resource depletion worldwide, which suggests that intergenerational equity requires intragenerational equity, or at least substantial moves towards it. The evidence of the impact of current levels of both wealth and poverty on natural resources suggests that unless the problem of inequity is solved, the opportunities of future generations will have been compromised.[10] Daly (1992b, p11) reaches a similar conclusion: "The real issue is the reluctance of the wealthy to accept the obvious implication that if further aggregate growth will not solve the global crisis, then the only option that will assure the survival of human civilization is a massive reallocation of existing global wealth. Unfortunately self-deception will not save us."

### Priorities

In the light of these calculations it is possible to specify in broad strategic terms what is needed to move towards sustainable development. Meeting the most urgent human needs in the South requires

- economic activity to be focused on meeting basic needs,

---

10. There is also the consideration that the growing numbers of very poor will not be prepared to accept indefinitely the degrading conditions the current economic system imposes on them.

- the latest ecologically efficient technology, and
- massive ecological regeneration and renewal.

The priorities are remarkably similar in the North despite the overwhelming difference in material standards:

- using economic production to meet the needs of the poor,
- the latest ecologically efficient technology, and
- conservation and restoration of natural capital (the boreal forests are under as great a threat as the tropical forests).

However, the difference in levels of consumption adds a crucial extra requirement of the North. In the name of equity and to meet the needs of the South we must also reduce imported sustainability — our reliance on the carrying capacity we have appropriated from the South. We can begin to do this in two ways, by gains in ecological effciency and by reductions in our material standard of living, guided by Brundtland's dictum that "living standards that go beyond the minimum are sustainable only if consumption standards everywhere have regard for long-term sustainability (WCED, 1987, p44).

## THE NEED FOR MEDIATION

"Obvious" solutions that are morally just or technically feasible are not in themselves able to guarantee their own adoption, any more than the development of a new technology ensures its application. Policy proposals designed to move towards sustainable development are no more exempt from political debate than any other policy proposals. Their supporters may find themselves confronted with the impasse so clearly presented by Wackernagel and Rees (1992, p16): "politically acceptable policies for sustainability would be ecologically ineffective, while ecologically meaningful policies remain politically impossible (if not heretical)". Nor should we trust in the emergence of the "political will" to bridge such a gulf, as Michael Carley (Carley and Christie, 1992, p144), fellow of the Centre for Human Ecology at Edinburgh University, points out: "except at the highest level of generality, there is no unitary public interest. Even the meaning and method of sustainable development will be vigorously and continually debated. Proposals that assume such unity of interest will never be implemented, attractive though they may be."

Change in the name of social justice, improved quality of life or long-term "ecological security" threatens the status quo at least as much as other social, economic and political changes. In societies that tolerate discussion of options for social policy, proposed changes lead to what is essentially political debate over social objectives and can only be accepted, possibly in some attenuated or watered-down form, after the resolution of conflicts arising from competing interests. Any analysis of the prospects for implementing sustainable development has to consider not only "just" solutions and available means, but entrenched interests and the conflicts of interest that inevitably arise. Thus the fate of policy proposals for sustainable development depends on mediation between competing and conflicting interests as Carley and Christie (1992, p47) point out:

> There are huge problems in adjusting market mechanisms and political values to such notions of sustainable development and carrying capacity ... all resources, including clean air, are now under threat from continuing unsustainable industrialism. Political mediation is the only alternative to war over these scarce resources, or to authoritarian imposition of sustainable activity. It is plain that a shift towards sustainable development within democratic systems will demand changes in behaviour that in turn will demand intense political debate and trade-offs in attempts to forge consensus.

Achieving sustainable development depends ultimately not on technical means, nor on economic mechanisms, nor predetermined blueprints, nor idealistic solutions, but on an essentially political process of protracted negotiation between conflicting interests to reach agreements that advance the twin goals of intergenerational and intragenerational equity. Carley and Christie (1992, p48) emphasize this point in their working definition of the process underpinning sustainable development:

> A continuing process of mediation among social, economic and environmental needs which results in positive socioeconomic change that does not undermine the ecological and social systems upon which communities and society are dependent. Its successful imple-

*mentation requires integrated policy, planning and social learning processes; its political viability depends on the full support of the people it affects through their governments, their social institutions, and their private activities.*[11]

## CONCLUSION

The steps that need to be taken to bring economic activity within the ecological boundary, and those that need to be taken to meet human needs equitably within such an arrangement, will involve change of several kinds: substantial technical changes in industrial and other processes that markedly improve the efficiency with which we consume natural capital; changes in economic arrangements at both national and international levels to allow these gains in ecological efficiency to be maximized; changes in the capacities of organizations to manage "environmental" problems that threaten environmental quality and human welfare; and changes in our views about the importance of material consumption, once material needs have been met, for quality of life and fulfilment of human need.

It is clear that the reduction of unsustainable impacts can be measured, that many technical changes that will achieve such reductions are feasible, and that economic inducements to adopt these have been devised. Ways also exist to facilitate the processes of mediating between conflicting goals, resolving conflict and building consensus (Carley and Christie, 1992). Yet the changes on which the implementation of these technical means depend — changes of attitude — may be the hardest to achieve. Why this should be so and what can be done to overcome this difficulty are examined in the next two chapters.

---

11. There are other reasons for regarding the process as being at least as important as the product in thinking about sustainable development — for example uncertainty, and the impossibility at present of defining precisely "the sustainable future": there are, in theory at least, many possible options for ecological sustainability and sustainable development scenarios, but we are unlikely to arrive at any of these unless we work through the process of mediation. Moreover, they remain options only for an unknown but finite period in that undue delay in progressing towards them — through the process of mediation — will mean that their range diminishes. There is of course no guarantee that mediation will result in a consensus that moves towards sustainable development.

# Part III

## Assessing the Obstacles

# Chapter 7 | OBSTACLES to SUSTAINABLE DEVELOPMENT

The most obvious obstacles to sustainable development — lack of awareness of the issues, the political unacceptability of "obvious" steps forward, the opposition of entrenched interests, and the inadequacy of institutional mechanisms for integrating environment and development — reflect the direction and priorities of the development path followed by Western societies for many generations.

Such obstacles are the product of ideas that have shaped Western society and dominated our culture, first in Europe and then more widely, ever since the age of geographical exploration and mercantile expansionism at the end of the Middle Ages. Among the most important of these ideas are a belief in progress, a view of the natural world as a resource to be exploited, and a belief in the special importance of scientific knowledge. Around them have developed a complex of assumptions about goals, strategies and procedures, which are frequently referred to as a paradigm, a set of "norms, beliefs, values and habits that form the world view most commonly held within a culture, and are transmitted from generation to generation by social institutions" (Engel, 1990, p8).

Many commentators believe these ideas have their origins in philosophical and scientific thinking since the Renaissance. Their roots can be traced in such antecedents as the investigations of Galileo; the empirical method of Francis Bacon (1561–1626) (who declared "knowledge is power"); the mechanistic science built on the distinctions between mind and matter, subject and object, made by René Descartes (1596–1650); the Enlightenment with its emphasis on ideas of reason, progress and freedom; the utilitarianism of Bentham; and the positivism of Comte.

Whatever the origins of the paradigm, it is possible to identify several powerful sets of values that dominate our thinking about social and political goals. These pervade many walks of life, for example business, politics, education and leisure, and perpetuate attitudes that lead to unsustainable development.

## PROGRESS

The idea of material progress has been closely associated with ideas of growth, which have underlain mercantile expansionism from at least the late sixteenth century. The fascination with growth can perhaps be traced back even further to the accumulation of wealth from the surpluses of settled systems of agriculture. Continued economic expansion became possible with the growth of scientific knowledge and technological innovation (which promised the speedy completion of the "conquest of nature"). The validity of notions of progress was confirmed by the "primitiveness" of non-Western peoples, those "lesser breeds without the law", hopelessly disadvantaged by their ignorance of Christianity, technology and European "civilization".

### Technocentrism

Our belief in progress is given a sense of new possibilities by technological advance. New technologies create new possibilities for faster growth, more consumption of natural capital and more ambitious development programmes. Their power has led to a set of attitudes which Tim O'Riordan (1981) calls technocentrism. The technocentric mode values the natural world as a resource rather than for its intrinsic value. Its approach to problems of environment and development is based on a faith in human abilities to use technology to control natural processes and manage resources for human ends, and on an assumption that if a problem can be identified, a technological solution can be found by applying techniques of "objective" appraisal and "efficient" management. Technocentrism breeds an optimism that appeals to those who equate growth, size and technological advance with improvements in human welfare. Rather than welcoming other approaches as complementary, it tends to disparage them, particularly if they include "subjective" or nonquantitative assessments or advocate simple, low-cost or "low-tech" solutions. This disparagement may extend to a reluctance to acknowledge the right of non-technologists to make significant contributions. Technocentricism's readiness to quantify problems and solutions and its forecasts of success make it attractive to decision-makers who may be ignorant of the complexities of issues filtered through viewpoints, interpretations and value judgements of which they may be unaware.

Technocentricism is reluctant to heed the truth of Garret Hardin's (1991) dictum that we can *never* do only one thing at a time. Technological solutions tend to create problems in their wake. Huge dams provide hydroelectric power and irrigation, but these gains are offset by very serious costs such as displacement of people, loss of soil fertility downstream and erosion of deltas. Nuclear power, with its problems of routine emissions, unplanned radioactive discharges, decommissioning and radioactive waste disposal, is another example. Despite these large-scale demonstrations of the limitations of technocratic solutions, a stream of expensive "end of pipe" solutions continues to focus on the effects rather than on the roots of the problem. These "solutions" frequently lead to further environmental costs, as in the case of catalytic converters. On a larger scale the US National Academy of Science (NAS) adaptation panel suggests we control global climate, not by reducing energy demand, but by massive engineering projects, fertilizing the seas, gigantic space mirrors and stratospheric dust, without seriously investigating the "side effects" of these proposals. Such examples illustrate Ehrenfield's (1978) law: "If a technology can be used for the worse, it will be."

At least one commentator sees such projects as stemming from "a misplaced confidence in human ability to effect desirable change in little understood natural systems", reflected in "the preference for massive intervention in global biogeochemical systems" rather than relatively small changes in relatively well-understood areas. Such a preference may undervalue the services provided by ecosystems, lead to the application of high discount rates to future environmental costs and damages, and may even cause irreversible damage resulting from especially unfortunate interference with ecosystems (Daily et al, 1991).

## Modernism

The continual advance of technology helps to promote modernist assumptions. Modernism can be defined as the view that ideas grounded in Western post-Enlightenment philosophy and science are sufficient for understanding our present situation. Modernism regards the religions, philosophies, wisdom and practical knowledge of other ages and non-Western cultures, such as those of India and the Far East as inferior, with few relevant insights to offer.

## Science and the Natural World

Underpinning technocentricism are assumptions about science as the key to the exploitation and mastery of nature. For centuries human civilizations drew on the plentiful resources of a world whose abundance was celebrated in the animist and pantheist religions of many cultures. However, the beginning of Western science introduced more exploitative attitudes to a world in which the many modes of supernatural being had already been reduced by Christianity. The new science seemed to offer a key to mastery of the natural world. Francis Bacon urged his contemporaries to make nature a slave and to "torture Nature's secrets from her" (quoted in Capra, 1983, p41). René Descartes also viewed scientific knowledge as a means of mastering nature and developed an analytical scientific method in which the observer, detached from the natural world, breaks down complex entities such as living organisms into their constituent parts. This methodology has proved very powerful. It has made possible the huge advances in medical science this century and complex technological achievements such as putting a man on the moon. But by encouraging the compartmentaliz-ation rather than the synthesis of knowledge, it has led to reductionism — "the belief that all aspects of complex phenom-ena can be understood by reducing them to their constituent parts" (Capra, 1983, p44). As a result it has played a major part in the destruction of the ancient view of nature as an animate, organic world with which human beings interacted: "for more than 99 per cent of human history, the world was enchanted, and man saw himself as an integral part of it. The complete reversal of the perception in a mere 400 years or so has destroyed the continuity of human experience and the integrity of the human psyche" (Berman in Sterling, 1990, p85). Instead science offers a view of a mechanistic, ordered world governed by unvarying physical laws and explicable in terms of the design and movement of its components. For many people today nature is, in the words of US environmental ethicist Holmes Rolston (1990, p70): "practically and prescriptively often pronounced to be valueless, except in so far as it can be used instrumentally as a resource. . . . The logic at the bottom of all this is that a valueless nature can be put to any cultural use we please".

In addition to eroding the animist view of the world, science claimed that its method of observation afforded special insights into reality: only the scientific method could lead to truth. Nineteenth-century Comtian positivism helped promote the view that scientific truth (based on the observation of reality "known" to us through the senses) is distinct from subjective interpretation by virtue of being objective and "value free", and therefore has a higher status than other forms of knowledge. Comte's view that there is no logical connection between fact, "what is", or action, "what can be", on the one hand, and principle, "what ought to be", on the other, may have contributed to a widely-held notion that the world of science is not necessarily bounded by, or interpreted within, a realm of ethical considerations and that when value judgements appear to conflict, science can play a role as an impartial arbiter. This view of science has of course been strongly contested. Polanyi has commented (quoted in Sterling, 1990, p79) on what he sees as a dereliction of moral responsibility: "Objectivism seeks to relieve us of all responsibility for the holding of our beliefs . . . the responsibility of the human person is eliminated from the life and society of man" and Gunnar Myrdal, the Swedish economist who won a Nobel prize for economics, has asserted (Ekins et al, 1992, p31; see also p184): "Values are always with us. Disinterested research there has never been and never can be. Prior to answers there must be questions. There can be no view except from a viewpoint. In the questions raised the viewpoint has been chosen and the valuations implied."

Western societies have an ambivalent attitude to science. While many people share the assumption (which is so powerful and pervasive as to have almost mythical force) that science can resolve many of the problems of environment and development, others acknowledge that it has a destructive potential. Holmes Rolston (1990, p71) suggests that unless the insights of science can be integrated with other values at a higher level of synthesis, conventional scientific and technological solutions are not the answer: "In a world without value except by human [exploitative or technological] preference, science-based values are not part of the solution; they are the root of the problem."

### Economic Growth

Technological advances based on the insights of science have facilitated economic growth as the means of pursuing material progress. At least one commentator attributes our readiness to rely on growth to a deep-seated fear of want. Others see it as an extension of attitudes that made sense in an "empty" world of small populations, abundant resources and insignificant emissions, when an increase in economic activity could improve both material standards and the quality of life.

Our attachment to growth pervades virtually every aspect of modern life in industrialized and industrializing societies. Governments depend on it to create employment, raise material standards of living and cure a range of social ills, on which it is assumed their continuation in office depends. Many of our institutions and practices have evolved, or been designed, to facilitate economic growth — interest-based finance (or usury as it was known in the Middle Ages when it was condemned by the Christian church); banking; the limited company with protected liability; development agencies; accounting; business schools; certain aspects of the legal system, as well as practices such as subsidizing resource extraction, cost-benefit analysis and the use of discount rates. Facilitated in these ways, growth feeds on itself. Increased production in the economy creates disposable income (at least for some), which further stimulates the demand for material goods and so leads to new production targets (which create further depletion and more pollution).

In the name of economic growth we allow resources to be used at greater and greater ecological cost for the manufacture of relatively trivial goods. We sanction the use of marketing techniques (including advertising, which conceals all information about the human and ecological costs of the goods) not only to ensure that goods are sold, but also to create a demand for new products, the existence of which could not have been predicted a short time before. So readily do we comply with such persuasion that shopping is now widely regarded as a leisure activity. Jointly we subscribe to the notion that growth is a good thing and honour those most closely implicated in it. Magnates are praised for creating business empires, tycoons are applauded for capturing shares of world markets, and executives are sought out for their ability to drive smaller and weaker enterprises out of business.

We persist in these attitudes despite much evidence of the negative consequences of growth — even greater oppression of the poor, a wide range of social costs, and degradation of the planet's resources to the point of threatening the life-support services they provide. Herman Daly, borrowing the term from the British economist E J Mishan, has labelled our obsession "growthmania" (Daly, 1992b, p183):

> *Economic growth is held to be the cure for poverty, unemployment, debt repayment, inflation, balance of payments deficits, pollution, depletion, population explosion, crime, divorce and drug addiction. In short, economic growth is both the panacea and the* summum bonum. *This is growthmania. When we add to GNP the costs of defending ourselves against the unwanted consequences of growth and happily count that as further growth, we then have hyper-growth mania. When we deplete geological capability and ecological life support systems, and count that depletion as net current income, then we arrive at our present state of terminal hyper-growthmania.*

The persistence of our belief in the importance of progress and growth (and our persistent disregard of such notions as equity, sufficiency and the rights of others to make their own livelihoods) seems to be related to very deeply rooted traits and forces — ambition, acquisitiveness, competitive striving, the desire for power, the urge to dominate nature, a fascination with both the physical means to these ends and advances in their power, the belief that "bigger" is "better" and that "more" means "good".

Such traits may also explain both our readiness to value individual enterprise more highly than co-operative efforts (as the means of providing welfare) and our inability to live in harmony with nature.[1]

One commentator even likens humankind's involvement in the dynamics of economic growth to a Faustian bargain in which the individual yields to the temptation of employing "the forces and potentialities of Nature to pursue the aim of finding ... economic bliss" and of becoming, "through unstoppable technical progress and infinite economic growth, creator of his own world" (Binswanger et al 1990). Daly (1992a, p153) also ponders our seemingly helpless attraction to material gains, but opts for a tragi-comic image, likening our predicament to that of the monkey in a south Indian fable, which put its hand into a monkey trap but would not let go its prize in order to gain its freedom.

Economic growth has an obvious appeal for political leaders in inequitable societies: the "trickle-down" effect will allow all to benefit from growth without disturbing the status quo, and particularly without threatening the power and privileges of the better off. An emphasis on growth evades the need to consider questions of distribution, or redistribution, of wealth, as Lester Brown of the WWI points out: "the vision that growth conjures up of an expanding pie of riches is a powerful and convenient political tool because it allows the tough issues of income inequality and skewed wealth distribution to be avoided" (Brown et al, 1991, p97). It is thus not economic growth *per se* that leads to an inequitable sharing of the fruits of growth, but rather "the abuse of legal and economic instruments based on an unfair allocation of power" (O'Riordan, 1981, p92).

Economic growth does not just evade the issue of inequity.[2] It also compounds the problem for two reasons. First, the unregulated operation of market forces in any society promotes inequity,

---

1. In his *Human Scale*, ironically a huge book, Kirkpatrick Sale, an American writer, accumulates evidence of the pervasiveness of 'bigness' in Western and particularly US culture. Sale attributes this to our having lost touch in modern times with a sense of sufficiency: "Because we do not really know how much is enough, we assume that bigger is better" (Sale, 1980, p70).
2. However, see Hirsch (1977) who points out that economic growth has renewed questions about distribution.

as Daly and Cobb (1990, p49) point out: "Last year's winners find it easier to be this year's winners. Winners tend to grow and losers disappear. Over time many firms become few firms, competition is eroded, and monopoly power increases." Even in the early stages of a market economy we can see forces at work that enrich some through impoverishing others, as Ruskin pointed out in 1860: "the art of making yourself rich, in the ordinary mercantile economist's sense, is therefore equally and necessarily the art of keeping your neighbour poor" (quoted in Daly, 1991a, p27).[3]

Second, once material needs have been adequately met, continued economic growth encourages accelerating consumerism, which gratifies wants rather than meets needs — with obvious implications for sustainability. Alhough, as research confirms, most people realize there is more to life than pursuing a higher standard of living, and feel reasonably content with their lot provided it matches the norm for their social group, they are reluctant to be left behind when others are improving their living standards (Hueting, 1986; Douthwaite, 1992). Thus continuing economic growth is always tempting us to form new aspirations — and feel new dissatisfactions, as Marx pointed out: "a house may be large or small, as long as the surrounding houses are equally small it satisfies all social demands for a dwelling. But let a palace arise beside the little house, and it shrinks from a little house to a hut" (quoted in Smith, 1991, p129).

The seriousness of this issue was addressed by an American professor of economics, Fred Hirsch (1977, p10), who noted that "addition to the material goods that can be expanded for all will, in itself, increase the scramble for those goods and facilities that cannot be so expanded". As economic growth provides more "positional" goods (by which people define their socioeconomic status relative to others, for example a country cottage), people have to consume at faster and faster rates to maintain their position relative to others. Ultimately the process is futile: there is

---

3. Robert Garioch's (1975) account of how entrepreneurship flourished in a prisoner of war camp in Germany illustrates the truth of Ruskin's insight. The successful entrepreneurs achieved their 'wealth' at the expense of others who had to do with less.

no advantage in standing on tiptoe if everyone in the crowd is doing the same. If there is more to life than material possessions, it is pointless to seek more material wealth. Economic growth encourages a kind of cognitive dissonance; people feel compelled to act in ways in which they do not wholly believe. There is a tendency for cynicism to set in: if material goods are up for grabs, why not? Such attitudes are deeply corrosive and quickly destroy consensus and tacit agreements about moderation and community, as was evident in Britain during the 1980s.[4]

## Wealth

Closely related to our belief in economic growth is our conception of wealth, which is increasingly thought of in material and financial terms. It is as if the exclusion from the economists' calculations of wealth of the many non-material "goods" that give life much of its meaning has constrained us into thinking in almost exclusively financial terms. The consumerist economy also encourages us to equate wealth with material possessions, or with the buying power that gives us access to them. The value of a commodity or service is equated with its price, the symbol and measure of its exchange value, rather than with its use value, the ultimate value for social and national wealth and for individual and community well-being. We "value" diamonds far more highly than water, though "if we were stuck waterless in the middle of a desert we would perceive a single liter of water to be worth more than all the world's diamonds combined" (Wackernagel and Rees, 1992, p7).

## Measuring Wealth

The use of per capita GNP as the measure of national wealth has several implications for sustainable development. First, the

---

4. On positional goods see Hirsch (1977, p23). He quotes Wicksteed, who wrote in 1910: "If an unequal distribution prevails, the richer man will price these rare things beyond the pocket of the average man; or if really equal shares prevailed, one would have to arrange a rationing system." Compare consumerist growth with the system of rationing in force in Britain during the Second World War, and perceptions of the social cohesion associated with each.

use of an average figure conceals information about the national distribution of wealth. Such a measure derives from the Benthamite principle of "the greatest happiness of the greatest number", but cannot accord with what Rawls calls "politico-moral obligations", which stem from an acceptance of the principle of maximizing the position of the least advantaged (see Hirsch, 1977, p134). Second, for several reasons GNP is not a very accurate index of average national wealth. It fails to value non-monetary goods, the many unpaid inputs of people's time and energy which support economic activity, such as the work of running a home and rearing children. Indeed, Robert Kennedy once said that GNP measures everything except the things that make life worthwhile. Third, GNP fails to deduct the costs of growth from the total product. The social costs of growth (treating poverty-related illness, for instance) and the ecological costs (for example, the cost of pollution-control equipment) are added to GNP rather than subtracted from it. Moreover, GNP fails to make any deductions for consumption of natural capital. A country can achieve dramatic growth through, say, the export of hardwoods, while destroying the source of its wealth — its stocks of natural capital. The insistence on a single monetary measure does not encourage the kind of valuation of stocks of different forms of natural capital (and other forms of wealth) that sustainable development requires.

## Development

Materialist notions of wealth underlie another important element in the paradigm — the notion of development. When a nation's economic growth has been slow, the modern assumption has been that development is required. The model of development underlying the initiatives of the UN Development Decades is relatively recent. A century ago development meant exploiting natural resources for economic gain, a meaning which survives in terms such as "development site" or "development opportunity". However, "development" began to acquire a new meaning in the years immediately following the Second World War. It came to mean not the exploitation of natural resources, but the end such an activity might serve — an increase in material prosperity and well-being usually, but not exclusively, at national level. A number of commentators have pointed to Harry Truman's speech on his inauguration as president of the USA in 1949 as a crucial moment in this shift. In his address Truman distinguished between the "developed world" and the "underdeveloped" countries in which the majority of the world's population lived, on the basis of the quantitative measure of national income — GNP. The speech emphasized that increased production was the key to prosperity and peace, and included an offer to help the underdeveloped nations to "relieve the suffering of these peoples" through "industrial activities" and "a higher standard of living" (Sachs, 1992a, p162).

The effect was to equate various forms of wealth with poverty simply because they could not be reflected in per capita GNP. Per capita measures of income had reduced what Wolfgang Sachs calls the "diverse and incomparable possibilities of human living arrangements" to poverty, endemic on a global scale. The wealth of a range of societies with flourishing cultures was simply ignored — for it could not be assessed in economic terms. As several commentators have pointed out,[5] many societies throughout the world, both in history and in our own time, have, at least until very recently, developed extremely rich cultural traditions at very much lower levels of consumption than those of the USA in the mid-twentieth century. For example, in illustrated talks on Ladakh, a high mountain-ringed plateau in the western Himalayas, Helena Norberg-Hodge shows a slide of a fine farmhouse, built in traditional style with ornate woodwork, standing amidst fields from which crops have just been harvested. The building symbolizes living traditions and a settled, successful way of life where people work hard and enjoy adequate rewards in a community in which until recently, she claims, the concept of poverty was unknown. Yet, by the criteria of the development era Truman ushered in, Ladakh is one of the poorest regions of the world (see Norberg-Hodge, 1992).

If high-income countries are "developed", countries with low income must require development, or so development thinking

---

5.  See, for example, the Norwegian philosopher Arne Naess (1990b) and Trainer (1989, p284).

runs. There is no attempt to discover whether there is some other explanation for a low GDP, as Sachs (1992c, p162) points out:

> *Wherever low income is the problem, the only admissible answer can be "economic development". There is hardly a mention of the idea that poverty might also result from oppression and thus demand liberation. Or that sufficiency might represent a strategy of risk-minimization, which is essential for long-term survival. Or even less that a culture might be directing its energies towards spheres other than the economic.*

Thus the diversity of human adaptations to the needs of survival and the challenge of creating community has been disregarded and devalued. Instead, the material wealth of the USA has set a simple standard for the rest of the world. However, the terms "developed" and "underdeveloped", or later "developing", are not simply descriptive, but judgemental. "Underdeveloped" comes to imply failure to achieve the features that characterize "developed", with its associations of progress, achieved targets and a completed process. "Underdeveloped" refers to a state that must be inferior because it can only be recognized from the more advanced position of the "developed" world: "development without predominance is like a race without direction. Thus the hegemony of the west was logically included in the proclamation of development" (Sachs, 1992b, p158). Almost without exception, the leaders of the South accepted the new value system: their "underdevelopment" was the problem, growth was the solution, even though rapid growth might require, as many World Bank and IMF reports have indicated, "structural readjustment", the wholesale overhaul of the institutions of nations, in which "traditions, hierarchies, mental habits — the whole texture of societies — [are] all dissolved in the planners' mechanistic models" (Sachs, 1992b, p159).

The construct of development that has prevailed for the best part of 50 years has represented, and continues to represent, a serious obstacle to sustainable development. In both North and South, development has meant an end to old habits of frugality, and, by its emphasis on industrialization, has also frequently destroyed the community resources on which frugality was based. It has swept aside the options for possible sustainable futures. It has created scarcity for the poor of modern times for whom money becomes increasingly important as a means of buying subsistence and, if possible, indulging some of the desires for the products of the growth machine.

## THE ECONOMIC SYSTEM

Economic growth and development are major features of an economic system that presents many impediments to sustainable development. Its obsession with the creation of new wealth to the virtual exclusion of questions of distribution and its tolerance of the domination of the economically weak by the economically strong affects many aspects of our lives, encouraging carelessness about both natural and human capital. Economic forces encroach on many areas of life, seeking commercial opportunities: marketing what were traditionally free goods; making money out of the celebration of non-monetary values; and encouraging consumerism through sponsorship, advertising and commercial control of the media. We live, as Weizsäcker (1994, p5) suggests, in the "Economic Century".

Even when the economic system provides the wherewithal for meeting needs, it does so largely on its own terms. Housing and health care are provided to meet the needs of a workforce. Educational syllabuses are devised to meet industry's needs. Only in the very early stages of education do we make a priority of developing talents and abilities that may not have an economic value. Only the very rich or the exceptionally gifted are free to develop their talents without having to satisfy economic criteria. We may pay lip service to the notion of developing each individual's potential, but the economic system does not permit us to treat such a goal as an end in itself.

The economic system provides for the fulfilment of human needs only to the extent that it values their potential — their economic potential — and ignores the needs of those whose potential contributions it does not value economically. As Ekins suggests, the forces at work in the economic system divide people into three categories: those who benefit from its workings, an elite who can sell skills that are valued in the market; a much larger group who "serve" the economy in humdrum jobs that offer few chances of personal growth and little more than a basic remuneration; and the vast "underclass" whom Ekins (1992a, p202) calls "the disposable people", the millions in the South who live in destitution and those in the North, estimated to be as high as 20 per cent of the population, who live below the poverty line.

By failing to meet human need, the economic system perpetuates massive human costs. Poor housing, unemployment, job insecurity, low pay, poor working conditions, bad diet and blighted neighbourhoods may singly or in combination be instrumental in creating the tragedies of child poverty, broken homes, serious emotional disturbance, ruined educational opportunities, addictions to drugs, alcohol or violence, homelessness, despair, unfulfilled lives and self-destruction. Such costs not only cause personal tragedies, but also deny communities the benefit of a vast supply of human resources — the inventiveness, resourcefulness, caring skills, co-operative abilities, in short the untapped potential of the many, many people economic forces worldwide consign to the scrapheap. The operation of the economic system destroys social cohesion and wastes the varied human abilities needed to form the social consensus on which sustainable development ultimately depends.

Not only does the system create destitution and deny many people a chance to contribute positively to the life of their communities, it also promotes a disinclination to remedy these sins against humanity. It diminishes our capacity to recognize the multiple poverties, for the more we live by material values the less we uphold spiritual or non-material values. Even when we recognize unfulfilled human need, the forces operating in our economic system make us less ready to acknowledge such need. For example, as John Kenneth Galbraith (1993) suggests in *The Culture of Contentment*, those who benefit materially from economic growth find it difficult to vote for the higher taxes by which their obligations to the poor might be fulfilled, as political developments in recent years in both Britain and the USA confirm. We all suffer what Daly calls the "corrosive effect of individualistic self-interest on the containing moral context of the community" (Daly and Cobb, 1990, p50). Paradoxically, those who have benefited from the economic system and become rich can no longer "afford" to meet the cost of attending to unfulfilled

human needs. The phenomenon operates at national, international and individual levels. Britain cannot "afford" nursery
education for all its young children. Inequity within a society
makes it more difficult to remove inequities between societies.
The countries of the North are generally too obsessed with their
relative economic standing to promote a more equitable
international economic order. Economic forces tend to undermine the moral framework on which is based the collective
restraint which is necessary if the market is to operate for the
common good. With regulation weakened, the corrosive effect of
free market policies sets in, as Daly and Cobb (1990, pp50–1)
describe:

> However much driven by self-interest, the market still depends
> absolutely on a community that shares such values as honesty,
> freedom, initiative, thrift, and other virtues whose authority will not
> long withstand the reduction to the level of personal tastes that is
> explicit in the positivistic, individualistic philosophy of value on
> which modern economic theory is based. If all value derives only
> from the satisfaction of individual wants, then there is nothing left
> over on the basis of which self-interested, individualistic want
> satisfaction can be restrained. . . . The market does not accumulate
> moral capital; it depletes it. Consequently, the market depends on
> the community to regenerate moral capital, just as it depends on the
> biosphere to regenerate natural capital.

Unless strictly regulated, the forces in the economic system work
against an equitable approach to meeting needs. Unless controlled, they create effects that give many the impression that we
serve the economy rather than have it serve us. These economic
forces operate locally, nationally and internationally. Internationally they work through the systems of trade, aid and debt
(briefly described in Chapter 1) to enlarge inequities and cause
much wasteful consumption of natural capital. Economically
weak or weakened nations have to survive within an integrated
international economic order which allows TNCs to exploit the
mobility of capital and so disregard national boundaries.

Such a system has obvious implications for sustainability, for it
imposes no constraints on the depletion of natural capital and
undermines self-reliance and local development initiatives. One

of its more insidious implications is that it weakens the national authority on which international agreements might be based, as Daly (1994, p187) points out:

> *To globalize the economy by erasure of national economic boundaries through free trade, free capital mobility and a free, or at least uncontrolled migration, is to wound fatally the major unit of community capable of carrying out any policies for the common good. That includes not only national policies for purely domestic ends, but also international agreements required to deal with those environmental problems that are irreducibly global (CO2, ozone depletion). International agreements presuppose the ability of national governments to carry out policies for their support. If nations have no control over their borders, they are in a poor position to enforce national laws, including those necessary to secure compliance with international treaties.*

## ETHICAL QUESTIONS

Elements of the paradigm may help explain our attitudes to ethical questions. The status of our moral judgements, and our belief in our capacity to make them and in the importance of doing so, is constantly under threat — undermined by the blandishments of advertising, denied validity by positivism, and assaulted by deterministic theories which explain our behaviour in terms of chemistry, psychology or social and economic structures. Also influential has been the utilitarian view that egalitarianism, based on the principle of equal opportunities for all, must defer to the principle of the pursuit of the greatest happiness of the greatest number, with no consideration of the needs of the inevitable remnant.

The combined impact of these influences may help explain our responses to many moral issues. We are often slow to uphold human rights. Our culture has very ambivalent attitudes to the application of moral principles. In many areas of human affairs, questions of right and wrong are subordinated to commercial gain or political advantage. Principled statements by public figures are often a gloss for policies or actions that do not stand up to moral scrutiny. Furthermore, society generally accepts a discrepancy between public and private morality, and appears to live happily with both inconsistency in the application of ethical principles and very definite limits to the areas within which we consider ourselves to have a moral responsibility.

## THE "ORTHODOX" VIEW

The paradigm both gives expression to beliefs and assumptions and reinforces these through the institutions to which it gives rise. Over time it establishes a dominant mode, a conservative force, which creates its own momentum and direction, which favours a "mainstream" view and tends to marginalize or discount alternative views.

Barring in this way serious challenges to its dominance, the orthodoxy protects its own fundamental assumptions. It may fail to submit ideas to a sufficiently rigorous critique or indeed to a simple process of validation by reference to reality. The paradigm approves or regards as self-evident ideas which, from other points of view, have only a tenuous justification. The continuing belief in the potential of growth is an obvious example. Other examples are not hard to find. The Indian physicist and feminist activist, Vandana Shiva, has pointed to the fallacy inherent in the assumption that the Green Revolution would not only mean abundant harvests and economic prosperity but would also, as a result of the reduction in scarcity, reduce social and political conflict. In reality, change led to an increase rather than a reduction in conflict. It is of course easy to be wise with hindsight, but a review of the effects of other distributions of new wealth in similar (and not so similar) societies would have indicated the improbability of reduced conflict.

The debt crisis of the early 1970s was another example of the failure to apply rigorous thought to the routine application of orthodox solutions. Financial institutions in the North, anxious to invest "petrodollars", were ready to lend additional sums to the South even though many Southern countries were finding it difficult to meet repayment schedules on existing loans. The "orthodoxy" of investment values overcame considerations of financial prudence, which might have been given more weight had evidence of the depth of many Southern governments' commitment to helping the poorest sections of their populations been examined. Difficulties created by these loans were compounded by the IMF's advice — to increase exports of primary products to earn the foreign exchange to meet debt service payments — which even a momentary recall of the law of supply and demand would have indicated was not in the interests of the South. Such examples bear out Gregory Bateson's view that finding solutions without figuring consequences is the paradigmatic condition of the age (Sale 1980, p27).

Norms within the paradigm seem to engender intellectual and moral confusion. Political leaders and electorates almost wilfully confuse the quantitative concept of material standard of living and the qualitative notion of quality of life. Means come to be treated as ends in themselves. Principles are lauded, but not implemented. The Brandt Report called for frank discussion of abuses of power by elites, but none took place. Economic forces are particularly oppressive for the weaker nations of the South, but there is silence in the North about the fact that these forces are the result of deliberate policy in the North. Kirstin Shrader-Frechette (1985, p97) suggests that "the worst environmental pollution is perhaps mind pollution, and the rarest global resources are well thought out ethical principles".[6]

## THE CONDITIONS OF MODERN LIFE

The forces of the paradigm have also created a way of life that discourages more sustainable practices. Our desire for the knowledge that might lead to an understanding of the crisis is blunted both by the challenge of mastering the technical complexities of many major areas of human activity (accessible only to experts) and by a flood of information and opinion from the press, radio and television. The media claim to keep us informed, but their reports are rarely set in context. They hunt dramatic stories but ignore long-term trends till catastrophe looms. Reports on serious issues are usually superficial and seldom tease out the connection between our lives and those of the victims, whose sufferings are assessed for their "news" value. For the most part we are content to remain incurious if events happen at a distance or if their impact does not immediately impinge on our lives.

---

6. "Mind-pollution" is what Conrad Waddington (1977), professor of animal genetics at the University of Edinburgh until his death in 1975, called, in lighter vein, "COWDUNG" — "the COnventional Wisdom of the DomiNant Group".

Though investigative programmes can awaken powerful moral responses, these are "contained" and limited by the context in which they appear — alongside great art, quiz shows, sports programmes, soap operas, films and possibly advertisements, all competing for the attention of a public expecting to be entertained rather than challenged. A moment of compassion may stimulate a generous cash contribution to an appeal fund, but the impulse is soon crowded out by other demands on our time and attention. Education also reflects the major forces of the paradigm. Increasingly dominated by pressures to transmit the expertise required in the complex modern world, it places little emphasis on the implications of our present treatment of people and the planet.

Modern urban life has weakened community bonds for many people. Social and economic forces destroy our opportunities to relate to each other as whole persons in small neighbourhoods. Changes heralded as progress seem increasingly to threaten livelihood, community and autonomy. Personal and communal bonds are weakened as organizations grow, firms amalgamate, constituencies expand and markets extend across the globe. Deprived of close community bonds and increasingly isolated socially, many people feel powerless to influence the large-scale impersonal changes that impinge on their lives but over which they feel they have somehow surrendered effective control.

Despite the most technologically advanced communication systems the world has ever seen, despite the spread of formal education, despite the relative ease of foreign travel, despite the prominence of human rights in the UN Charter and the real, if limited, success of many campaigns for the rights of disadvantaged social groups, despite the value we place on creativity and imagination, despite the very high standards of care displayed by many individuals in both their private and occupational roles, and despite many generous contributions to aid appeals, we are rarely able to summon up the collective will to begin to undo the inhumane and ecologically unsound effects of unsustainable development.

## PSYCHOLOGICAL IMPACTS OF THE PARADIGM
The paradigm may have an even deeper impact at a psycho-

logical level. Individually and collectively we share a capacity to refuse to face the seriousness of the crisis. The individual or collective psyche may well prefer to ignore reality rather than face changes that threaten security. Our defence mechanisms include evasion and displacement. We plead pressure of other commitments, lack of time, lack of knowledge, a reluctance to intervene in others' affairs. We declare our willingness to support solutions, but make our contribution contingent on similar conditional commitments by others, and continue in the meantime in ways we cannot justify.

The most powerful defence mechanism is denial. We deny the seriousness of the situation, afraid to admit to ourselves that prevailing practices are wrong or inappropriate, and are even more obstinately defensive when others confront us with evidence of the need for some amendment of our normal ways. Denial operates at the institutional as well as the individual level. For instance, Daly (1994, p185) interprets the World Bank's silence on the need to achieve sustainable development in the North as "a continuing psychology of denial regarding limits to growth". Similarly, denial explains the role of Northern financial institutions in the development of the debt crisis. It is the denial of inconvenient aspects of reality, the refusal — or inability — to admit that standard ways of operating are not a "sufficient response" to the complexity of a situation to which they were not intended to apply, which underlie unimaginative, unadaptive responses, bureaucratic inflexibility, narrow views, facile optimism, and institutional cynicism.[7]

---

7.  Many commentators describe the psychological effects of the paradigm. For example, Al Gore (1992), vice-president of the USA, explains denial in terms of "dysfunctional civilization". Like children denied unconditional love in dysfunctional families, we "quietly internalize the blame for our civilization's failure to provide a feeling of community and a shared sense of purpose in life", resulting from the destruction of the bonds with the natural world. Conditioned to feel utterly dependent on our civilization instead, we internalize "the pain of our lost sense of connection to the natural world". We consume the resources of the earth in an attempt to distract ourselves from this pain, unable to alter our behaviour, for "many of the unwritten rules of our dysfunctional civilization encourage silent acquiescence in our patterns of destructive behaviour towards the natural world" (see Gore 1992, pp232–7).

Whatever the precise mechanisms by which they create their impacts, the deep-seated forces that have shaped Western society still largely determine social goals, cultural values, political possibilities and institutional objectives and practices. Moves away from unsustainable policies and practices and towards sustainable alternatives will be greatly facilitated by a modification of the norms these dominant ideas have helped create. We shall consider how we can attempt to achieve such a formidable task in the next chapter.

# Chapter 8 | OVERCOMING the OBSTACLES

The magnitude of the changes involved in any transition to a sustainable social and economic system should not be underestimated, as W D Ruckelshaus (1989, p115), adviser to two US presidents, has pointed out:

> Such a move would be a modification of society comparable to only two other changes: the agricultural revolution of the late Neolithic, and the Industrial Revolution of the past two centuries. These revolutions were gradual, spontaneous and largely unconscious. This one will have to be a fully conscious operation guided by the best foresight society can provide — foresight pushed to the limit. If we actually do it, the undertaking will be absolutely unique in humanity's stay on the earth.

Other commentators have suggested that to achieve such a transition we need to replace the ideas and values that underlie the formidable complex of obstacles described in the last chapter with a new set of shaping ideas and values. To do this, they argue, we need not just a modification but a revolution in our thinking — what has sometimes been called a "paradigm shift" However, it is not obvious quite how such a change can be achieved given the unsustainable paradigm's ascendancy. How is it possible to develop a new socioeconomic-political-technological framework that will allow us to tackle the interlocking problems of the global *problématique*?

Pressure for change is generated by the tensions the

unsustainable paradigm creates, as J Ronald Engel (1990, p9) has observed:[1]

> *The Ottawa conference [1986] was one more expression of the growing consensus — broadly shared among the conservation community and increasingly recognized in the international development community — that not simply this or that part of the present global development pattern needs to be corrected, but that the entire model of modern industrial development is seriously awry. Not only the economic values of competition and consumption, but the expectation of unlimited material growth; not only the prevalence of technology but the view of the world as a machine; not only the hierarchies of power, wealth, status or sex, but the idea of hierarchy itself; not only the dichotomy of resource conservation versus ecocentricism, conservation versus development, humanity versus nature, theory versus practice, intrinsic versus extrinsic values, but the need to think in dichotomies at all. In other words the basic world view or image of social and cosmic reality, in terms of which scientific, moral, political and most other questions have been asked and answered since the beginning of the modern industrial era, is being questioned.*

Moreover, he asserts, such questioning is taking place, "especially because failure is being primarily experienced as failure to provide a fulfilling and sustainable life, a *good life*, for all" (Engel, 1990, p9).

The shorthand of "paradigm shift" tends to obscure the fact that the paradigm is neither a monolithic entity that has to be dismantled nor a deterministic framework allowing only standard and uniform responses, but a complex of ideas, assumptions and social practices which individuals consciously or unconsciously endorse. Though there may be a dominant consensus, this is continuously open to amendment through processes of communication and mediation. Differences in individual values are growth points for change, and diversity in individual viewpoints and group attitudes represents a form of debate within the paradigm. Individuals and social groups can — and do — adopt

---

1.  See also Brown (1981) on tensions within the paradigm.

new values even while the established paradigm remains dominant.

## ACHIEVING THE NEW PARADIGM

Radical changes in the ideas that shape our way of life come about through processes of gradual change as new ideas gain acceptance, are put into practice, and modified in the light of results. The problems involved in bringing about a paradigm shift are the problems of changing any orthodoxy — of winning acceptance for ideas that are not generally accepted and that seem to challenge established wisdom. Progress can only be made through protracted arguments and negotiations within social groups at all levels in societies that permit discussion of social and economic priorities. To facilitate such processes we can set intermediate objectives such as raising awareness of the issues, arguing the importance of change, discussing the feasibility and advantages of change, persuading people it is to their advantage to change and creating an interest in alternatives and a desire for change. Efforts to achieve such goals become means to further goals. We can identify a number of instruments of change that can be used to advance the process of sustainable development.

## THINKING HOLISTICALLY

Holistic thinking is a particularly important means of change for sustainable development; to use Bateson's phrase, it attempts to figure the consequences. Holistic approaches try to anticipate the problems "simple" solutions create and to identify more satisfactory structural solutions. Holistic thinking led one farmer in Kenya, sickened at having to shoot the elephants ruining his crops, to adopt an alternative form of land use, accommodating not only his own interests, but also those of the elephants, of tourists who wanted to see the elephants and of local people who could supplement their subsistence economy with an income from tourism. When a crossing to the Isle of Skye in northwest Scotland was proposed, holistic thinking led to a proposal for a causeway which linked communities directly and incorporated a tidal electricity-generating scheme, in preference to a bridge that bypassed the communities and increased the costs of travelling between them. (The Scottish Office opted for the bridge.)

Holistic thinking is based on the recognition of two principles (Savory, 1988, pp30, 32):

- "Since greater wholes have qualities and character not present in any of their constituent wholes (parts) one must seek to understand the greater whole in order to understand its parts, not vice versa"; and
- "wholes have no defined limits".

Holistic thinking recognizes that problems may be symptoms of deeper causes, that connections may be complex, that inter-actions between different forces may be dynamic and that structural solutions that acknowledge these complexities are preferable to "fixes" that may incur large costs (often con-veniently over the horizon or not likely to be borne by the present generation). Holistic thinking pursues connections and leads to integrated approaches that try to accommodate different sectoral interests (in the economy, government and society generally). It recognizes that any intervention in a system has impacts other than those originally intended. Holistic awareness complicates the issue of choosing goals in the short term, but leads to greater clarity in long-term planning and can operate at all levels — locally as in analysing city traffic problems; nationally as in integrating policy on land-use planning, energy and transport; and internationally as will be required in devising a new international economic order.[2]

## THE VISION OF THE NEW PARADIGM

Also important are visions of alternatives to current policies and practices. These enlarge our sense of the possible, and stimu-late thinking about how to achieve it, for as Weizsäcker (1994, p175) points out: "Realpolitik alone tends to become dull and meaningless without a vision of what could be different and how one would *wish* things to be. ... The new century, the Century of the Environment, will also need a compelling, global vision."

---

2. One example of a holistic approach is systems analysis. See, for example, Donella Meadows (1992) on properties of complex systems that affect change.

How such a vision can be translated into practical reality may not always be clear, but visions of the future do not arrive unsuspected out of nowhere any more than paradigm shifts happen overnight. Accordingly the following sketch includes, as pointers to and precursors of a sustainable future, examples of current practice and of ideas that have already been developed.

Though we cannot predict with certainty what form a new sustainable society will assume, it must differ from the unsustainable paradigm in at least five important respects:

- its conception of progress,
- its regard for the natural world,
- its respect for humans and its valuation of human potential,
- its conception of wealth, and
- its view of economic activity.

*The New Progress*

The new progress will have clearly defined objectives — not of growth and aggrandizement through expansion, domination and competition, but of sufficiency, equity and security founded on co-operation rather than competitiveness; participation rather than token consultation, oppression or exclusion; empowerment rather than deprivation and dispossession; and self-reliance rather than dependence.[3]

Acceptance of the principle of sufficiency will mean an end to the cult of size. The unrestricted growth of an economic enterprise or of the economy itself will be seen as a threat to both sustainable utilization of resources and others' rights of access to them. Small-scale enterprises will allow close control over their ecological impacts and provide social and human benefits, giving people more opportunities to contribute creatively than they have in large systems. Small scale will also be the most ecologically efficient option, given, as some commentators suggest (see, for example, Brown, 1981), the provision of energy on a local basis. There will also be wide support for policies of demand management, based on the awareness that we can learn to do

---

3. Without an overriding principle of sufficiency the ecological efficiency discussed in Chapter 6 will not of itself guarantee sustainability.

without wants as well as endlessly trying to satisfy them. What Wolfgang Sachs (1992c, 164) calls "comfortable frugality" will replace conspicuous consumption as the norm.

There will be a general acceptance of the need for more equitable distribution both nationally and internationally, based on a general awareness that there is only a finite amount of wealth to be shared. An entitlement to a share of resources and the opportunity to utilize them productively (for example, equitable access to money for productive investment at local level) will be regarded as more important than a share of the dubious net benefits of the trickle-down effect of conventional economic growth.

A sustainable society will provide a far more valuable form of security than the kind governments have sought through massive arms spending, which, far from guaranteeing security, has consumed resources, created costly international tensions and been likened to "dismantling a house to salvage materials to erect a fence around it" (Michael Renner of the WWI in Ekins, 1992a, p58). The security a sustainable society will offer will have three aspects and will require:

- maintaining the integrity of the ecological systems of the biosphere and restoring these where they have been degraded,
- managing these so as to sustain human livelihoods, and
- maintaining communities and their cultures in such a way as to allow people to fulfil their aspirations as fully as possible.

### Respecting the Natural World

Of fundamental importance for any sustainable future will be a new respect for the natural world. Some commentators see this as a matter of recovering a relationship with the natural world which was eroded as industrialization created urban societies.[4] Though we obviously cannot return to a preindustrial mythological view of nature, ecocentrists advocate that instead of

---

4. In 1870 only 3 per cent of world population lived in cities. By 1950 the figure had risen to 29 per cent. By 2025 it is estimated that 60 per cent of an estimated world population of 8.5 billion will live in cities. See Johnson (1993, p181).

exploiting the "neutral stuff" of nature, we should respect the intrinsic value of the natural world and attempt to preserve its remnants. Some ecocentrics argue for a morality with a greater imperative than a people-centred morality: "Examine each question in terms of what is ethically and aesthetically right, as well as what is economically expedient. A thing is right when it tends to preserve the integrity, stability, and beauty of the biotic community. It is wrong when it tends otherwise" (Leopold, 1987, p224). However, such an ethic opposes so much of current economic activity and in a way often seen as unrealistic, at least within the constraints dictated by current assumptions and values of the unsustainable paradigm, that it is able to offer few solutions that are considered either feasible or politically acceptable.

To our modern, urbanized consciousness, the two modes of valuing nature — reverential and utilitarian — tend to seem mutually exclusive. We need to develop a public awareness that is not split between mainstream, "practical" technocentrism and marginalized, "idealistic" or even "unrealistic", defensive, protectionist eco-idealism. It will not be enough to acknowledge our dependence on the natural world on a notional or theoretical level. We will be on a truly sustainable path only when our awareness of that dependence informs all our thinking about using natural resources and all our practices in every form of economic, social and cultural activity. That awareness must permeate our thinking and influence our practices as thoroughly as it did in isolated rural societies, in places such as Ladakh and the Outer Hebrides, which until recently depended almost completely on meagre local resources with no expectation of compensating external inputs should these be depleted.

Such an awareness would help us to integrate economic and ecological considerations, and would stimulate in us the determination and ingenuity required to reorder our priorities so as to minimize the sacrifice of natural capital still possible under "best practical" options. The Brundtland Commission and Rio Summit did try, however imperfectly, to encourage such integration. The Duch government has taken this thinking much further in its *National Environmental Policy Plan*. Several countries are showing an interest in strategic environmental assessment, as they attempt to bring ecological concerns into high-level decision-making and ensure vertical integration of policies, plans, programmes and projects. In Canada, a Cabinet-level committee considers the environmental implications of government policy. Such moves will remove the contraints frequently placed on environmental impact assessment by decisions taken at a higher level and end such anomalies as the conclusion that the only significant environmental impact of a proposed nuclear power station would be that an approach road would threaten a rare plant community.

These policy moves are paralleled by a growing interest in fully integrating economic activity with ecological integrity, thus enabling us to meet needs without cost to the environment — not only in varieties of permaculture, organic farming and sustainable forestry, but also in less well-publicized efforts by dedicated individuals to conserve locally-adapted plant varieties, such as drought-resistant millet and maize in Ethiopia and Zimbabwe and bere barley suited to the cool summers of northern Scotland.

Respect for the natural world will also shape the assumptions of those engaged in science and technology, as Schumacher (quoted in Capra, 1983, p443) suggests: "Wisdom demands a new orientation of science and technology towards the organic, the gentle, the nonviolent, the elegant and beautiful". Scientists will accept that their relationship with the natural world is inevitably an interactive one, that "the knower is implicated in the known", and that even "detached" analysis cannot lead to "objective" truth.[5] A new awareness of the interdependence of phenomena and the complexity of reality will lead to a reassessment of the understanding which scientific knowledge provides.

Two US scientists, R R Wallace and B G Norton, of the School of Public Policy at the Georgia Institute of Technology, suggest that Lovelock's Gaia hypothesis implies abandoning the ideal of a "value free" science that leads to comprehensive objective "truth". With its insight into hierarchical global systems, Gaian

---

5. Patrick Geddes (1992), the pioneering Scottish human ecologist, suggested that only those who develop a delight in the natural world during childhood should be allowed to carry out scientific research.

theory has meant a shift from unitary to pluralistic systems of analysis:

> *Both epistemological and physical theory have been driven, despite enormous intellectual energy expended to avoid it, toward the conclusion that there exists no single, uniquely correct description of the physical world. The problem, however, is not that no consistent and accurate descriptions of the world exist; rather, there are too many. The world of experience is unavoidably complex, and there are many valid perspectives and scales upon which to describe and evaluate it. There is no unitary picture of reality against which a paradigm can be compared. To choose a paradigm is to choose one way of describing the world, and the choice cannot be determined descriptively. A determination of scale and perspective first requires a determination of goal — a value-laden decision.*
>
> (Wallace and Norton, 1992, p115)

They also point out that choosing an approach to the management of resources is a value-driven decision which depends on social priorities: "Until the public develops and articulates both economic and ecological goals, science alone is inadequate for choosing a perspective from which to study the system. Science, guided by deeply felt obligation not to destroy the options of future generations, can, however, delineate a horizon of concern and a time perspective in which to address a given problem" (Wallace and Norton, 1992, p115).

One commentator (Rolston, 1990) has suggested the need to divide science into "ecoscience", which studies nature for itself, and "technoscience", which would be as much about defining and respecting limits to the exploitation of the natural world as about devising means of drawing down stocks. Technoscience thus has an explicitly ethical dimension, which would be integrated into the process of making decisions about using scientific insights to exploit the natural world. It represents the kind of feedback which, had it been available earlier, might have dramatically altered the path of research in nuclear physics.

Aware that science cannot be neutral and that facilities available to researchers reflect economic and political objectives, scientists will readily accept a share of the responsibility for their work. Ernst Ulrich von Weizsäcker suggests they should accept responsibility for working on the problems of the modern world, including those science has helped to create, and if necessary make a conscious commitment to work in the political arena. As he points out, organizations such as Pugwash, International Physicians for the Prevention of Nuclear War, and the Society for Social Responsibility in the Sciences already demonstrate the readiness of some scientists to take a stand on issues in which they feel implicated (Weizsäcker, 1994, pp190–1).

A new general awareness of the impossibility of a "value free" objective truth will not make science any less fascinating. Weizsäcker suggests there will be numerous opportunities in a world of uncertainties and other constraints to work on "complex applied problems" even more challenging than much current research. The criteria of sufficiency, equity and security will require the development of ingenious, beautifully "simple", effective, low-cost technologies that work in harmony with nature and that, once installed, will immediately begin to reduce ecological damage. Already many developments point to the future — renewable energy systems, biological pest control, integrated pest management, agroforestry, permaculture, organic agriculture, techniques for restoring degraded ecosystems, and "ecologically engineered" waste disposal systems such as reed-bed technologies. Integrating disinterested enquiry with ethical and human considerations and technological challenges may reverse the rejection of science by a substantial proportion of able students — which has been a feature of our culture for at least 20 years.

### Valuing People

A sustainably developing society will permit neither the classification of people into Ekins's categories (see p142) nor the subordination of welfare to economic forces. It will insist on each individual's right to fulfil his or her needs and on the provision of equal opportunities for all to develop their abilities, and it will allocate resources accordingly.

It will provide a supportive framework for all those on whose love, care and creativity the welfare of the disadvantaged, the young, the aged and the infirm depends. Guided by the recognition that the welfare of each individual depends on the fulfilment of the needs of many others (for example, parents, neighbours, teachers, carers, supervisors, employers, colleagues), the sustainable society will support all its citizens in caring for each other, cherishing the dimension of "relationality" and mutuality in human existence, for as Harrison (1990, p204), a feminist theologian in the USA, puts it:

> We literally build up the power of personhood in one another. It is within the power of human love to build up dignity and self-respect in each other or to tear each other down. We are better at the latter than the former. However, literally through acts of love directed to us, we become self-respecting and other-regarding persons, and we cannot be one without the other.

There will also be a new recognition that we can ill afford to do without the human potential that is wasted when needs are not met. It will be widely accepted that we are more likely to solve development problems if we nourish and make use of the creative potential of the mass of people and give priority to economic production that liberates that potential. In particular we will value the diversity of individuals' talents, aptitudes and skills and the variety of different cultures' technologies (in the broadest sense) as "resources" on which we will have to draw if we are to maintain progress towards a sustainable society, resources which will be lost if not maintained in use. As we have seen, the negotiations involved in achieving progress towards sustainable development will demand resourcefulness, imagination, flexibility, generosity, responsibility and co-operation.

## New Wealth

The "sustainable" conception of wealth is implicit in the recognition of the prime importance of human needs, the full range of which can be fulfilled only if a number of "goods" are available and equally accessible to all people. We need a broad, human-centred conception of wealth. Money may be a useful means of exchange and a convenient way of storing some forms of wealth. However, it is not wealth itself, which is founded not on material consumption but on maintaining stocks of a wide range of the goods — physical and nonphysical — on which human welfare depends. Such goods are both economic and noneconomic and include health, family life, livelihoods or jobs, working conditions, income levels and income distribution, leisure, the state of the environment and security, including confidence about the future.

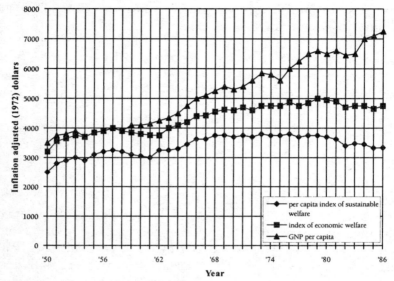

Source: Daly and Cobb (1990, p420).

**Figure 8.1** *Alternative measures of economic welfare*

We will need new indicators of welfare to replace GNP, which is widely used for this purpose although it measures something else — the size of the financial flows in the economy. A number of alternative indices have already been proposed, for example, the Physical Quality of Life Index, developed by the Overseas Development Council, which gives equal weighting to infant mortality, life expectancy and literacy in an attempt to measure the contribution to quality of life of welfare provision and living conditions generally. In 1990 the UNDP initiated its Human Development Index, updated annually in the UNDP's *Human Development Report*, which is also a single index based on per capita GDP adjusted for purchasing power, adult literacy and life expectancy. Both these indices have been recently extended to take account of the extent to which human rights are respected — in the UNDP's Human Freedom Index and in the Authentic

Socio-Economic Development Index of Mark Lutz, professor of economics at the University of Maine. Most interesting of all is Daly and Cobb's Index of Sustainable Economic Welfare (ISEW) which combines 20 indicators of welfare. This shows that despite continued growth in GNP, economic welfare has declined in the USA since a peak in 1979 (see Figure 8.1).

## The Economy

Founded on this broad conception of wealth, the new economics will take a much wider view of the economy than conventional economics, which ignores all aspects that cannot be valued in monetary terms. It will acknowledge the contribution to social wealth of the informal or non-monetary economy as well as the formal economy, which is restricted to business and government. Particularly important here, because so often overlooked, is the contribution to the national economy by households, especially through unpaid work at home, work without which many activities within the formal economy could not function as they do at present. Some estimates value household "production" in industrialized countries at around 30 per cent of GNP. The informal economy also covers the range of contributions to wealth from barter, from the "unreported" economy of, for example, street trading in many Southern countries (as well as such illegal activities as "moonlighting" and drug-dealing). Local exchange trading systems (LETS) are one attempt to promote the informal economy in ways that benefit the community and particularly its financially poorest members. Sustainable economics will also take into account the work of voluntary organizations, other community associations and community-based activities which also create non-monetary wealth, as Ekins, Hillman and Hutchinson (1992, p68) point out

> It is arguable that such groups do as much for our quality of life as the formal business sector. Human rights groups safeguard our basic freedoms; peace groups confront the arms race; environmental groups work for a secure future; women's groups give gender solidarity and provide the backbone of community life in many countries. Mutual aid groups of all types, often of some of the most disadvantaged in society, bring succour and support to their members and those farther afield. Development groups either raise

*awareness about, and money for, Third World problems, or set about directly solving those problems.*

A new broader view of the economy will end the distinction between those with a job and the unemployed. If we maintain technological advance we will reach the point at which a very small proportion of the population will be required to produce material goods for everyone. We will then be faced with a choice between foregoing purely technological efficiency, which we may have to do anyway on ecological grounds, and revising radically the notion that only those with a job contribute to the economy. The evidence of the last two decades suggest that nations with industrial economies already suffer from "structural" unemployment, which has highlighted the dependencies that traditonal patterns of work and non-work create. Promoting a concept first suggested over 70 years ago, the Basic Income Research Group proposes that all individuals should receive from the state a basic income which would replace existing unemployment benefit, other benefits and tax relief. This would guarantee people a basic livelihood and allow them to contribute to society in ways that allow them to use their abilities most effectively, and prevent them suffering the stigma of being unemployed and feeling a burden on the state.

A future sustainable society looking back to the twentieth century will find our inability to devise economic arrangements to meet human needs virtually incomprehensible, for its citizens will understand that economic systems are not founded on unalterable natural law, but are human constructs which communities, given power, can amend to suit their needs. In a future sustainable society the economy will serve people rather than perpetuate a system in which the welfare of the majority is subordinated to profit, market share and competitive advantage. A sustainable economy will aim "to bring forth the goods and services needed for a becoming existence" (Schumacher, 1973, p45) and arrange to do this in ways that meets people's individual and commnunity needs. Economic growth will be used as a carefully controlled means of meeting specific needs within sustainability constraints.

A sustainable economy will inevitably be a regulated one.

Guided by criteria of sufficiency, equity and security, govern-ments anxious to develop sustainable economies will

- set limits to the extent to which powerful economic interests can dominate the market. (Sustainability does not require the abolition of markets that can organize production efficiently);
- ensure that prices reflect the "full" costs of production and in particular that the externalities of production, such as environmental and social costs, are included in prices;
- carry out a redistributive role where the operation of past mar-kets has resulted in unfair distributions of economic power;
- support local economies that function primarily to meet local needs and that use the resources of local people and their communities. Such support will be required to prevent the centralization of economic power and profits by groups that treat outlying regions as "extractive" economies.

### The International Economic Order

At the international level, governments will defend national economic interests against the impact of supra-national economic forces, such as shifts of capital by TNCs to low-wage economies; and negotiate adjustments to the national economy in the light of international agreements about the protection of global ecological resources and redistribution of wealth between North and South.

The sustainable future will have an equitable international economic order with no debt crisis, effective and relevant aid programmes and genuinely free trade. Achieving it will require complex negotiation, but steps towards it have already been suggested. Susan George (1992) proposes cancelling debts on the grounds that they have in effect already been repaid by a combination of interest payments and low commodity prices. It has also been suggested (see Ekins, 1992a, p62) that money spent on armaments should be used to solve the debt problems of the poorest countries. Further aid will be made available to poor nations in a manner that will help them fulfil human need and achieve ecological sustainability. It will take various forms — resources, cash, technology transfers — and may operate in similar fashion to the Global Environmental Facility (GEF) but on a much enlarged scale. On international trade Herman Daly

(1994, p187) recently suggested that "ten years from now the buzz words will be 'renationalization of capital' and the 'community rooting of capital for the development of national and local economies'". Such moves could be a first step towards returning to a system of exchange in which nations trade surpluses to obtain goods and resources they cannot produce themselves within a policy framework of increasing their self-reliance and respecting other nations' rights to do the same.

## Measuring Wealth

The new system will require a better measure of economic success than the purely monetary evaluations of conventional economics; for example, GNP will be replaced by a more comprehensive and multifaceted form of acccounting for sustainability. In the UK, David Pearce and his colleagues have already called for GNP to be reformed so that it takes into account the depreciation of natural resources, defensive expenditures (against the costs of growth) and loss of capacities and life-support services (Pearce et al, 1989). It needs to be widely accepted that income from natural resources is only true income if it can be sustained indefinitely and does not eat into capital. The Dutch government's Central Bureau of Statistics is working on an index of such income. Its work complements that in other countries, for example Norway and France, to include accounts of natural resources in national accounting.

Sustainable resource management will also amend such price-based means of evaluating projects as cost-benefit analysis, with its reliance on discounting that discriminates against future generations. It is a tool of conventional development and will not survive without major modification. We need a broad, multi-dimensional assessment of all costs and benefits using a wide range of criteria (economic certainly, but also distributional, social, environmental, scientific, technological and risk analytical) and possibly also sustainability constraints. The analysis will present not a single monetary or other quantitative index, but a range of relevant information. It will make explicit any suggested trade-offs and should be available to all those involved in making, or affected by, decisions about the wealth of the community. It will also point out that, even with such a broad approach, there is still a risk of some costs and benefits being ignored because they cannot be quantified, for example, the cost of the loss of wilderness or community amenities.

## Economics

A new discipline of economics is required to study the creation, distribution and consumption of wealth (as more broadly defined above) and particularly the best allocation of scarce resources in a finite world so that needs can be met with as little cost as possible.

In presenting options for achieving economic objectives economists will need to abandon their claim to neutrality and function as the servants of larger ends, being explicit about the values and assumptions behind alternative policies. Three criteria will apply in selecting options:

• ecological sustainability,
• reduction of inequity, and
• the participation of people in the process of development, thus giving them opportunities to fulfil their needs rather than treating them simply as consumers of the end products of increased economic activity.

"Sustainable" economics will be based on an awareness of ecological reality and an adequate understanding of human need rather than on ecological ignorance and a model of *homo economicus* that ignores modern psychological and sociological insights into human behaviour.

The new economics will mean a reappraisal of such basic economic concepts as allocation, distribution and scale. The criteria for the optimal allocation of resources will be those of ecological efficiency rather than the considerations that determine optimality in neoclassical economics. The Pareto distribution will also have to be amended, for any sustainable system that meets needs will involve a reduction in consumption by those who exceed their share of natural capital and will make some people "worse off". As we have seen, the issue of scale will assume fundamental importance.

Many economists are already building on the work of

Boulding, Georgescu-Roegen and Herman Daly. Their work has received valuable support from a number of economists exploring "new" or "real-life" economics, including Paul Ekins and Manfred Max-Neef. Particularly important is the development of ecological economics — an attempt to build a new discipline on a new framework incorporating the insights of ecological science rather than simply extending neoclassical theory as in environmental economics.

### A New Ethic?

The values of sufficiency, equity and security will contribute to a new "sustainable" ethic, which many see as based on a new relationship with the natural world. We may, however, have less need to find a new ethic than to practise the cardinal virtues of the world's religions, which have much in common with the values of sufficiency, equity and security. The fact that the survival of all will depend on the systematic application of the criterion of sufficiency may help to bring about a more consistent approach to ethical questions, for, as Ronald Higgins has observed, morality operates in all walks of life or none at all. A sustainable society will reject Keynes's famous plea (quoted in Schumacher, 1973, p82) that: "For at least another hundred years we must pretend to ourselves and to everyone that fair is foul and foul is fair; for foul is useful and fair is not. Avarice and usury and precaution must be our gods for a little longer still."

Business and commerce will see a revival of the values of family businesses, which considered providing a fair deal and giving service to customers as important as making profits — indeed regarded one as impossible without the other. The way forward is signposted by the activities of groups like the Briarpatch organization in California and Traidcraft in the UK.[6]

### PUBLIC DEBATE

Any sketch of a new paradigm has a utopian quality. Despite developments that point the way forward, it is unclear how we attain a society that embodies many of the more desirable features

---

6.  On the Briarpatch organization, see Ekins (1986, pp272–82); on Traidcraft, see Chapter 10, p211–12.

we envisage. Therefore, as John Proops (1989, p62) of the Department of Economics at the University of Keele points out, such accounts are not "images to which we should strive: rather they are imaginings against which we can judge likely outcomes". They are just one contribution to a much wider debate about our objectives as a society and the means we employ to achieve them.

As we have seen, our ideas about the ends "progress" serves are vague and are obscured by our reliance on economic growth. The pace of technological advance and the power of the economic interests that exploit it have blurred our distinctions between means and ends. As Einstein (quoted in Savory, 1988, p4) pointed out, "perfection of means and confusion of goals seem ... to characterize our age". The technical means at our disposal enable us to solve many problems, especially those which Alan Savory calls "mechanical" and Schumacher calls "convergent". We are less successful in solving problems relating to what Alan Savory (1988, p24) calls "the non-mechanical world of complex relationships and wholes with diffuse boundaries" (see box on next page). These Schumacher calls divergent problems. Solving them involves "overcoming or reconciling opposites" and finding answers that cannot be supplied from factual, intellectual or technical knowledge. Schumacher (1973, p81) attributes our lack of success to the fact that having "to grapple with divergent problems tends to be exhaustive, worrying and wearisome". However, grappling is essential if we are to reach some public resolution of conflicting views.

Public debate ideally takes place in many different social groups and can be conducted in a variety of ways, for example through government consultation, political discussion, the media planning in a wide range of sectors, and education. It takes many forms (though formal debates are rare) and can be stimulated and informed by inputs which range from government white papers through NGO campaigns to action by committed individuals. From time to time inputs make a special impact, such as the report *Transport and the Environment* (Royal Commission on Environmental Pollution, 1944) or the activities of "direct action" groups such as Earth First at the Twyford Down motorway site in the summer of 1994. Debate can take place at any level — international conferences, local initiatives (the Sustainable Seattle

## SUCCESS IN PROBLEM-SOLVING

| Mechanical | Nonmechanical |
|---|---|
| *Development of:* | *Management of:* |

**Mechanical**
*Development of:*

- Transport
— air
— land
— water
- Communication
— radio
— television
— telephone
— satellite
- Weapons
— conventional
— nuclear
— laser

- Space Exploration
- Computer Technology
— artificial intelligence
— robotics
- Home Building and Home Appliance Technology
- Energy Plants
— nuclear
— hydroelectric
— etc
- Medical Technology
— brain scanners
— eyeglasses/contact lenses
— medicines
— etc
- Genetic Engineering
- Chemical Technology
— soluble fertilizers

**EVER INCREASING SUCCESS TESTIFYING TO THE MARVELS OF SCIENCE**

**Nonmechanical**
*Management of:*

- Agriculture
- Rangelands
- Forests
- Air Quality
- Fisheries
- Water Supplies & Quality
- Erosion
- Economies
- Wildlife (including insects)
- Human Relationships
- Human health

**EVER INCREASING PROBLEMS TESTIFYING TO OUR LACK OF UNDERSTANDING**

*Source*: Savory (1988, p25).

project tried to encourage wide public participation in selecting sustainability indicators for the city) and environmental fora set up by private individuals wishing to claim a "space" in which to discuss issues of mutual concern. Agencies of various kinds can stimulate the debate and set the agenda in a number of ways, such as courses, publicity and the allocation of resources.

The significance of such debate lies at least as much in the discussion itself as in the conclusions that emerge. Unlike formal debates, discussions of this sort widen awareness, modify opinions (including preconceptions about "obvious" solutions) and facilitate mediation between the different interests on which progress to sustainable development depends. For example, by bringing together representatives of many different interests, the Canadian Round Table movement encourages a broader understanding of the key issues. As Wendy Simpson Lewis of the Canadian State of the Environment directorate, points out, "The more people you have round the table, the more you have to be open to other points of view."[7]

To be effective such debate must:

- be adequately resourced;
- engage the population as a whole, including those who are not normally active in the decison-making process, but who have interests to represent and a positive contribution to make;
- be informed (participants must be aware of the nature and dimensions of the problems); and
- be conducted openly and in good faith with no hidden agenda, and reach decisions openly.

## DEMONSTRATING PROGRESS

Practical examples of sustainable solutions both complement and contribute to wide-ranging public discussion. Reports of projects should inform the debate and modify opinion. For example, the fact that Namibia, a newly independent country, has established a sustainable fisheries policy is relevant to the debate and should not be lost on the participants in it (Wightman, 1994).

---

7. In a speech at the NEF/FOE/SANGEC conference on sustainability indicators, Edinburgh University, April 1994.

Primary environmental care (PEC) is an important example of progress towards sustainable development. It is an approach developed by IIED, Oxfam and UNICEF in which local communities organize themselves with outside support to use their own skills and knowledge to meet their needs for basic livelihoods in ways that care for the local environment and resources on which they depend. It is distinguished from other rural community development projects by the explicit recognition of the need to integrate three sets of goals — meeting material needs, enabling communities and making the best sustainable use of the environment. It depends for success on the abilities of local groups to develop initiatives and on "outside institutions that empower the local community by way of political support and open access to information, and that take an adaptive and flexible approach if they provide resources" (Holmberg and Sandbrook, 1992, p32). Although first designed to raise the productivity and welfare of the poor in rural development in the South, PEC is equally valid in both rich and poor countries and can be used in both rural and urban settings.

Successful alternative projects may, however, have to cope with the psychology of denial. Alan Savory (1988) speaks of the conflict generated by what he took to be the "successful" completion of a seven-year trial to prove the effectiveness of a system of grassland management in Zimbabwe, an outcome he attributed to a psychological inability to accept change.

## PUTTING PEOPLE FIRST

We need constantly to assert people's right to welfare (which no more implies dependence than equity implies handing something for nothing to the lazy and unscrupulous). We need continually to challenge the thinking that accepts that "at the end of the day economics will decide". The frequency with which we use such a phrase clearly illustrates how we have surrendered responsibility for control of the forces that should generate benefits for people (as they did, up to a point, in Europe in the immediate postwar years through the Marshall Plan). (Ruckelshaus (1989) points out that in 1989 US foreign aid was running at $37 billion per year, which would have had to become $127 billion, at 1989 prices, to equal US spending on the Marshall Plan.) Putting people first means quite simply valuing people for themselves, for what they are, rather than for what they can do, or how they can perform in the service of some interest whose ends may be quite radically opposed to the meeting of human need.

Asserting the primacy of human need does not on the face of it seem a difficult intellectual, moral or imaginative feat. What is striking about Chambers's account of the poor's priorities (see Chapter 4) is how much it has in common with the list we would draw up for ourselves in the North: a secure livelihood providing physical and social well-being and minimizing the chances of sickness, early death and impoverishment; and a good command of assets. Such assertion may seem superfluous till we remember how unscrupulously those with economic power can oppress those without. Examples come only too readily to mind — child slavery, sweatshops and the failure of the asbestos industry to modify its processes even after the danger to workers' health became known.

## EMPOWERMENT

Putting people first also means empowerment — the process by which those who are or feel excluded from decison-making are enabled to participate in it. It involves the transfer of power from those in authority to smaller groups. In some countries this has to begin with establishing or re-establishing political rights and other basic freedoms. (A recent example is the return to free elections in Malawi and Kenya.) Only then can a start be made to provide education and training to raise awareness and allow people and communities to play an effective role in the political process. However, as R Sharp (1992, p43) of the International Institute for Environment and Development (IIED) points out, "since those who hold power are seldom ready to relinquish it, some commentators have suggested that empowerment may need to mean the struggle of the disadvantaged to achieve it". Empowerment thus also refers to what Paulo Freire, the Brazilian educationist, calls "conscientization" or education for consciousness, by which communities and individuals become aware of the reasons for their poverty and oppression and begin to discuss what they themselves can do about it without enabling action by the authorities.

# EDUCATION

Education — whether formal or informal — is a powerful means of promoting changes in awareness and attitude. There has been a number of attempts to promote "environmental education" internationally,[8] though much of the thinking behind these initiatives reflects the values of the prevailing model of development. Education for sustainable development must not only create an awareness of the global crisis, but must place it at the heart of the curriculum. It must be "ecological" rather than "environmental", encouraging broad holistic thinking, teaching the need for structural change and promoting the correct application of reductionist thinking to specific technical problems.

It will embrace all the means of change discussed above (which will operate in many contexts other than education) and alert students to the feasibility of alternative practices. More importantly, it will not only inform students but allow them to participate in the processes that promote change; it will not only teach them about holism but require them to think holistically; it will not only acquaint them with others' visions but stimulate them to formulate their own. Students will be encouraged to debate the issues themselves and to confront the need "to clarify our central convictions". They need practice in distinguishing between ends and means and in assessing the significance of important assumptions in the light of larger goals. We need an education that not only teaches science (among other subjects) but that also encourages, in Schumacher's (1973, p81) words, an "awareness of the presuppositions of science, of the meaning and significance of scientific laws, and of the place occupied by the natural sciences within the whole cosmos of human thought".

Ecological education will not only teach about empowerment, but will enable students to fulfil their aspirations by helping them develop their full range of abilities (without implying that any of these are inferior to a facility in mathematics or verbal

---

8. There have been conferences in Nevada in 1970, Belgrade in 1975 (the year in which the International Environmental Education Programme was established), in Tiblisi in 1977 and in Moscow in 1987. Since then the Council of the European Communities has twice called on member states to advance environmental education in all sectors of education.

reasoning). By paying equal attention to emotional and intellectual development, it will teach the basic life skills people need to establish identities and grow as individuals. By encouraging creativity, commitment and initiative, it will equip students to take responsibility for themselves and their futures and thus avoid the kinds of dependency large organizations are keen to promote. It will also focus on relationships and teach what Harrison (1990, p203) calls the "work of human communication, of caring and nurturance, of tending the personal bonds of community", which enhances our ability to relate to each other, not just on the level of day-to-day "communication skills", but more importantly by acknowledging each other's identities and rights.

The new education will initiate a process of lifelong growth in awareness and aspiration. An individual's readiness to participate in that process, at however lowly or rudimentary a level, will be more important than acquiring impressive qualifications, for, as Paulo Freire (1972) points out, we are all "unfinished" human beings with a commitment to improve "unfinished" reality.

Without the opportunity to develop their potential, individuals cannot participate fully in discussions and initiatives on which progress to more sustainable development depends. Properly resourced and directed, education will ensure that *all* students become the beneficiaries of the care, concern and skills of others. They will not only become aware of the issues (and be able to act on that awareness) but will be equipped with the skills required to contribute effectively to the debate — they will learn to plan, organize, communicate with others, develop strategies and create alliances. In a world where the challenge of sustainable development is an imperative rather than an option, we cannot afford to debar people from participating by making them feel failures — whether academic failures as a result of the rigid application of elitist standards, or social or personal failures as a result of inadequate valuation of both their needs and their potential.

## POLITICAL PRIORITIES

Identifying the instruments of change is one thing. It is quite another matter to gain wide social and political agreement for their use. The dominance of the prevailing paradigm means that governments are unlikely to commit sufficient resources to facilitating debate, empowerment and education. Progress towards sustainable development will thus depend on the actions of NGOs and committed individuals, for whom two other means of bringing about change — campaigning and networking — become particularly important.

However, governments' priorities reflect individual choices and values. Politicians' views of what constitutes "political suicide" reflect the electorate's collective view of social and economic priorities and of the legitimacy of possible constraints and sanctions on their activities. As Ronald Higgins (1980, p180) points out in his book *The Seventh Enemy*, "The inertia of governments derives in large measure from the self-imposed helplessness of individuals." The paradigm then is not an imposed constraint, but a structure we have inherited, if not actually built for ourselves. It reflects our current values and will change as individual values change. Unless we subscribe to a fatalistic, deterministic view (which of course the prevailing paradigm encourages us to adopt in many insidious ways), we can change social and political arrangements to bring them into line with new perceptions and values. Ultimately it is not the economic system that controls our lives, but we who determine the nature of the economic system by our individual choices. It is not technological advance that dictates change, but we who choose how technology will affect our quality of life.

Our readiness to be fatalistic about economic forces and social structures can be explained partly by Higgins's "self-imposed helplessness" and partly by lack of knowledge of the linkages within the *problématique*. Even more crucial, however, is a lack of a different form of knowledge — of self-awareness, of the kind of understanding without which we are blind to our involvement in the way the world is. As Higgins (1980, p180) points out, "despite the world's evident atrocities, greed, lies, neglect and cruelties, most of us cannot accept that we are in any fundamental way party to them, that in practice or in spirit we all in some degree participate in the evils".

Such an understanding transcends the knowledge of issues and problems we acquire from academic study or some other source. It creates within us a new perspective, as Max-Neef (1991, pp102–3) points out:

> *In the realm of understanding, problem posing and problem solving do not make sense since we deal with transformations that start with and within ourselves. It is no longer the "we are here and the poor are there and we have to do something about it, so let us devise a strategy that may solve the problem". It is rather the "we are part of something that has to be transformed because it is wrong, and, since I share the responsibility for what is wrong there is nothing that can stop me from starting the process by transforming myself".*

Such personal transformations enable us to commit our energies and abilities to campaign for changes that express the values we tell the opinion pollsters we believe in. In the absence of prompt effective action at the national level they will persuade us of the need to work — arguing, protesting, lobbying, campaigning and using our power of choice as "consumers" (or more appropriately "conservers" or "sustainers") — to build broad support for moves that will produce distinct if limited improvements.

Progress to more sustainable pathways depends on political change. However, there is little point in trusting to political solutions in which we have not invested, just as it is futile to try to build sustainable development on resources to which we are not entitled. The catalyst for political change is our individual participation in action to influence decision-making in ways that use our energies most effectively.

Thus ends become means and means become ends. We can only enlarge others' awareness of the need for change by acting on our own awareness of the need for change. We can only create a higher respect for individual human beings by acting on our own feelings of respect, care and concern. We can only hope to reform the economic system by asserting the values we know it fails to uphold. It is only by our commitment to the resolution of Schumacher's "divergent problems" (1973, p80) that we can bring about meaningful change, for divergent problems "demand, and thus provoke the supply of, forces from a higher level, thus bringing love, beauty, goodness and truth into our lives."

# Part IV

## Developments since Brundtland

# Chapter 9  |  THE RIO SUMMIT

By certain standards UNCED was clearly a success. An event which looked to be heading for disaster just two or three months before, with preparations in such disarray that it was dubbed the "Summit of Hypocrisy", ended with the signing of five "Earth Summit" agreements and was hailed, admittedly by one of the two conference newspapers, as "an elaborate programming tool that could set the planet on a new course towards global sustainable development" (Johnson, 1993, p3). Over 100 heads of state attended the final two-day meeting, and overall 178 governments were represented. During the two weeks of official meetings over 500 NGO groups met at the parallel Global Forum to discuss a range of topics related to the central themes of environment and development.

At the beginning of June 1992, 30,000 people flooded into Rio, including 7000 journalists and 1500 officially accredited representatives of NGOs, to attend what has been called the largest international conference ever held. The widely publicized events of the first two weeks of June — the Earth Summit itself — were, however, only the culmination of months of preparations, which had involved "literally several million people, some working on specific substantive issues, some on the organization of the event, and some, directly or indirectly, on the creation of a broader public awareness" (Weizsäcker, 1994, pp168–9). Many international meetings involving governments, UN agencies and NGOs were held in the two years leading up to June 1992, and most governments responded positively to the invitation to submit reports on their environment and development in time for Rio.

These preparations were set in motion when the UN General Assembly, acting on a recommendation in the Brundtland Report, passed Resolution 44/228 in December 1989. Brazil's offer to host the conference was accepted and the date was set to coincide with the twentieth anniversary of the Stockholm conference. Maurice Strong, the Canadian industrialist, was asked to be secretary general, as he had been at Stockholm. A secretariat was set up in Geneva, and a series of four five-week preparatory committee meetings (prepcoms, in the jargon) were held in Nairobi, Geneva and New York between August 1990 and March 1992. These were to prepare many matters, including the drafting and negotiating of the texts of the major documents to be signed at the conference.

At the start of the process Maurice Strong hoped for agreements in five major areas:

* conventions on climate, biodiversity and forests,
* an earth charter,
* a global action plan, Agenda 21, outlining priority issues for the twenty-first century (hence the title)
* an agreement on new financial resources to implement the recommendations of Agenda 21, and progress on transfers of environmentally sound technology from North to South, and
* a strengthening of international institutions, especially the UN, to facilitate the achievement of these aims.

However not all his hopes were to be realized.

## THE OUTCOMES
### *The Climate Convention*
The work of the inter-governmental panel on climate change, which had its first meeting in 1988, indicated a need for an agreement on carbon dioxide emissions, and the success of the Montreal Protocol on substances that deplete the ozone layer in 1987 suggested that a Climate Convention was a realistic target. The work of the prepcoms resulted in a Framework Convention on Climate Change, signed by 153 national governments and the European Community (as the European Union then was), a legally binding agreement on a framework for dealing with the

threat of "global warming". It accepts the reality of the problem and the need for a precautionary approach. However, it is weakened by its failure to reach firm agreements on targets for reducing emissions, though it does generally aim to stabilize emissions of carbon dioxide and other greenhouse gases at their 1990 levels by the year 2000. (Attempts to negotiate both specific targets and timetables were hampered by the USA, which took a stand against any agreement committing it to reduce its $CO_2$ emissions). Nor does the convention include binding agreements on finance, although it includes an agreement that the North will meet the cost of action taken by Southern countries as a result of their signing the convention.

The convention requires governments to report on the impact of their abatement policies. Moreover, it sets up a mechanism for reviewing the adequacy of national commitments in the light of new scientific information. Much will therefore depend on the quality of the reports nations submit and the extent to which they try to honour the spirit of the agreement. The convention does mean that nations have to face the issue, but does not of itself guarantee they will make swift progress on it.

## The Biodiversity Convention

The Convention on Biological Diversity is based on previous discussions about the conservation of biodiversity and about how the North, with its interest in biotechnology, can ensure access to the diversity of species in the South, over which individual countries assert sovereign rights. The convention gives some support to the South by asserting that individual states have sovereign rights over their own "biological resources", as well as responsibilities for maintaining diversity and making use of it in a sustainable manner. It agrees on the need for finances to do this more effectively, the bulk of which will come from the North. It also agrees in principle to an equitable exchange of genetic resources in return for access to, and transfer of, technology to the South. However, it is couched in terms that water down commitments with such loopholes as "as far as possible".

The Biodiversity Convention was also weakened by the stance of the USA, whose principal objective was to protect its bio-technology industry. The convention pays more attention to access to species, technology transfer and biotechnology as a solution to loss of biodiversity than it does to the need to protect both the biodiversity on which people depend for livelihoods (for example in tropical forests) and the indigenous knowledge and culture of the people themselves. As a result it says nothing about practical ways of preserving biodiversity. It neither specifies a programme for international action to reduce species loss (or even a framework for such a programme) nor highlights the areas or species that should receive urgent attention.

### The Forest Principles

The attempt to prepare a forests convention in time for Rio has been declared "an unmitigated disaster" (Johnson, 1993, p7). Widespread concern in the North about the rate of *tropical* deforestation was seen in the South as an attempt by the North to conserve a "sink" for emissions of carbon dioxide and so evade responsibility for reducing greenhouse gas emissions. In addition, several countries in the South resented strongly the idea that the rest of the world should see fit to tell them how to manage their forests, particularly after the North's exploitation of its own forests over many centuries. Malaysia called for all countries to accept that they should maintain forest cover over at least 30 per cent of their territory or provide funds to allow this to happen elsewhere — a jibe both at the North's record on managing its own forests and its involvement in the exploitation of the South's.

What emerged from the discussions held before and at Rio was a non-binding statement of "principles of forest management", which avoided any reference to principles or obligations on controversial issues. Much of it relates indirectly to the importance of forests for biodiversity and climate (and therefore ultimately to the desirability of some form of international management). It also emphasizes the importance of the participation of local people in the planning of forest policies and the management of forests. The statement ranges over such themes as the importance and roles of forests; national sovereignty; full economic valuation; and the need for international co-operation. But it makes so many generalized and sometimes unclear observations and recommendations that the result is "a document with something for everyone, without any clear message of direction" (Sullivan in Grubb et al 1993, p166). Al Gore, vice-president in the US Democratic administration, which signed the Climate Convention after coming to office in 1993, saw the weakness of the forest agreement as directly related to the stance on carbon dioxide emissions taken by the USA under President Bush.

## The Rio Declaration

Before Rio, Maurice Strong proposed as a foreword to Agenda 21 an earth charter setting out the basic principles required to progress towards sustainability. He envisaged a brief, positive introduction to the plan of action. What emerged — the Rio Declaration on Environment and Development — is a bureaucratic synthesis, "a distillation of the political and conceptual arguments dogging the North–South debate. Far from a timeless ethic, it was now a snapshot of history" (Grubb 1993, p85).

## Agenda 21

Agenda 21, the action plan for sustainable development, includes details of both the finances and technology transfers required for its implementation, and of institutional arrangements at the UN for overseeing the process. Officially the Programme of Action on Environment and Development, it has 40 chapters covering 500 pages. It is divided into four main sections:

- social and economic development (chapters 1–8),
- the conservation and management of resources for development (chapters 9–22),
- strengthening the role of major groups involved in achieving sustainable development (chapters 23–32), and
- means of implementation (chapters 33–40).

Of these the first section is the most important with its treatment of fundamental issues such as the inequities between rich and poor, wasteful consumption, the population explosion and the integration of environment and development. The second section, however, is by far the longest, being almost as long as the other three put together.

Agenda 21 bears the marks of a negotiated document, several

sections of which were "bracketed", during the prepcoms process, that is, marked off as requiring further negotiation and compromise at Rio itself. The signing of the final document was therefore regarded as something of a diplomatic triumph. Inevitably it bears the marks of its genesis. Even in the first section some of the chapters (for example chapter 8, on the integration of the environment and development) are much more succinct than others (for example chapter 4 on changing consumption patterns). Vagueness and ambiguity vary with contentiousness, as Roger Levett (LGMB, 1992, p3) has commented: "Some of these disagreements [for example about population control, the reduction in use of fossil fuels, and the damaging nature of North–South debt and much trade] were only resolved by the adoption of intentionally meaningless or self-contradictory forms of words. The worst drafting in Agenda 21 is therefore often on the most crucial issues."

Nevertheless, commentators have acknowledged that Agenda 21 does try to integrate environment and development and point out the connections between specific problems. It sets few specific targets but calls for the setting up of a UN Commission for Sustainable Development, preparations for a convention on desertification, and conferences on small island states (particularly threatened by global warming) and fish stocks. It also makes estimates of the costs of its recommendations.

Agenda 21 has been described as "the most thorough and ambitious attempt yet to specify what actions will be needed to reconcile development with environmental concerns" (LGMB, 1992, p1). Matthias Koch of the Technische Universität in Berlin and Michael Grubb of the Royal Institute of International Affairs in London suggest it is "perhaps best seen as a collection of agreed negotiated wisdom as to the nature of the problems, relevant principles, and a sketch of the desirable and feasible paths towards solutions, taking into account national and other interests. It stands as a grand testimony and guide to collected national insights and interests pertaining to sustainable development" (Grubb et al, 1993, pp97–8). They consider it "will form the key intergovernmental guiding and reference document on the issues for the rest of the decade", an assessment broadly endorsed by other commentators (Grubb et al, 1993, pxv).

However, it is not legally binding and has therefore been described as "toothless" (Middleton et al, 1993, pp11, 25).

Several themes are given major emphasis. The importance of the role of national governments in promoting sustainable development is stressed. Each government should prepare a national strategy for sustainable development, which should build on and integrate existing sectoral policies. All governments should integrate development and environment policies at all levels and in all sectors. They will need to develop management systems in order to do this. In addition, governments should aim to build a national consensus and, in the South particularly, devise ways of "capacity building".

Capacity building is one of the major themes of the fourth section — Means of Implementation. It involves "developing the abilities and resourcing of institutions to manage the various changes and activities required of them" (LGMB, 1992, p5). This can be done in a number of ways such as developing "human resources", strengthening the capacities of existing institutions in research and development and "programme implementation", and coordinating reviews of sectoral needs in the light of national strategies. Capacity-building also involves addressing issues of technology transfers and the terms on which these might be made, and negotiations over intellectual property rights. According to Roger Levett (LGMB, 1992, p5), capacity-building "is a crucial part of the Agenda 21 philosophy. It is as much concerned with enabling people and organizations to make the necessary changes as with the changes themselves". Governments are asked to include reviews of their needs for capacity building in their first national sustainable development strategies.

Agenda 21 envisages national sustainable development strategies as very different from national development plans of the past with their top-down approach and their frequent reliance on expensive, aid-sponsored "prestige" projects. Instead, Agenda 21 places a strong emphasis on people and on their communities and organizations (including NGOs) in an approach which can be broadly described as "bottom-up" and which stresses the needs of the poorest. There are frequent references to the rights of the poor and the disadvantaged, not just to food, clothing, health and shelter but also to education and personal development, to a role in decision-making, and to participation in planning and capacity building.

Thus sustainable development is not just the concern of governments. People are acknowledged to have a role too. Agenda 21 stresses that the most effective planning evolves gradually through a participatory process that allows different social groups to debate the gains and losses in reconciling development and environment. The role of women in local development is stressed, as is the need to respect indigenous cultures. The rights of a range of social groups and organizations, including women, young people, indigenous people, workers and NGOs, are acknowledged. Commentators agree that many of the sections that advocate the importance of such "bottom up" approaches to development are the outcome of intensive lobbying by NGOs at the prepcom stage. However, there is less certainty about how extensively they will be adopted: "What is less clear is whether governments have taken on board what participation actually means in practice ... progress will hinge on the availability of equitable political and public institutions attuned to participation by the most needy" (Holmberg et al, 1993, p10).

Other themes recur throughout the document: the importance of "open governance" (that is open, accountable and participatory democracy); the need for more information (but not at the expense of delay); the importance of "cross-cutting" institutions that transcend sectoral divisions and attempt to deal with the forces underlying linkages between specific problems; the need for governments to achieve a balance between environmental regulation and market mechanisms; and new emphases on international co-operation and international trade beneficial to the poorer nations within a sustainable framework. However, there is almost no mention of such intractable problems as international debt; the arms trade and the impact of armed conflict on the potential for sustainable development; nor of the unsustainable nature of nuclear power.

Despite its positive features, Agenda 21 is a far from perfect document. It has been seen as failing to meet the original objectives of UNCED. For example, Adil Najam (quoted in Holmberg et al, 1993, p35), points out that it is weakest on the very things Resolution 44/2288 stressed most — financial arrange-

ments, institutional arrangements and technology transfers —
and concludes that on these matters it is no advance on
Stockholm.

Holmberg et al (1993) have a number of other reservations.
Agenda 21 gives estimates of the necessary finances (US$ 600
billion annually, of which $125 billion would come from foreign
aid) which are subject to large uncertainties and so do not
provide a credible basis for debate. It reveals a built-in bias in
favour of Northern perspectives, its emphasis on the role of
poverty in creating environmental problems obscuring the fact
that economic growth creates a number of very serious problems,
including poverty. It is seen as naïve or wilfully ignorant in that it
emphasizes community empowerment, land redistribution and
re-afforestation yet fails to point out that attempts to implement
such initiatives have proved difficult in the face of political
realities and that communities are often riven by conflicts
between different social groups. Holmberg et al also see Agenda
21 as tending to assume too much faith in the UN's capacities to
promote sustainable development when the level of bilateral aid
had been running at three or four times that of multilateral aid
over the previous decade.

Agenda 21 has surprisingly little to say about business and
industry in view of the general assumption that economic growth
should remain a prominent feature of future development and the
prevalence of the dubious proposition that growth is necessary to
generate the resources required to protect the environment.
Though there are signs of a trend away from planned and towards
market-based economies, there is support for the idea that economic instruments, including "environmental pricing", should be
set within a broad framework of regulation devised by government. The desirability of such a framework seems to be
confirmed by the balance of opinion of two publications submitted to UNCED by business organizations. One, the *Business
Charter for Sustainable Development* produced by the International
Chamber of Commerce (ICC, 1992), which represents several
hundred major companies, favours self-regulation. The other,
*Changing Course*, from the Business Council for Sustainable
Development, a smaller organization headed by the Swiss industrialist Stephan Schmidheiny (1992), questions the efficacy of

self-regulation on the grounds that there are limits to what any one company acting on its own can achieve without weakening its competitive position. It also argues that in the long term the most successful companies will be those with the most environmentally sound policies. Stephan Schmidheiny called for new partnerships between business and government and there were signs of a willingness on both sides to develop new relationships.

## RIO — THE WIDER VIEW

It is important to consider a number of broader themes in assessing the contribution of Rio to progress towards sustainable development.

### Process and Product

Any assessment of Rio must consider the almost complete absence of a set of binding agreements about, say, reductions in emissions or contributions to funding, for which some onlookers had hoped. The political complexities thwarting progress to satisfactory agreements are illustrated by the fact that the South opposed the drawing up of lists of endangered species, seeing such an exercise as an infringement of their sovereignty. However, the lack of binding undertakings is to some extent compensated for by agreements to initiate or maintain processes, for example, agreement in the Climate Convention to monitor progress on reducing emissions and the agreement in Agenda 21 to set up the CSD (Commission on Sustainable Development). These are just two examples of a number of processes initiated at Rio intended not only to share knowledge and widen perceptions but also to lead to new institutional responses, networks and alliances. Much as "talks about talks" may seem a modest (but in retrospect essential) step forward in other negotiations, so new processes may be necessary preliminaries to the process of sustainable development itself. However, process alone is not enough, as Michael Grubb (Grubb et al, 1993, p25) points out: "Commitments cannot always be eschewed in favour of new processes; the evasion of key measures has to stop, and the procreation of new processes cannot continue indefinitely. What is required are processes which (foster the political conditions required to) spawn a steady accretion of effective and meaningful commitments."

Holmberg et al (1993) attribute some of the emphasis on process, as opposed to commitment, to the design of the conference itself. They suggest that broad agendas, drawn up in recognition of the need for a holistic approach to deep-seated issues, are not in fact a good basis for arriving at specific action plans, targets and other commitments. Almost inevitably the complexities of the negotiating process become the focus of attention rather than the desired substantive outcomes. This tendency is strengthened by the importance the UN attaches to achieving consensus, which can depend on the skill of diplomats to find words to which all parties can append signatures. The UN convention which allows individual states to append notes of dissent or express reservations can at times make consensus appear like the protracted negotiation of the status quo. More might be achieved with simpler agendas, more realistic expectations, more emphasis on specific, detailed outcomes and a revision of the consensus convention.

## NGOs

Some of the key players in the Rio negotiating process were NGOs. With Maurice Strong's encouragement they negotiated the right to make written submissions to the prepcoms. Though barred from negotiations at these meetings they contributed in a number of ways, which were generally welcomed by government delegations (more readily by those from the North, at least in the early stages). Some NGO representatives were official members of government delegations, some negotiated on behalf of their governments, some had close links with the secretariat and some played a role in producing national sustainable development strategies. NGOs also made substantial contributions to parts of Agenda 21, such as those of women's organizations to the theme of people's participation in decision-making. Their role after Rio is discussed in Agenda 21, which urges international organizations, governments and NGOs to co-operate in the "fullest possible" way. At Rio itself, however, their impact was less clear: the global forum (of NGOs) met at a distance from the official proceedings; national delegations concentrated on diplomatic negotiations; and the NGOs found it difficult to speak in unison. Though NGOs generally earned new respect from both governments and UN agencies at Rio, Michael Grubb predicts that as they become more influential the differences between them will become more distinct, as will their limitations.

## North–South Relations

The North–South divide was probably the most important of the wider issues addressed at Rio. As Michael Grubb (Grubb et al, 1993, p26) puts it: "The central issue with which all future attempts to promote globally sustainable development will have to grapple is that which formed the most pervasive feature of UNCED, namely the division between rich and poor, developed and developing, North and South." As at Stockholm, the South feared that the North would impose new constraints on their development, but hoped that they would be given help towards more sustainable development in the form of commitments from the North on debt relief, official development assistance, access to international liquidity, better commodity prices and better access to markets in the North. But these hopes were not fulfilled, for the North was unable or unwilling to provide the finances to meet the estimated cost of implementing Agenda 21.

North–South inequity was reflected in the conference agenda. Northern concerns were given a higher priority than vitally important Southern issues, such as improving the quality of water (contaminated drinking water is still the main cause of infant mortality in the poorer countries).

The reluctance — indeed refusal — of the USA (and the readiness of other Northern countries to take advantage of its intransigence) to make any commitments that would oblige it to reduce its levels of consumption tended to generate an equally uncompromising response in the South. Michael Grubb quotes Tariq Osman Hyder, a leading participant in the negotiations leading to the Climate Convention (Grubb et al, 1993, p27):

> It is difficult for most of the developing countries to accept the proposition that they should enter into commitments which would adversely bind them, either now or later on, for the sake of a problem caused by the developed countries — who neither wish to

> *equitably share the remaining emission reserves in the atmosphere,
> nor to share (even in a small way) the benefits and resources that
> they have built up by plundering the world's greenhouse gas
> capacity.*

The impasse was reinforced by other factors. Both North and
South had genuine difficulty accepting the validity of each other's
political constraints. The South underestimated the strength of
the North's assumption that it would be electorally unpopular to
introduce taxes to fund development in the South; while the
North found it hard to appreciate the South's unwillingness to
allow them to attach conditions to or monitor any offers of aid.

North–South differences also arose in discussions about
population, which as we have seen is an important factor in
progress towards sustainability. Despite the sensitivity of the
issue, many Southern countries readily acknowledged the need to
discuss policies to arrest population growth and achieve the
demographic transition. Nevertheless, the countries of the South
were quick to point out that the North — with just 20 per cent of
the world's population — is responsible for by far the larger
portion of ecological degradation. They therefore insisted on
linking the issues of population and resource consumption,
which meant that the two chapters addressing these topics in
Agenda 21 (chapters 4 and 5) were negotiated together, with
trade-offs between the two.

Agenda 21's approach to the issue of consumption also reflects
UNCED's Northern bias. Many sections are devoted to how the
South might achieve sustainability, but there is virtually no
discussion of how the North might also accomplish it. This is due
partly to the North's success in influencing the agenda and partly
to the South's reluctance to accept that the sustainable development path might not lead to the levels of material wealth enjoyed
by the North. Michael Grubb puts the matter very clearly (Grubb
et al, 1993, pp32–3, emphasis added):

> *Yet there was a fundamental paradox in the fact that UNCED
> participants almost universally interpreted the "D" (development) to
> mean the process of poor countries getting richer, along an economic
> path similar to that followed by the industrialized countries, whilst
> the whole point of the "E" (environment) was to encourage such*

*countries to "leapfrog" that path of development to a wealthy but sustainable state. If the end-point is supposed to be so radically different from the current resource-intensive pattern of industrialized countries,* a central question has to be how the already industrialized countries are supposed to develop towards such a state. Sporadic attacks by some developing countries on the consumption patterns of the North, and the need to encourage cleaner technologies did not amount to any clear vision of alternative paths for Northern development — such questions were simply not addressed in detail. There seemed little recognition of the fact that the UNCED agenda was incoherent unless "development" was broadened to include questions about the future development of industrialized countries. . . . *Indeed, if the developed countries did start to address such issues about their own future development more seriously, it could have seriously strengthened their moral position and thus increased pressures on the developing countries to accept more responsibility towards altered development goals. Only in the closing stages of negotiations did it seem that some NGOs began to argue the fundamental importance of addressing questions of Northern development within UNCED.*

Until this inconsistency is addressed, the North–South relationship will be at best an uneasy one. The mistrust which has persisted since Stockholm may intensify as gaps widen and global politics change. Holmberg et al (1993, p10) believe the North–South relationship has already entered a new phase: "Following the dissolution of the Soviet Union, the East/West confrontation is dead. The fault line has shifted 90 degrees from East/West to North/South, and bitter divisions of wealth and poverty marked many of the most acrimonious debates during the UNCED process."

Although the difference in income between rich and poor countries continues to widen, the South's contribution to global pollution will increase with further development, making the issue more acute. The South's bargaining power is also likely to increase as the North grows keener to have access to the genetic capital stored in the tropical forests. However, it would be a mistake to regard the blocs in North and South as united. The countries of the South maintain a united front by virtue of their common interest in finance, but can have radically opposed concerns (for example Bangladesh and Egypt, with extensive low-lying territory, deplored the weakness of the Climate Convention, while Saudi Arabia and Kuwait, seeing their oil revenues threatened, refused to sign it). In the North, Japan, the USA and the European Union differed in their approaches to several issues, while "Canada, Australia, New Zealand, as well as the Nordic countries tended to form different groups again, generally more sympathetic to developing country concerns" (Grubb et al, 1993, p33). Meanwhile, the countries of the east (both in Europe and further afield) take various positions towards North and South.

## THE AFTERMATH OF RIO

At its meeting in December 1992 the UN General Assembly broadly supported UNCED's work and urged members to implement the agreements made there. More specifically, it endorsed the establishment of a Commission for Sustainable Development as a means of monitoring progress on the implementation of Agenda 21. It accepted the other recommendations in Agenda 21, including a desertification convention, a small islands conference, a fish stocks conference and the UNDP's capacity-building programme, Capacity 21. It approved the setting-up of a "high-level advisory board" of independent experts to report directly to the secretary-general, an "inter-agency committee" (with representatives from the main UN agencies in an attempt to improve and co-ordinate sustainability initiatives within the UN) and a new secretariat within the UN. There were protests from the South about finance and technology transfers, but the immediate reaction was generally favourable: "The overall impression, however, is that far from being an attempt to downgrade or weaken the issue of sustainable development as some had feared, the negotiators sought to ensure that the integration of environmental issues with enhanced development efforts will form a central part of the UN's agenda over the forthcoming years" (Grubb et al, 1993, p22). The six months following Rio confirmed that UNCED was "about much more than education, public relations and media hype" (Grubb et al, 1993, p22).

## ASSESSING UNCED

Almost three years on, it is hard to assess the achievements of Rio. In a sense it is too early to do so, for the outcomes of the many discussions held at UNCED and elsewhere are still incomplete. Preliminary assessments of its success depend very much on the criteria applied. For those caught up in the complexities of negotiating agreements and achieving consensus there were many local successes, sometimes achieved in dramatic fashion late in the day and against all apparent odds. However, as Holmberg et al (1993, p37) have remarked: "Getting agreement is the diplomat's sign of success, irrespective — it seems — of content."

Optimists point to a number of achievements: the wide publicity and its importance in raising awareness of the issues (though some commentators claim it impeded rather than aided certain negotiations); the success, as represented by signed agreements, in resolving deep conflicts between different interests; the focus on national sustainable development strategies; the creation of the CSD; the emphasis on community participation in development and on the role of NGOs; the agreement on new World Bank funds; and the endorsement of agreements by the UN General Assembly — all achieved when circumstances were not exactly propitious (with a recession in the North, uncertainty in eastern Europe and in the former Soviet Union and with many governments reluctant to expand their commitments).

Pessimists caution against undue optimism, pointing out that not one of the issues identified at Stockholm has been resolved. In the intervening 20 years many problems have become more serious and new problems have made global impacts. They argue that Rio has done little to address the most urgent priorities directly and that the poorest countries will derive least benefit from its agreements. The majority of rich countries have still to make unequivocal commitments to raise aid to the poor countries to the 0.7 per cent of GDP recommended by the UN. There is no indication that the North is prepared to reduce levels of consumption in the interests of international equity, and little sign of readiness in either the North or South to discuss the possibility that integrating environment and development may require a more radical rethink than simply trusting technology to produce the efficiencies in resource use that will prolong business as usual indefinitely.

Little was done directly to ease conflicts between the North and South over such issues as consumption levels, population pressures, funding, technology transfers, and intellectual property rights. Such conflicts may well continue for as long as we have "unending references to the special situation and needs of developing countries ... [which seem] more akin to a global apartheid. ... This was not imposed, or opposed, by any group; it was quickly established as a consensus approach from which there was hardly any dissent because it was clear that rich and poor could not be treated alike. Yet it seems a poor basis on which to build a 'global partnership for sustainable development' in the twenty-first century" (Grubb et al, 1993, p33).

Grubb also doubts the adequacy of the outcomes of international diplomacy and bureaucracy:

> As the culmination of such an extensive process itself, building on the 20 years since the Stockholm Conference and the five years since the Brundtland Commission, the lack of clear policy commitments must be recognized as troubling. The agreements are hardly convincing demonstrations that countries are yet ready to tackle seriously the major changes required to bring sustainable development much closer to reality.
>
> (Grubb et al, 1993, p24)

Yet some indications suggest that Rio will be succeeded by more conventions, each possibly spawning new additions to institutional machinery.

There is also the issue of credibility. How seriously are governments committed to "bottom-up" approaches, participation by NGOs and "open governance" with its emphasis on participatory democracy and accountability, all of which entail some sharing of power if seriously implemented? Grubb and Koch (Grubb et al, 1993, p154) comment that "such references seem to have received little opposition, even from those countries which clearly do not practise such principles. Agenda 21 thus seems to represent on paper the much vaunted global triumph of the ideas of participatory democracy". This issue underlies the serious question of the tension between national interest and international responsibility, which was not handled directly. Many governments responded to general pressure to declare their support for the integration of environment and development by signing non-binding agreements (including the establishment of a monitoring process) even though these might conflict with their perception of short-term national and political interests. Thus, as Mark Imber (1993) of the Department of International Relations at St Andrews University points out: "Governments expect "the UN" to "co-ordinate" policies for "sustainable development" that governments themselves do not pursue." Three years after Rio, it is still uncertain how positively governments will respond to the agendas generated by the processes they have collectively established. Without some positive response, all the investments in what was a momentous exercise in raising the awareness, both of political leaders and of the people of the world through television, will have been largely wasted.[1]

Optimists, Holmberg et al suggest, tend to look at what governments can be expected to achieve and welcome "first steps", whilst pessimists apply the criteria of human and planetary needs. They themselves (Holmberg et al, 1993, p7) conclude that "it is difficult to escape the conclusion that the Conference has set in motion some very large, if slow-moving wheels". However, in a speech to a plenary session of the conference, Mustafa Tolba, the Egyptian director of UNEP till his retirement in 1993, cautioned about prematurely sanguine assessments: "Contemporaries are very fond of designating "turning-points". History is a much harsher judge. Probably it will take us several years before we ascertain that this meeting in Rio has entered that select pantheon of events which truly marked a turning point in the affairs of mankind" (quoted in Johnson, 1993, p8).

---

1. It was especially appropriate that UNCED was held in Rio de Janeiro. Brazil has not only one of the largest differences in income between rich and poor, but is also considered to have one of the highest rates of species extinction of any country in the world.

# Chapter 10

ON or DOWN
from the
SUMMIT?

If it is difficult to estimate the achievements
of the Earth Summit, it is even harder to gauge progress since
June 1992. There have been encouraging initiatives, but many of
these highlight missed opportunities. There is also much
evidence that the forces most opposed to sustainable development have not begun to slacken significantly. It is therefore hard
to know whether individual steps are blips in trends that will
continue to dominate our treatment of people and planet, or
whether in retrospect the first half of the last decade of the
twentieth century will prove to have been a turning point.

The urgency of the need for rapid progress towards sustainable
pathways has clearly not diminished. The most recent statistics
provide little evidence that the tide has begun to turn (Brown et
al, 1994). Ecological damage continues to increase: areas of farmland and forests are shrinking; fish catches are declining; species
loss continues, while $CO_2$ emissions to the atmosphere continue
to rise. Meanwhile, as world population grows, the number of
poor continues to rise, the gap between rich and poor widens and
"Third World debt" continues to climb. Armed hostilities are not
confined to the well-reported conflicts in the former Yugoslavia,
Rwanda and Chechnya, but are now endemic with a host of
"local" wars. At home in 1994 the New Economics Foundation
(NEF), together with the Stockholm Environment Institute,
applied Daly and Cobb's ISEW to the UK and found an almost
continuous decline in sustainable economic welfare since 1974

and a quality of life no higher than in 1950. Other recent reports document the social costs of growth. [1]

## INTERNATIONAL NEGOTIATIONS

Against such a backdrop, international responses may seem ponderous and ineffectual. Yet it would be wrong to overlook the amount of activity since 1992, much of it set in motion by the Earth Summit itself. Several important agreements have been concluded. The Biodiversity Convention was ratified (on being signed by 50 countries) in December 1993. A year later, as its first Conference of Parties was about to be held, around 90 countries had signed, most of them anxious to safeguard their claim to a share of the commercial value of genetic material to the industries of the North.

The Climate Convention was ratified a little later, in March 1994, by which time most signatories had prepared climate strategies. NGO assessments suggest that most plans will fail to meet the goal of stabilizing $CO_2$ emissions at 1990 levels by 2000. However, as we have seen (page 110), the concentration of greenhouse and other gases in the atmosphere will have to be reduced to much lower levels. European countries and the USA have made tentative suggestions that the convention needs to be strengthened. However, the first meeting of the Conference of Parties held in Berlin in April 1995 failed to reach agreement on swift and decisive action, despite a graphic reminder only a few weeks earlier of the seriousness of the possible impacts of global warming when a huge iceberg split away from the Antarctic icecap.

International action on CFCs shows how much (but also how little) can be achieved in reaching and implementing international agreements. The original Montreal Protocol has been strengthened twice (at London and Copenhagen) since September 1987, and production of CFCs in the North must now be halted by 1996. These measures have led to a 60 per cent drop

---

1. For the ISEW study, see Jackson and Marks (1994). See also the reports of the Commission for Social Justice (1994) and the Rowntree Foundation (1995).

in CFC emissions since 1988. However, a drop in CFCs in the atmosphere will depend on all countries complying in full with the London and Copenhagen agreements, and on the willingness and ability of countries in the South, particularly India and China, to end production by 2006, the end of the concessionary period for the South. Even if the most optimistic projections of reductions in emissions are fulfilled, the levels of chlorine in the atmosphere will mean increased ultraviolet radiation for many years to come, with impacts which are not yet fully known.

In June 1994 a third convention — the treaty on desertification — was agreed in Paris, and was quickly ratified, with 87 countries signing by October of that year. The convention provides a framework for action to restrict the spread of land degradation and desertification, which afflicts about 25 per cent of the earth's terrestrial surface and threatens the livelihoods of almost 1000 million people.

Another convention — the Convention on the Law of the Sea — was also ratified in 1994, after alterations to the original treaty to make it acceptable to the industrial North. This enshrines the twin principles of national sovereignty over "exclusive economic zones" extending 200 miles offshore and national responsibility for the ecosystems within them. It incorporates many previous agreements on dumping at sea and the regulation of shipping and fisheries, which now become binding on signatories. The UN has also taken action on "straddling" fish stocks (namely those that "straddle" boundaries between exclusive economic zones), which are not covered by the Law of the Sea but which were discussed at Rio.

International agreements since Rio have not been confined to environmental issues. In September 1994, the UN International Conference on Population and Development in Cairo, attended by representatives from over 160 countries, rejected "top-down" coercive family planning programmes. It was agreed that the problem of population growth could not be solved without also solving the social problems that cause it to persist. The conference approved a World Population Plan of Action designed to prevent world population rising above 9.8 billion, an ambitious target given earlier UN projections (see Chapter 1). The plan sees stabilizing the world's population as a socioeconomic rather than medical issue, and looks at population growth in the context of the empowerment of women, the role of the family, reproductive rights and health, and migration. It calls for a threefold increase in spending on both family-planning programmes and projects to raise the status of women by changing social and economic conditions. The North was asked to supply just over a third of the funding ($5.7 million) and to strengthen existing UN programmes to increase literacy and improve women's health.

The succession of international meetings continued in March 1995 with the UN Conference on Social Development held in Copenhagen, which focused on poverty, unemployment and social exclusion. The draft declaration committed governments to national targets "for the substantial reduction of overall poverty and the eradication of extreme poverty" and called on the World Bank and IMF to modify structural adjustment programmes in the light of sustainable development goals. The conference thus resumed discussion of development concerns dating from at least the early 1960s (see Chapter 3). However, it failed, despite being heralded as the "Social Summit", to attract either the publicity of the Earth Summit or, significantly, the support of several leaders in the North.

The Copenhagen agenda included a proposal from UNDP to tackle the skewing of aid towards military and other prestigious expenditure and away from spending on human needs. The "20:20 Compact on Human Development" proposed that countries in the South agree to commit 20 per cent of their resources to meeting human needs on the understanding that countries giving aid earmark 20 per cent of their funding for the same purpose. The agenda also included the issues of alleviating debt burdens and reforming unfavourable terms of trade, which were not properly addressed at Rio.

The Copenhagen Summit was followed by at least two other important meetings in the year that marked the fiftieth anniversary of the founding of the UN. In July the G7 countries devoted their economic summit to a discussion of the framework of institutions needed to bring about sustainable development, and in September the UN World Conference on Women was held in Beijing.

## The UN Commission on Sustainable Development

The CSD, created by the UN General Assembly in December 1992, began work in 1993. The commission, which consists of 53 diplomats drawn from both Southern and Northern countries (including the UK), meets annually in May and ends with an assembly attended by ministers of the environment from national governments, of whom 50 were present in 1994. Working groups on finance and technology meet in February each year.

Though some commentators at the Earth Summit were doubtful about the CSD's ability to fulfil a rather large and vague remit, their most pessimistic predictions have not come true. At its 1993 meeting the CSD developed an outline for the years to 1997, when there will be a review of progress on the implementation of Agenda 21. Since 1993 it has discussed a range of issues from Agenda 21 at its annual meetings, concentrating on specific themes each year — health, human settlements, freshwater resources, solid wastes and sewage, and toxic chemicals and hazardous (including radioactive) wastes in 1994; land (including forestry and biodiversity), poverty, population, and indicators of sustainability in 1995. Climate change, air pollution, oceans and trade are the topics scheduled for 1996. A review of Agenda 21's eighth chapter, "Integrating Environment and Development in Economic Decisions", is also on the agenda for 1995 along with a discussion on national accounting systems.

The CSD has followed the example of Rio where NGO representatives outnumbered official government ones by two to one, and encouraged a considerable amount of NGO participation. More than 500 NGO groups are permitted to observe CSD meetings and make contributions under certain conditions. The CSD's policy is an important consequence of Agenda 21's emphasis on the participation of a range of social groups and has meant that representatives of community organizations can, with help from major NGOs, challenge other interest groups and influence decision-making at CSD meetings.

The CSD is responsible for coordinating the formulation of national sustainable development strategies and for receiving annual reports on these strategies from national governments and a range of other bodies. These include UN agencies such as the World Health Organization (WHO) and UNEP; other multilateral bodies such as the IMF, GATT and the World Bank; the conventions on biodiversity and climate change; and treaty organizations such as the Montreal Protocol on Ozone Depletion. The CSD also encourages the submission of reports by the nine major groups given prominence in Agenda 21 — NGOs, business groups, trade unions, local authorities, women's (but not men's) organizations, youth groups, farmers, academics and indigenous peoples. The CSD has also given detailed guidance on the preparation of reports and strategies to help it collate (and submit to ECOSOC and the General Assembly) an overview report based on the national reports it receives.

Despite these activities, the CSD has achieved less than its supporters had hoped. This is partly because of its very large remit, but also because it has received insufficient support from individual countries to facilitate an exchange of ideas on sustainable development and to create an international climate in which nations feel obliged to demonstrate their progress towards it. Although over 100 countries had set up national sustainable development commissions by the May 1994 meeting, only half the CSD's member nations and only ten other countries submitted strategies. As a result, the Inter-Action Council (an independent group of former heads of governments) has proposed that independent experts report to national governments and then, within the UN, to the secretary-general rather than to ECOSOC.

## SUSTAINABLE DEVELOPMENT INDICATORS

Pressure on the CSD has stimulated discussion about indicators for sustainable development. Simple statistical indices would provide a measure of progress towards sustainable development and highlight areas where there is insufficient progress. They would not only make the CSD's job easier but would also give it credibility, particularly in view of the planned review of progress in implementing Agenda 21 due in 1997. If widely accepted, they would heighten public awareness of sustainable development, possibly becoming as significant in the public mind as such economic indicators as growth rates, unemployment figures, balance of payments figures and the *Financial Times* share index. Their "simplicity" and convenience also makes them highly appealing to the bureaucratic mind.

Attempts to devise widely acceptable sustainable development indicators are being made by a range of organizations. These include multilateral bodies such as the United Nations Statistical Office (UNSTAT) and several UN agencies (FAO, UNICEF, WHO, UNEP and UNDP) as well as the World Bank; regional agencies such as the OECD, the United Nations Economic Commissions for Europe (UNECE) and Africa (UNECA) and the Asian Development Bank; several national governments (the Netherlands, Canada, Norway, Denmark and the USA); various NGOs including IUCN, WRI, WWI, WWF, Milieu Defensie, NEF and UNA; and various research institutes. Local authorities are also trying to develop their own indicators.

At the national level the Netherlands has probably done more work on indicators than any other country, taking six years to decide on policy targets and potential sustainability limits for the impacts on seven environmental features of six key groups in the economy (three more are planned).

There has been considerable criticism, largely from NGOs, of the sets of indicators produced by multilateral organizations. First, they concentrate on environmental indicators. They give little attention to "social concerns" and to the problems of the South, failing to address directly the issue of human needs. Second, they have tended to neglect such key areas as patterns or levels of consumption, trade, participation in decision-making and ecological footprints. Third, unlike the Seattle project, multilateral organizations have made little or no effort to encourage wide public participation in the choice of indicators. Fourth, there is a lack of technical coordination between some sets of indicators and policy targets and objectives. And fifth, doubt has been cast on whether the information on which indicators are based is available in some parts of the world, particularly in Africa, and even on the validity of some of the information that is available.

There have also been problems in reaching a consensus over indicators. These are partly due to the number of agencies involved, the different approaches they have developed and their lack of openness to other groups; but they are also partly due to the difficulty of ensuring that potential indicators are accepted as accurate, reliable and relevant. Other reasons derive from the status of any indicators that are chosen. They will be regarded as very important sources of information; for example, they will be able to highlight a government's failure to implement sustainable policies. Their potential power may mean that unsuitable indicators or ones that can be used in a misleading way are selected. Reaching agreement on indicators involves resolving conflicts of interests. Ultimately, our choice will reflect our values, as Hazel Henderson (1986, p37) has pointed out: "We must never forget that, in the most scientific sense, reality is what we pay attention to. Indicators only reflect our innermost core values and goals, measuring the development of our own understanding."

## OTHER MULTILATERAL INITIATIVES

Agencies outside the UN have also been active in promoting sustainable development. The IUCN and IIED have contributed to the post-Rio process by issuing a guide to preparing national sustainable development strategies (NSDSs) (see IUCN/IIED, 1993 and 1994). They suggest that successful strategies are likely to have certain features in common — they will concentrate on the priority issues and the most effective ways forward, and will monitor and then improve chosen programmes of action: "A national strategy for sustainability is a participatory and cyclical process of planning and action to achieve economic, ecological and social objectives in a balanced and integrated manner" (IUCN/IIED, 1993, p3). Strategies should integrate different sectoral approaches and involve all the main groups affected. They should be adaptive, for outcomes are often uncertain and conditions, capabilities and preferred policies change over time. Strategies are, however, difficult to implement successfully. The concepts of sustainability, cross-sectoral thinking and integration are still relatively unfamiliar and methods have still to be worked out or proved effective. The strategy process depends on a tradition of open critical discussion and on building a broad consensus, practices that may not be strongly established in some countries. It may be impossible to sustain the process when there are deep conflicts over issues or when external forces (such as terms of trade or external markets) limit practical options. Because they need to be comprehensive and involve many interests, strategies cannot be developed quickly, especially when resources are limited. Expectations should therefore remain real-istic: "A strategy is not a panacea. It is a difficult undertaking no matter how well-equipped the country" (IUCN/IIED, 1993, p22).

Of fundamental importance for the success of an NSDS, according to the IUCN, is participation, which means the full involvement at every stage of the process of all the groups likely to be affected. Participation is not simply consultation. Full participation requires a dialogue "in which each party provides information and receives and considers the information of others" (IUCN/ IIED, 1993, p43). It is important for several reasons: it increases the chances of the strategy being put into practice; it allows people to identify with the strategy process and so build support for the strategy itself; it makes more information and opinions available; and it leads to a broader debate on priorities, options and trade-offs.

Participation needs time to be done well and can therefore be expensive. However, it engages people in the process and allows them to feel they have a share in it. It increases awareness of the issues, helps create sympathy for the long-term aim and encour-ages a realistic understanding of the options. It is in fact crucial to success: "The question of who participates and how is the key to the success of any strategy" (IUCN/IIED, 1993, p43).

## TOWARDS SUSTAINABILITY

Another important agreement is the Fifth Environmental Action Programme adopted in late 1992 by the then European Community. Entitled *Towards Sustainability* (Commission of the EC, 1993), it goes beyond the emphases in previous EC environ-mental action programmes on pollution control and habitat protection, and calls for progress on integrating sustainable development into all areas of policy-making. It regards environ-mental issues "not so much as problems, but as symptoms of mismanagement and abuse. The real 'problems' which cause environmental loss and damage, are the current patterns of human consumption and behaviour" (Commission of the EC, 1993, p3, paragraph 17). It calls for a reversal of what until recently have been normal assumptions about meeting demand, and sets a policy of reducing or restraining demand. Practical requirements for sustainability include facilitating optimum levels of reuse and recycling, rationalizing the production and consumption of energy, and altering consumption and behaviour patterns. The report recognizes a particularly urgent need for significant reductions in the environmental impacts of five sectors of the economy: industry, energy, transport, agriculture and tourism. Weizsäcker (1994, p34) sees the inclusion of transport and energy as particularly significant, describing them as "previously sacred cows of an expansion-oriented Community". The report also specifies the main strategies in each sector: for example, improvements in technical efficiency and the adoption of less polluting, cleaner technologies in industry and energy.

## SUSTAINABLE DEVELOPMENT: THE UK STRATEGY

Britain played "a leading role" in the development of *Towards Sustainability* — so we are informed in *Sustainable Development: The UK Strategy*, published in February 1994 along with *Biodiversity: The UK Action Plan, Climate Change: The UK Programme, and Sustainable Forestry: The UK Programme.*[2]

*Sustainable Development: The UK Strategy* has four sections. Section 1 describes the context, scope and preparation of the document and the principles of sustainable development. These do not refer to human needs directly, though "a healthy economy is better able to generate the resources to meet people's needs". What constitutes a "healthy economy" is significantly not defined. The document refrains from identifying sustainable development with economic growth, but does little to discourage those who do, or to emphasize the problems of integrating environment and development ("new investment and environmental improvement often go hand in hand"). However, it does affirm, in rather guarded fashion, important principles: sustainable development requires that "decisions throughout society are taken *with proper regard to* their environmental impact"; "precautionary action *may* be necessary"; "ecological impacts must be

---

2.  See UK Government (1994a, 1994b, 1994c and 1994d).

*considered*, particularly where resources are nonrenewable or effects may be irreversible" (emphasis added).

Section 2 reviews the state of the British environment, identifying "the likely pressure points over the next 20 years", but without comment on clearly unsustainable long-term trends and projections. Section 3 contains 12 chapters, each reviewing a sector of the economy and each identifying key issues for sustainability, but gives only the most general indications of how unsustainable activities might be reduced.

Section 4 ("Putting Sustainability into Practice") fails to supply what might reasonably be expected — some account of specific policies, targets and deadlines and the resources required to meet them. Instead, it reviews, in very broad terms, some considerations to be borne in mind in developing policy. It accepts that all sectors in society — central government, local government and other agencies, including citizens — have a role to play in promoting sustainability, and that sustainability requires changes in lifestyle from everyone. It is aware of wide public concern about the environment and notes that "people do not or cannot always make the changes they say [in opinion polls] they are willing to make". However, it shows no awareness that government policy, or the lack of it, may have a bearing on this. It discusses, without any apparent awareness of the irony, the UK government's commitment to promoting sustainable development internationally and in particular in the South.

On the face of it the document represents an important advance in stated policy. However, the title is something of a misnomer, for the document does not set out a strategy, but provides a general survey of some of the considerations to be taken into account in formulating one. It glosses over areas of policy that do not meet sustainability requirements and presents modest progress as major contributions to sustainable development, exemplifying the comment of Hilary French (1995, p182) of the WWI: "Because governments are reporting on their own actions, these documents tend to be long on self-congratulation, and short on substantive analysis of remaining challenges."

Contrary to the IUCN's advice, a rather top-down strategy process was adopted, as reflected in the preparation of the document itself in which participation was limited to consultation.

Following a conference at Green College, Oxford, in July 1993 (Green College Centre for Environmental Policy and Understanding, 1993), the Department of the Environment sent a draft document to 6000 organizations, of which 500 responded in ways that led to substantial improvements in the final document. The extent to which this tapped public interest can be gauged from the fact that about 8000 *Daily Telegraph* readers returned a questionnaire on sustainability.

Despite its lack of detailed policies and targets, *Sustainable Development: The UK Strategy* can be seen as a positive step, if only because it establishes a baseline for thinking about environment and development for government departments. The document will function as a position paper on which more detailed and ambitious policy can be built. Its value lies as much in the processes by which it was produced as in the document itself, for these represent the first steps in a programme of gradual ecological conscientization of all sectors of society, including government. Opinions differ over whether the pace need be quite so slow and whether the programme extends the process widely enough.

### Legislating for the Environment

After such a guarded fulfilment of the commitment to produce a sustainable development strategy, it is hardly surprising that the UK government's record on the protection of the environment should also leave room for improvement. In October 1994 it announced the setting-up of the Environment Agency, an integrated body to replace separate control of pollution of rivers, air and areas around waste dumps (by the National Rivers Authority, Her Majesty's Inspectorate of Pollution and local waste regulation authorities). The draft legislation requires that the new body must have regard not only to the "desirability of conserving and enhancing natural beauty", but also to "costs and benefits in exercising its powers" and to the need to "minimize the burden on industry". It appears that the proposed watchdog will have fewer teeth than the ones it replaces. The *New Scientist* comments,[3]

---

3. "Gummer leaves environment agency toothless" and "Reneging on Rio?", *New Scientist*, 22 October 1994.

"The absence of the word 'protection' from the title is no mere accident."

Two months later the government announced it had decided to repeal the unimplemented section of the Environmental Protection Act of 1990, which provided for public registers of contaminated land. This decision was apparently in response to pressure from property developers, who were fearful that registers would mean a drop in the commercial value of "development" sites, and from insurance companies anxious to avoid huge liabilities. The government announced an alternative system that will prevent members of the public having access to information about the whereabouts of contaminated land and also reduce the obligations on landowners and developers to clean up pollution.[4]

## Local Agenda 21

Local government in the UK has responded much more positively to the challenge of sustainable development. The Local Government Management Board (LGMB) has made a commitment on behalf of the local authorities it represents to set targets for quality of life, to create partnerships with all sectors including central government and to share expertise and good practice with local authorities in other countries (for example, by providing training and support for Local Agenda 21 initiatives in several African countries).

However, as the fate of a report by the Association of County Councils (1991) on a policy for sustainable transport showed (its recommendations have been largely ignored by central government), local authorities face severe constraints on the extent to which they can move towards sustainable policies without government support. The LGMB has called on central government to remove restrictions on local authorities' powers to make decisions about policy and spending; to give local authorities stronger powers to implement strategic environmental management and promote the use of high environmental standards in contracts; to implement the EU's Fifth Environmental Programme; and to develop "sustainable" policies on a wide range of issues.

---

4.  "Gummer buries list of poisoned land", *New Scientist*, 3 December 1994.

Local authorities are committed to developing Local Agenda 21 initiatives in time for the CSD meeting in 1996 and to forming networks with local authorities in other countries. Preparation of a local Agenda 21 has at least six aspects:

- improving the local authority's own performance on environmental issues,
- integrating sustainable development goals with existing policies and practices,
- raising local awareness,
- encouraging the participation of the public,
- forming partnerships with a range of interests, and
- monitoring and reporting on progress.

In addition to work on Local Agenda 21 initiatives, local government's current programme includes further work on environmental auditing, on developing indicators for local authorities, and a wide range of other initiatives (LGMB, 1993a).

One particularly impressive example of local government commitment to sustainable development was "Global Forum '94", which was held in Manchester during the summer of 1994 to examine the implications of Agenda 21 and to look at seven key issues for sustainable cities. The conference was attended by around 800 delegates, 750 of whom represented 63 cities around the world. They were drawn equally from local authorities, trade unions, business and industry, and NGOs and community groups, and joined forces with 50 "international experts". Together they made around 300 recommendations on sustainability in cities, which they forwarded to the CSD and those involved in preparations for the Social Summit. Perhaps its key achievement was to demonstrate that the four sectors that were represented could be brought together to achieve consensus and find innovative solutions.

## Other Developments

Sustainable development has also made some impact on the business community. There is room here for only a few random examples. As a contribution to Local Business Agenda 21, the National Westminster Bank, together with the WWF, is working to try to demonstrate to small and medium-sized businesses that ecologically sound practices are essential to business success. Many companies, such as Marks & Spencer, insist on their suppliers following an environmental code, and B & Q, the do-it-yourself chain, has published a booklet, *How Green is My Hammer?*, giving information about products and materials imported from abroad. Meanwhile 35 per cent of people in the UK are said to care about "ethical consuming", and a new organization, Out of This World, "will encourage them with a chain of shops, built, designed, stocked and run in environmentally sound and ethical ways" (CAT, 1995, p7).

At a time when individuals make speculative gains from sales of public assets, and competitiveness is invoked to justify both large-scale redundancies and huge salary increases, one company has shown that there is another way to do business. Traidcraft, which imports most of its stock from the South, supports small and disadvantaged producers by paying more than other buyers and acting to promote security of livelihood. In 1994 Traidcraft instigated a "social audit" to examine the impact of every aspect of its operations from packaging to its corporate ethos.

The audit includes a commitment by both directors and share-holders to pioneering new standards in company reporting. The company's annual report gives information about prices paid to suppliers, profit margins, job descriptions (revised in the interests of equity) and grades, equal opportunities within the company, policy on the chief executive's salary (which at under £20,000 is only 2.6 times that of its poorest-paid employee), and comments by suppliers, staff and customers. Traidcraft, which was founded in 1979 and is based in Gateshead, sent copies of its annual report to the top 100 private limited companies in the country in an attempt to persuade them to adopt a similar style of reporting (*Guardian*, 16 August 1994).

There are also many interesting initiatives in academic and research institutions. Besides developing new courses, several British universities are developing environmental management and audit systems. Edinburgh University began a "green initiative" with a comprehensive review of practice in the three sectors of teaching, research and administration. The Council for the Greening of Higher Education facilitates the exchange of information among universities and also disseminates information about work in other countries. In the USA a number of colleges and universities have not only conducted environmental audits and adopted environmental management schemes, but have also involved students in these projects or responded to student initiatives in these areas. One student project investigated the energy and other costs of transporting over long distances the food consumed in college residences and eating-houses and the feasibility of replacing "imported" food with local produce. There are also innumerable research projects into many aspects of sustainability. Some of the most interesting of these are the investigations of ecological footprints and "appropriated carrying capacity" (Wackernagel and Rees, 1992); the calculations of ecological rucksacks (Bringezu et al, 1944); and the computer modelling of enhanced carrying capacity options (ECCO) developed by Malcolm Slesser and Jane King of the Centre for Human Ecology at the University of Edinburgh (Slesser et al, 1994).

Other groups have also been researching sustainable policy. At its 1994 conference the Labour Party approved an impressive document, *In Trust for Tomorrow*, based on the work of the Socialist Environment and Resources Association (SERA). The Green Party and the Liberal Democratic Party also have environmental policies.

There are many other initiatives, too numerous to be listed here: projects in sustainable agriculture and rural development; projects in agroforestry, soil conservation and voluntary flood protection schemes; projects based on indigenous knowledge and the selection of traditional crop varieties; urban neighbourhood improvement schemes in which local people work in partnership with such organizations as IIED, the ETC Foundation and Oxfam; campaigns, not only by prominent organizations such as Greenpeace and Friends of the Earth (FOE), which now links organizations in many countries, but also by many other local voluntary groups; networking by groups that share an interest in reducing unsustainable practices (for example, the Save the Cairngorms Campaign brings together over 20 NGO groups); environmental audits; and eco-labelling. Meanwhile, at meetings and conferences attended by delegates drawn from chambers of commerce, voluntary organizations, local government and other groups, speakers invoke Agenda 21 in calling for action to reverse unsustainable trends, support local communities, revive local economies, fund ecological restoration, rebuild nature and build awareness. In both official and private capacities, vast numbers of individuals are trying to create movement toward sustainable development. Indeed Ernst Ulrich von Weizsäcker (1994, p34) estimates that millions of European citizens are now engaged in active environmental work.

Even far-from-ideal developments or initiatives can have a positive effect. For example, in its first report in January 1995, the elitist Prime Minister's Panel on Sustainable Development not only called for action on overfishing, reform of the CAP and the taxing of environmental pollution, but also endorsed Greenpeace's call for better monitoring of the continuing damage to the ozone layer.[5]

However, for every citizen who participates in "green" action there are hundreds, perhaps thousands, who do not. Even as Sustrans announces plans for an extended network of cycle routes, the lobby against windpower gathers strength. For every small organization campaigning for change there are hundreds of larger organizations that see little advantage in altering the status quo. For every loan for a small solar energy project made under the GEF there are plans for massive investments in coal-fired power stations funded by World Bank loans. For every sustainability initiative there are dozens of routine practices that continue to degrade resources or deprive the poor (and others) of access to them.

In the business world there has been some interest in, but few positive responses to, Traidcraft's innovations. Only The Body Shop — not included in the companies to which Traidcraft sent copies of its report — has announced plans to carry out a social audit. Robert Gray (1994, p21), professor of accounting at Dundee University, calls for radical changes in the framework of

---

5. The members of the Panel on Sustainable Development are: Sir Crispin Tickell (chair), warden of Green College, Oxford; Lord Alexander of Weedon, chairman of the National Westminster Bank; Sir John Houghton, chairman of the Royal Commission on Environmental Pollution; Dr Anne McLaren, vice-president of the Royal Society; and the Earl of Selbourne, chairman of the Joint Nature Conservation Committee.

reporting to incorporate concepts of stewardship and account-ability not just to other financial institutions, (which do not at present "express anything other than the very mildest concern for the social and environmental effects of organizations they own and lend to") but also to society, to the communities affected, and to future generations. Such changes will not come about, he believes, if companies are left to adopt "sustainability" reporting procedures voluntarily. This is an important issue: if markets are efficient and respond to new information, as economic theory assumes, then "sustainability" reporting should influence the way capital is allocated. However, although many companies have schemes similar to Marks & Spencer, the "overriding view" in the financial world is that the "fiduciary duty" to make as large a return as possible on an investment conflicts with any obligation to society to take a wider view.[6] Such evidence confirms the words of a BP executive at a conference on sustainable development: "Find an individual to take responsibility, companies don't."

Some political parties may have impressive policy documents, but in the autumn of 1994, John Major, prime minister and leader of the Conservative Party, announced that it was his ambition to see GNP double again in Britain over the next 25 years, without making any attempt to educate the public about the need for greater resource and energy efficiency and productivity. About the same time the Liberal Democratic Party quietly dropped its proposals for basic income on the grounds that they were an electoral liability.

And perhaps most significant of all, while a growing number of individuals attempt to find alternatives to unsustainable systems, the vast majority of the population are unaware of, or unaffected by, both the initiatives with which the minority persevere, and the compelling reasons why they do. Much progress is required in three crucial areas — business, education and the media.

Without a serious campaign at the national level to increase public awareness it is difficult to see how to initiate wide public

---

6. See "Emerging markets fail to see the green light", *Scotland on Sunday*, 24 August 1994.

debate about sustainable development. However, three different kinds of initiative may help to bring that debate nearer and to inform discussions when it begins to take place.

The first of these are initiatives aimed not only to develop public awareness but to encourage participation in discussions about local resources by those not normally involved or unsure about how to convert their interest into effective action. The Scottish Rural Development Programme, designed to complement a Forests and People in Rural Areas Programme promoted by government agencies, is one such example. This has used techniques of participatory rural appraisal (PRA), developed in and for the South, to help four rural communities in Scotland assess their local forestry resources and their potential contribution to community welfare. The project demonstrates what is required to convert the principle of people's participation into practice in Northern countries (IIED, 1994).

The second type of initiative demonstrates ways of fulfilling environmental targets (for example, reducing carbon emissions) without threatening livelihoods. These are important, because "long-established economic policies and practices on which hundreds and thousands of jobs depend cannot easily be reversed" (Gordon, 1994, p34). Such projects are often thought of as urgently needed in the South, but they are equally relevant in the North. The Glasgow City Council Housing Department plans to spend £157 million over two years to convert poorly-insulated, condensation-ridden tenements into energy-efficient housing. Not only will this contribute to Britain's efforts to reduce $CO_2$ emissions, but it will also enable tenants to afford adequate heating, thus immediately improving their physical welfare and reducing the associated human costs of poor housing — such as childhood asthma, malnutrition and family breakdown — which afflict those who are unable to heat their homes properly even when spending a disproportionately large proportion of their income on fuel.

The third type of initiative is designed to increase public awareness of the inequities built into levels of consumption in the North. Milieu Defensie, the Dutch FOE group, has calculated the per capita share of common commodities and resources to which each of us is entitled on the basis of a fair share for each person on the Earth. Its Action Plan for a Sustainable Netherlands (Milieu Defensie, 1992) is based on the concept of "environmental space" (the total quantity of natural resources available under sustainable management) and is designed to demonstrate to the Dutch public (and other Northern consumers) that they can still have an acceptable quality of life even if they alter consumption patterns so that the world's natural resources are shared equitably among the world's population. Milieu Defensie have calculated shares for the year 2010, when it is estimated world population will reach seven billion. Equitable shares will mean considerable reductions in current Northern rates of consumption of many natural resources. The per capita share of farmland will drop from the present 0.45 hectares to 0.25 hectares, of which 0.19 hectares will be needed for basic food supplies, while the consumption of timber, including wood used for paper, will have to be reduced by 60 per cent. However, levels of consumption do not have to fall as much as levels of resource extraction if resources are used very efficiently and there is a great deal of reuse, recycling and repair of materials. The number of trees felled for paper, for example, can be reduced by 75 per cent if paper recycling is increased from its present level of 37 per cent of all paper used in the Netherlands to 75 per cent, and if the manufacture of paper can also be made more efficient. This approach is being taken up by FOE groups in other countries in association with the Wuppertal Institute.

## CONCLUSION

There have been a number of sustainable development initiatives since Rio (at international, national and local or NGO levels), many of which would not have happened without the stimulus of UNCED. The numerous international negotiations have served several ends. First, they have contributed to the extensive campaign to raise awareness, of which Rio, which has been described as a very expensive educational exercise for diplomats and bureaucrats, was itself a part. Second, they have enabled smaller nations to build coalitions for change, which can isolate and put pressure on single large nations (such as the USA at Rio). Third, through the "soft law" of voluntary agreements they have put moral pressure on governments unwilling to accept binding commitments. And fourth, the presence of NGOs at such negotiations has both increased internal and external pressures on national governments and countered lobbying by other interests.

Such negotiations have resulted in 170 international environmental treaties (two-thirds of which have been negotiated in the 20 years since Stockholm), and a total of over 800 environmental agreements (French, 1995, p172). According to Jackie Roddick (1993) of Glasgow University, progress at the international level should not be underestimated:

> *Perceptions that there has been no progress since the Earth Summit are over-stated. A great deal has been happening: a massive effort at putting in place the institutional machinery needed to cope with the world's problems of sustainability, at levels from local government to the UN. What is lacking is the upsurge of public concern which would make it possible for this creaking assemblage of bureaucratic machinery to generate real change.*

The lack of a parallel growth in public concern cannot be explained simply by the media spotlight switching away from Rio. There is unlikely to be any dramatic increase in public concern until governments put as much effort into raising public awareness, particularly awareness that "environmental" problems are symptoms of deep-seated forces, as they have done into reaching international agreements. Only then will governments give substance to international agreements and build the capacities — through allocating resources and enabling people — to put ideas for more sustainable alternatives into practice.

Without public concern Rio would not have happened, nor would most of the initiatives reviewed in this chapter. Without continued public concern governments are unlikely to feel impelled to reach new international agreements, which in turn create new pressures on governments, stimulate innovative projects and broaden individuals' awareness. Governments should not be content — and electorates must not allow them to be content — to wait until public concern is refuelled by disquiet and outrage at new revelations about what is happening to our planet and its people. Instead they must play a proactive role to give further momentum to the process of change — and electorates must insist that they do. Public concern and enabling government action are key factors in the complex dynamic of individual, national and international action, and must reinforce each other in a creative way. If they do not, governments are likely to ignore the international agreements they have signed. The limited achievements of the Copenhagen Summit and the Berlin Climate Convention Conference can be explained by the absence of such a synergy. As one commentator (French, 1995, p171) confirmed a couple of years after Rio: "The reality is that the international momentum generated by UNCED is flagging, and the global partnership it called for is foundering due to a failure of political will."

If national governments take sustainable development seriously they can do much, even with limited resources, to build on public concern, but they need clear indications that they have a mandate for such action. They are of course unlikely to receive this until the general public is sufficiently aware of the need to make this a priority. Until we resolve this deadlock, progress toward more sustainable options is likely to continue to falter. The concluding chapter considers the impasse more fully.

# Chapter 11 | SUSTAINABLE DEVELOPMENT in the mid-1990s

Revising an article first written soon after the publication of the Brundtland Report, Tim O'Riordan accepts that sustainable development has achieved a currency and status he would not have predicted for a concept he had contended "was deliberately vague and inherently self-contradictory so that endless streams of academics and diplomats could spend many comfortable hours trying to define it without success". Five years on, he concedes, "the term has stuck. ... Like it or not, 'sustainable development' is with us for all time" (O'Riordan, 1993, p37).

He attributes its persistence to such phenomena as the impact of green consumer campaigns, the increase in number and stringency of environmental regulations and the desire for a more sustainable future, "latent in most emancipated individuals". However, he suggests that for "true sustainability" five conditions "that are still far from any political consensus" have to be met:

(i)   *a form of democracy that transcends the nation-state and the next election, namely that alters the meaning of "self-interest" and "sacrifice";*

(ii)  *guarantees of civil rights and social justice to oppressed peoples the world over, so that they are allowed to consume resources in an equilibrium manner, and appreciate the intrinsic rights of nature;*

(iii) *commitments of resources, notably technology, intellectual property generally, and cash, to impoverished and environmentally vulnerable regimes, many of which are run by politically unstable and inherently corrupt governments (as indeed are many rich nations);*

(iv) *eliminations of debt where debt is induced by unfair terms of trade and a historical legacy of exploitation;*

(v) *establishment of a variety of public-private and non-governmental mechanisms for delivering resources, training and management techniques to areas and communities in need, in such a way as to be socially acceptable and democratising.*

(O'Riordan, 1993, p39)

As O'Riordan (1993, p39) points out, these are not novel suggestions, having been "promoted in official and quasi-official reports for generations".

He goes on to illustrate the nature of the forces ranged against sustainable development as revealed in a recent case of official forecasts of demands for aggregates. Produced in secret by working parties made up of representatives of central and local government and the aggregates industry, these forecasts reveal a lack of interest in options for reducing demand or for reusing or recycling aggregates; a secretiveness common to both industry and regulators; and "insidious connections with the road industry, the car lobby and the whole paraphernalia of promoting new motorspace at the expense of less mobility, more effective public transport. and an energy conservation priority" (O'Riordan, 1993, p42).

For O'Riordan (1993, p43), the case illustrates that "all our institutions, whether they be extractive, administrative, regulatory or economic (in the broadest sense), are effectively geared to depletion, to passing on third-party costs and, above all, to the comfort of not having to think and act sustainably".

In short, our institutions suit ruling elites and large commercial organizations, with their linked interests in political and economic power, for they have been shaped by, are protected by and promote the values of what has been called "the nexus of state and commerce" (Middleton et al, 1993, p209).

This alliance of political and economic power has fostered and shaped to its own ends an economic system that not only depletes natural resources in an unsustainable way, but also refuses to accept that labour is different from other factors of production, as Daly and Cobb (1990, p61) point out:

> *Labour is not just a commodity like any other, to be priced by supply and demand. The price of other commodities can approach or*

*become zero if necessary to clear the market. The wage of labour*
*cannot fall below a subsistence minimum, which may be defined*
*biologically in poor countries or by custom and social standards in*
*wealthy countries.*

Despite this, the system subordinates human needs to capital (or
to the authority of the state in the communist system). It has
always placed a higher value on capital than on labour, on profits
than on people. We can see this clearly in times of recession: if
profits are threatened, workers are discarded.[1]

The convergent interests of state and commerce form an
alliance which has rarely been interested in equity. From before
the middle of the last century until quite recently, it was the
representatives of labour who fought for and achieved, if not
social equity, at least the substantial mitigation of the unre-
generate capitalist system. This resulted in the basic welfare
provisions of the modern democratic state — housing, health-
care, education and pensions, as well as some control over wage
levels and working conditions.[2] It is therefore hardly surprising
that the elites who wish to retain or extend their economic or
political power have responded equivocally to the concept of sustainable development, for, as O'Riordan (1993, p39) points out,
sustainable development "confronts modern society at the very
heart of its purpose".

There are, of course, many people at all levels of society who
recognize, consciously or unconsciously, that their interests are
aligned with those of the "nexus". They are, in the words of
Ulrich Loening (in an unpublished letter to the September 1994
conference of the Balaton Group):

*"the wreckers": those who exploit while the going is good; for*
*whom the principles of sustainability, however formulated, however*
*understood, and even agreed on, crumble in the face of the drive to*

---

1. It is a feature of the competitive global market that workers are made
   redundant even when firms are doing well.
2. The struggle for such improvements in welfare were, of course, abetted by
   industry's demand for an increasingly well-equipped work force, but it is
   arguable that without the campaigns of the Chartists, and later the trade
   unions, capitalism would have collapsed in competition with more socially
   responsible systems.

*forge ahead. When evaluating our ideas we may overlook that most of the world does not seem to want ecological sustainability. The wreckers may not necessarily be wicked. There is a wide spectrum from outright corruption to the best of intentions, which nevertheless lead to trouble. . . . "Apathy" would be sufficient . . . to continue the damage. Equally damaging and more concealed, seems to be the unconscious intelligence behind most of trade and commerce and government. People recognize how their bread is buttered.*

Entrenched economic interests have prospered in the political and economic climate of the years since 1983, when the Brundtland Commission began the work which was to give worldwide publicity to the concept of sustainable development. The same can hardly be said for the common good. The relaxation of market controls has threatened the welfare provision achieved through the political struggles of the previous 150 years. Reductions in welfare services have been accompanied by a decline in public investment in social welfare projects and in the renewal of social and economic infrastructure, and the sale of public assets, including major utilities, to private individuals and companies. Meanwhile, the electorate values the short-term, individualistic gains of tax cuts more highly than the public and social benefits derived from maintaining social welfare policies. The results, as we have seen, have included fewer jobs, poorer working conditions, greater social inequities, growing social problems (associated with deprivation of various kinds), less environmental protection, and a less cohesive and increasingly polarized society.

Unregulated economic forces thus discourage consensual approaches, which, it has been shown (see Weizsäcker, 1944, p142), favour progress in environmental protection and thrive best in the social democracies.

The effects of unregulated market forces can also be seen in other countries, perhaps most graphically in the former Soviet Union where, for example, Russia, having abandoned centralized state control of commerce and industry in favour of a "free-market" economy, finds it lacks the institutions it needs to protect the common good against unscrupulous entrepreneurs.

These changes at the national level are paralleled on a larger scale in the international economy. In the absence of any effective system of international regulation, TNCs move their capital about the world, driving down wages and standards. Over the last decade powerful economic interests have been at work on the international scene to establish larger free trade areas in Europe (during this period the European Community of ten member states became the European Union of 12, and then 15 in 1995 with the addition of Sweden, Austria and Finland); in North America (where the USA, Canada, and Mexico have formed the North American Free Trade Area); and globally through the General Agreement on Tariffs and Trade (GATT).

Advocates of these groupings invoke the ideology of free trade and free markets and argue the economic benefits of membership for smaller, less wealthy and peripheral nations, but the reality is that without carefully designed safeguards the economically powerful will dominate. Economically less powerful countries are left with unsatisfactory alternatives. Their chances of building self-reliance are small if they have to trade among giants. If they join a large trading area, they inevitably do so from a position of weakness. They are as disadvantaged as a weak province in a prosperous nation with no regional economic policy, as Schumacher (1973, p60) pointed out:

> In a mobile, footloose society the law of disequilibrium is infinitely stronger than the so-called law of equilibrium. Nothing succeeds like success, and nothing stagnates like stagnation. The successful province drains the life out of the unsuccessful, and without protection against the strong, the weak have no chance; either they remain weak or they must migrate and join the strong; they cannot effectively help themselves.

The growing consumerist international economy exacerbates what is happening on a much smaller scale as rural economies become urbanized: "urbanization and trade have the effects of physically and psychologically distancing urban populations from the ecosystems that sustain them. Access to bio-resources produced outside their home region both undermines people's sense of dependence on "the land" and blinds them to the far-off social and ecological effects of their consumption" (Rees and Wackernagel, 1992, p9). We import without compunction beans and potatoes from a nation like Egypt, which cannot feed its own population; food from Ethiopia during a famine there; and flowers grown in Kenya using pesticides banned in Europe and applied with little or no concern for the health of the workers.

*Table 11.1 Overseas development aid as a percentage of GNP*

|  | 1970 | 1980 | 1990 |
|---|---|---|---|
| Norway | 0.33 | 0.90 | 1.04 |
| Sweden | 0.41 | 0.85 | 0.97 |
| Netherlands | 0.60 | 0.90 | 0.94 |
| Denmark | 0.40 | 0.72 | 0.94 |
| Canada | 0.41 | 0.47 | 0.44 |
| Australia | 0.59 | 0.52 | 0.38 |
| Japan | 0.23 | 0.27 | 0.32 |
| UK | 0.42 | 0 43 | 0.31 |
| USA | 0.31 | 0.24 | 0.15 |
| Average for industrial countries | 0.33 | 0.35 | 0.32 |

*Source*: UNDP (1991, p53)

Trends in the 1990s offer little prospect of ameliorating the most serious impacts of the economic system. The continuing internationalization of world trade, the conversion of GATT into the Multilateral Trade Organization (MTO), and the creation of larger trading blocs will exacerbate the current inequities of the economic order. Though new agreements may increase trading opportunities for some Southern nations, they will do little to ease the burdens (such as debt repayments) many of the poorest nations carry, and little to improve the lot of their rural populations, whose alternatives will be no more satisfactory than those of their national leaders, as Schumacher (1973, p61) pointed out: "their only choice is either to remain in their miserable condition where they are, or to migrate into the big city where their condition will be even more miserable. It is a strange phenomenon indeed that the conventional wisdom of present-day economics can do nothing to help the poor." As we have seen, the North offered little at Rio to supplement current aid contributions which, with the exception of those from the Netherlands and the Scandinavian countries, still languish far below the UN's recommended levels (see Table 11.1).

Meanwhile, Northern capital, responding to the force of economic "logic", abandons its already largely token efforts to meet Southern needs, attracted by the possibility of higher returns elsewhere. In the West, industrialists see the inefficient and polluting industries of eastern Europe as lucrative markets for improved technology. Similarly, banks and governments see eastern Europe as a more worthwhile candidate for aid than the "underdeveloped" economies of many African, Asian and Latin American countries, which offer less enticing prospects of economic return. Brisk business in eastern Europe, built partly on further depletion of Southern assets, will further widen the North–South divide. And China, with a vast labour force, a high proportion of manufactured goods among its exports and in recent years growth rates sometimes exceeding 10 per cent, looms as a threat to other economies and to international attempts to reach agreements on emission controls.

With the ending of the Cold War and the courting of eastern Europe by the West, the stage is set for a further heightening of tensions and conflicts between North and South. Economically there may be one "interdependent" world, but it will be a hierarchical world of beneficiaries, servants and "the disposable" (see p142). In the poorer countries of the South we can anticipate a substantial increase in the already vast underclass of people who, like the unemployed victims of automation and technology in the North, have simply been jettisoned: having no relevant role to play in the economic scheme of things, they have been abandoned.

As differentials continue to widen and as competition for resources intensifies, the alienation between the affluent North and the dispossessed South will increase. Economic interests in the North, dimly conscious of the inequities on which their advantage is founded but reluctant to concede wealth or power, will be forced into adopting more extreme measures to hold what it has — the USA showed little hesitation in building an alliance to fight a "resource" war against Iraq. Continuing ecological degradation will affect the South most directly, the North (in the

West, at least) cushioned by its wealth unless directly affected by a major ecological collapse. Growing numbers in the South see migration to the North as the most direct way of improving the welfare of themselves and their families. In response both Britain and other countries have tightened immigration controls.

Some commentators predict the emergence of a fortified, beleaguered North, anxious to preserve access to the resources that will allow it to maintain the levels of consumption it believes it cannot do without. Whether or not such predictions are fulfilled, a future world will inevitably be a diminished one, with more loss of biodiversity and the already shrinking diversity of cultures subject to further serious erosion. Already around 6000 languages throughout the world are said to be under threat, largely from the spread of English in the wake of the forces of progress.[3]

Such developments will make us all poorer — not simply through the loss of material welfare, which an international community with a published declaration of human rights might be thought able to prevent. They will also mean a diminution of our common welfare through the waste of unfulfilled human potential that results from denying people opportunities to develop their aspirations to the full. In this respect Brundtland's analysis of the linkages between development and the environment, between development and poverty and between poverty and the environment (see Chapter 3, p57) is incomplete in one significant detail. While it correctly shows the two-way interactions between development and the environment and poverty and the environment, it fails to indicate that just as development can generate poverty, so poverty in all its forms can degrade development. A development model that extends economic domination, imposes external solutions, measures progress in materialist rather than human terms, degrades the planet and impoverishes people, is itself impoverished. Successive phases of national and international development programmes have lacked the enrichment of inputs from individuals and communities able to offer diverse and innovative ideas. As Sachs puts it, they have been

---

3. See also "One World" in Sachs, 1992a.

deprived of suggestions for "social changes which take their inspiration from indigenous ideas of the good and proper life". As a simple example he points out that Agenda 21 fails in its section on transport to suggest any means of reducing the number of vehicles on the world's roads. Indeed, suggests Sachs (1993, p17), "the development syndrome has dangerously narrowed the social imagination in the North as well as the South".

Thus development recreates humankind in its own image. A World Bank official can talk of exporting more hazardous wastes to "underpolluted" countries (*Guardian*, 14 February 1992) and an economist can point to the economic costs of honouring human obligations (Hirsh, 1977, p77). Market forces erode not only the social virtues on which they depend, but ultimately the human qualities which alone can generate these social virtues. Competition in an unregulated economic system not only drives down costs in the market, but also depresses our readiness to think highly of one another, to see each other as spiritual beings rather than simply as economic agents, to give each other time, and to respect mutuality and reciprocity. It makes us — rendered ignorant by the physical separation that the distances in the global economy create, and made callous by the illusion of non-interdependence — predators on one another. Ultimately we are all degraded by the destitution we allow to persist.

Dominant economic and political interests have also shaped much of what has happened in the name of sustainable development since the publication of the Brundtland Commission's *Our Common Future*. Despite its concern about the impact of development on people, Brundtland's emphasis on economic growth and its faith in an amended international economic order have provided the elites who dominate the international community with a pretext for viewing sustainable development as the latest version of "development", rather than as a new concept that challenges orthodox assumptions and means a radical departure from conventional thinking and practices.

The agenda of the Earth Summit five years later was primarily an economic one, concerned particularly with how dominant economic interests could be maintained within ecological constraints, as Richard Sandbrook (1993), director of the IIED, has pointed out: "This was not a conference about the environment at all, it concerned the world's economy and how the environment affects it."

Major events since Rio have done little to alter the impression that we are content to allow sustainable development to become ecological sustainability. To major economic interests, ecological sustainability ("saving the planet") appears to be a more compelling challenge than sustainable development ("meeting people's needs, today and in the future"). For example, not all Northern leaders regarded the agenda of the Copenhagen Summit as sufficiently important to warrant their attendance, or perhaps they simply wished to avoid awkward questions about the increase of poverty in the North. National sustainable development strategies will concentrate, if the UK's is anything to go by, on the environmental aspects of sustainable development to the almost complete exclusion of any discussion of human need, just as the debate on indicators has focused, at government and international agency level, on ways of indicating progress to save the planet.

In their bid to make the world safe for further development, the dominant interests will increasingly make use of the findings of environmental science. The instruments and insights of ecological research — which in the past strengthened NGO protest — will now also inform a global system of ecological management which will be presided over by Northern economic interests. Therefore, Sachs (1993, pxvi) suggests, it has become "necessary to focus on the political, social and cultural implications involved in different environmentalist designs", for "after nearly everybody — heads of state and heads of corporations, believers in technology and believers in growth — has turned environmentalist, the conflicts in the future will not centre on who is or who is not an environmentalist, but on who stands for what kind of environmentalism."

Sustainable development is thus contested territory with its ownership disputed by forces with very different interests. It is difficult to foresee any slackening of the efforts of those who will continue to attempt to impose development to suit their ends, invoking "modernity, national integration, economic growth or a thousand other slogans" (Adams, 1990, p199). On the other hand, there is a considerable consensus about what must be the essential characteristics of the "emerging paradigm" (Jacobs et al, 1987, p20) of sustainable development if it is to meet the criteria of Brundtland's definition. These characteristics can be summed up here as:

- integration of conservation and development,
- satisfaction of basic human needs,
- opportunities to fulfil other non-material human needs,
- progress towards equity and social justice,
- respect and support for cultural diversity,
- provision for social self-determination and the nurturing of self reliance, and the
- maintenance of ecological integrity.

Sustainable development — "development which meets the needs of the present without compromising the ability of future generations to meet their own needs" — cannot then be delivered by any agency that represents a national or international alliance of political and economic power, for sustainable development has to be (as any development ought to be, it could be argued) "what human communities do to themselves" (Adams, 1990, p199). Sustainable development cannot be imposed "top-down", or implemented according to a blueprint in which the majority of the people have had no say. Instead it should evolve, growing organically from people's responses to the changes in the world around them. It will depend on the "continuing maintenance and creation of political and social spaces within which people's power can be effectively exercised" (Ekins, 1992a, p208), and build on the knowledge people already have.

Sustainable development thus challenges the values of conventional development, which we may take to be very close to the heart of society's purpose. The process of sustainable development is not just about managing and allocating natural capital. It is also about deciding who has the power both to do this and to institute whatever social, economic and political reforms are considered necessary. Progress towards sustainable development will depend on maintaining the challenge at every opportunity and at every political level. Neither glowing visions of the sustainable eco-society nor an explicit green political agenda will be sufficient, as Middleton et al (1993, pp10–11) point out in their book, *Tears of the Crocodile*:

> *So there is a dilemma to be faced. It is not difficult to envisage a series of important agreements in which the world's resources are divided up on a more equitable basis and it would be straightforward enough to devise means for their implementation. Indeed the Global Forum [of NGOs, at Rio] went some way towards formulating the sorts of treaty that would produce a more equitable world. But such a programme can only serve as a counsel for perfection; it is not clear that, even as a hidden agenda, campaigning for a whole complex of such agreements could make practical political sense. Instead it is necessary to fight, inch by inch, for every single agreement which goes towards improving social justice, and the fight is against entrenched, labyrinthine social, financial and political interests and each battle itself will modify the circumstance of the next.*

Support in that struggle comes from an unexpected quarter. Despite the drift from Brundtland's initial concern with the effects of development on people to the Rio agenda dominated by the priorities of Northern economic interests, and despite the lack of binding commitments in Agenda 21 (it has been described as "the softest of soft law" (Johnson, 1993, p6)), UNCED's action plan for the twenty-first century takes up themes of participation and community-based action first stated at Cocoyoc and in *What Now? Another Development* in the 1970s, and restates them with an emphasis which was lacking in the Brandt Reports. Middleton et al (1993, p11) comment: "Governments have committed themselves to support certain generalized positions which may yet be fleshed out in myriad local and national campaigns for justice. In Agenda 21 governments reluctant to disturb the status quo have possibly offered one hostage to fortune too many. It is there that our scintilla of hope may live."

John Gordon of the Global Environmental Research Centre at Imperial College, London (Hughes and Lee, 1993, p1) expresses a common reaction: "What in fact were our usually hard-nosed diplomats and politicians up to when they negotiated and signed up to UNCED? Were they playing at being Greenpeace supporters? Were their fingers crossed behind their back? Or were they genuinely convinced that fundamental changes were needed and determined to see them through?" The immediate explanation is that the inclusion of these statements is the fruit of long campaigns by NGOs in North and South to have them there. However, it is not entirely clear why governments should have yielded to such pressure when it commits them, on the face of it, to sharing power, and when "sustainability is not regarded seriously by those who really count, namely those at the top of political structures and those who control the flows of national and international capital" (O'Riordan, 1993, p54). It is easy to incline to rather uncharitable interpretations of their action, for instance to see it as a cynical calculation by those who are confident of their hold on power. It is more tempting, however, to believe that it represents both a genuine aspiration by at least some individuals in the senior levels of government for a better world order and an acknowledgement that adequate solutions to major problems are unlikely to emerge from within the conventional development discourse and depend on the injection of moral concern and innovative practice that NGOs can supply.

It may also indicate that, despite the insistence on the need for growth throughout the development decades, some kind of institutional learning has taken place. Holmberg and Sandbrook (1992, p33) point out that one of the major lessons of a wide range of development projects in many countries over the last two centuries is that "development to be sustainable requires the active involvement of the people themselves in the design and implementation of activities designed to improve their welfare. Empowerment of the people to take increasing charge of their own development is the key ingredient, combined with a clear knowledge of environmental constraints and of requirements to meet basic needs."

However, there is a danger that institutional learning may not go far enough and that participation may become the latest flawed orthodoxy (like growth through industrialization and the basic needs approach), for the validity of the principle depends on a number of provisos which tend to be overlooked. The point is illustrated by the wide acceptance of the slogan that local people are the best guardians of forest resources, which may be true if local people are able to protect them against other interests and if certain other social conditions are met.

Participation can only effectively contribute to the struggle Middleton et al define when it is backed by supportive government action of the kind Holmberg and Sandbrook describe (see Chapter 8, p172). If bottom-up approaches are to lead to change at higher levels, governments need to devolve power and give local people a greater say in the ownership of resources.

Local Agenda 21 initiatives in the UK show that attempts to encourage local participation run against the grain of the assumptions generating (and generated by) centralized, top-down development and welfare provision. In the absence of the support only a higher level of government can provide (for example, educational inputs, community development initiatives, land reform, changes in planning law and regional economic policy), it is hard to convince people that they can translate a newly-discovered interest in sustainable development into action, and that they can engage in meaningful bottom-up participation in ways that will ensure that "when local progress is constrained by factors beyond the control of the community concerned, public pressure will grow to amend the national and eventually also the international context" (Tony Britain, quoted in Holmberg and Sandbrook, 1992, p31).


The introduction to this book posed several questions. From our standpoint in the mid-1990s it seems possible to answer only the first two with a clear affirmative. Despite many uncertainties we *can* talk of progress towards more sustainable systems. There are guidelines for policies to achieve such progress, and the financial commitment that would be required is not impossible. It is the availability of other essentials that is in question, as Johann Holmberg and Richard Sandbrook (1992, p37) point out: "The means required in financial terms are not necessarily very large, but the shifts in political power and patronage, and into foregoing achievable consumption, amount to a sacrifice in favour of an uncertain future."

Public opinion is not generally in favour of sacrifice, as Patricia McConalogue (1995, p6) was reminded on her return from the Fourth World Family Congress in New York in September 1994:

"The general feeling [is] that people don't want to change their attitudes. It is not that they don't care, it's just that they are so comfortable they don't want to change or they don't want to know." And, of course, it would be unrealistic to think of voluntary reductions by those who are not "comfortable", even if some evidence suggests that they may be willing to engage in the issues.

As a result many, perhaps all, Northern governments, aware that there are few votes in either Third World issues or radical alterations to the status quo, are reluctant to mobilize their resources behind sustainable development, and we await the "upsurge of public concern" on which change depends.

We need action on several levels, as Holmberg and Sandbrook (1992, p37) point out: "People can help to bring about sustainable development only if the local, regional and national government policy framework is propitious to that end. But the reverse is equally true: sustainable development will not come about without active involvement of the people concerned." The path of development has led us to the point where the resources we need to make a transition to more sustainable ways are in short supply. In its efforts to meet international agreements, a government is unlikely to have the active support of an informed and concerned electorate if it has failed to promote social justice, create an awareness of global realities and nourish a public social conscience and social imagination. Such failures at government level can be attributed in large part, in democracies at least, to electorates not insisting on the prior claims of human needs and not pressing for educational resources, freedom of information in the widest sense, awareness-raising campaigns and resources for skills training and capacity building.

Therefore sustainable development confronts, not just society, but each of us at the heart of his or her purpose. It invites us to give practical support to the values of social equity, human worth and ecological health; it questions our readiness to involve ourselves in the struggle for change; it challenges our willingness to contribute in greater measure to the activities of NGOs and dedicated individuals who campaign on our behalf; and it asks us to accept that the small beginnings from which so many successful campaigns have started reside within ourselves.

Progress towards sustainable development depends ultimately on removing what Laszlo (1989, pp46–7, quoted in Claxton, 1994, p72) calls the "inner constraints on our vision and values":

> There are hardly any world problems that cannot be traced to human agency and which would not be overcome by appropriate changes in human behaviour. The root causes even of physical and ecological problems are the inner constraints on our vision and our values. . . . Living on the threshold of a new age, we squabble among ourselves to acquire or retain the privileges of bygone times. We cast about for innovative ways to satisfy obsolete values. We manage individual crises while heading for collective catastrophes. We contemplate changing almost anything on this earth except our-selves. . . . A new insight must dawn on people: you do not solve world problems by applying technological fixes within the frame-work of narrowly self-centred values and short-sighted national instruments. Coping with mankind's current predicament calls for inner changes, for a human and humanistic revolution mobilizing new values and aspirations, backed by new levels of personal commitment and political will.

The seeds of the competitive, expansionist, technocratic model of progress lie within ourselves, but so equally do the sources of the changes that can replace them. In the final analysis it is not, as Ulrich Loening points out, resources or the planet we have to manage, but ourselves. The most important changes may be less obvious and harder than we think, for as Laszlo put it, "we con-template changing almost anything on this earth except our-selves". However, they may be easier than we suppose, for each of us can make them and no one can prevent us from doing so, as Max-Neef (1991, p113) explains:

> I have reached the conclusion that I lack the power to change the world or any significant part of it. I only have the power to change myself. And the fascinating thing is that if I decide to change myself there is no police force in the world that can prevent me doing so. It is just my decision and if I want to do it, I can do it. Now, the point is that if I change myself, something may happen as a consequence that may lead to a change in the world.

As such an awareness becomes more general, sustainable development *will* be regarded seriously by the people who really count — not just O'Riordan's elites, but people generally. Then progress will be more certain, for as Holmberg and Sandbrook (1992, p37) state, "when the policy makers are ready, the requisite knowledge is available".

# References and Further Reading

Abernethy, V (1993) "The Demographic Transition Revisited: Lessons for Foreign Aid and US Immigration Policy", *Ecological Economics*, 8, pp235–52

Adams, N A (1993) *Worlds Apart: The North/South Divide and the International System*, London and Atlantic Highlands, NJ, Zed Books

Adams, P (1991) *Odious Debts: Loose Lending, Corruption and the Third World's Environmental Legacy*, London, Earthscan

Adams, P and L Solomon (1991) *In the Name of Progress: The Underside of Foreign Aid*, London, Earthscan

Adams, T, J Carruthers and S Hamil (1991) *Changing Corporate Values*, London, New Consumer

Adams, W M (1990) *Green Development*, London and New York, Routledge

Ahmad, T J, S El Serafy and E Lutz (1989) *Environmental Accounting for Sustainable Development*, Washington DC, World Bank

Aiken, W (1992) "Human Rights in an Ecological Era", *Environmental Values*, 1, pp191—203

Altvater, E, K Hubner, J Lorentzen and R Rojas (eds) (1991) *The Poverty of Nations: A Guide to the Debt Crisis — from Argentina to Zaire*, London and Atlantic Highlands, NJ, Zed Books

Amin, S (1990) *Delinking: Towards a Polycentric World*, London and Atlantic Highlands, NJ, Zed Books

Angell, D J R, J D Coomer and M L N Wilkinson (eds) (1990) *Sustaining Earth: Response to the Environmental Threat*, Basingstoke, Macmillan

Association of County Councils (1991) *Towards a Sustainable Transport Policy*, London, ACC

Ayres, R U (1993) "Cowboys, Cornucopians, and Long-Run Sustainability", *Ecological Economics*, 8, pp189–207

Banuri, T and F A Marglin (eds) (1993) *Living with the Forests: Knowledge, Power and Environmental Destruction*, London and Atlantic Highlands, NJ, Zed Books

Barnet, R and J Cavanagh (1994) *Global Dreams: Imperial Corporations and the New World Order*, New York, Simon & Schuster

Barney, G O (ed) (1980) *The Global 2000 Report to the President*, Harmondsworth, Penguin

Barton, H and N Bruder (1995) *A Guide to Local Environmental Auditing*, London, Earthscan

Bateson, G (1972) *Steps to an Ecology of Mind*, San Francisco, Chandler

Bello, W (1990) *Brave New World: Strategies for Survival in the Global Economy*, London, Earthscan

Bennet, J (1995) *Meeting Needs: NGO Coordination in Practice*, London, Earthscan

Bergh, J van der and J van der Straaten (eds) (1994) *Towards Sustainable Development*, Washington, DC, Island Press

Binswanger, H C, M Faber and R Manstetter (1990) "The Dilemma of Modern Man and Nature: An Exploration of the Faustian Imperative", *Ecological Economics*, 2, pp197–223

Binswanger, H C (1994) *Money Magic (A critique of the Modern Economy in the Light of Goethe's Faust)*, Chicago, University of Chicago Press

Blaikie P, T Cannon, I Davis and B Wisner (1994) *At Risk: Natural Hazards, People's Vulnerability and Disasters*, London and New York, Routledge

Blowers, A (ed) (1993) *Planning for a Sustainable Environment*, London, Earthscan published in association with the TCPA

Boulding, K (1966) "The Economics of the Coming Spaceship Earth", in H Jarrett (ed) (1966) *Environmental Quality in a Growing Economy*, Johns Hopkins University Press. Reprinted in A Markandya and J Richardson (eds) (1992) *The Earthscan Reader in Environmental Economics*, London, Earthscan

— (1991) "What Do We Want to Sustain? Environmentalism and Human Evaluations", in R Costanza (ed) *Ecological Economics: The Science and Management of Sustainability*, New York, Columbia

— (1992) "The Economics of the Coming Spaceship Earth", in A Markandya and J Richardson (eds) (1992) *The Earthscan Reader in Environmental Economics*, London, Earthscan

Braidotti, R, E Charkiewicz, S Häusler and S Wieringa (1994) *Women, the Environment and Sustainable Development: Towards a Theoretical Synthesis*, London and Atlantic Highlands, NJ, Zed Books in association with the UN International Research and Training Institute for the Advancement of Women

Branford, S and B Kucinski (1988) *The Debt Squads: The US, the Banks, and Latin America*, London and Atlantic Highlands, NJ, Zed Books

Braun, E (1994) *Futile Progress: Technology's Empty Promise*, London, Earthscan

Bringezu S, F Hinterberger and H Schütz (1994) "Integrating Sustainability into the System of National Accounts: The Case of Interregional Material Flows", Proceedings of an International Symposium "Models of Sustainable Development. Exclusive or Complementary Approaches of Sustainability?" held in Paris, 16–18 March, pp669–80

Brown, L R (1981) *Building a Sustainable Society*, New York, Norton

— (ed) (1990) *State of the World*, New York, W W Norton (annual reports from 1984 on progress towards a sustainable society)

— (ed) (1995) *State of the World*, New York, W W Norton (annual reports from 1984 on progress towards a sustainable society)

Brown, L R and H Kane (1994) *Full House: Assessing the Earth's Population Carrying Capacity*, Worldwatch Environmental Alert Series, London Earthscan

Brown, L R, C Flavin and H Kane (1994) *Vital Signs: The Trends that are Shaping our Future*, London, Earthscan. (Annually since 1991)

Brown, L R, C Flavin and S Postel (1991) "From Growth to Sustainable Development", in R Goodland, H E Daly, S El Serafy and B von Droste (eds) *Environmentally Sustainable Economic Development: Building on Brundtland*, Paris, UNESCO

— (1992) *Saving the Planet: How to Shape an Environmentally Sustainable Global Economy*, Worldwatch Environmental Alert Series, London, Earthscan

Brown, M B (1993) *Fair Trade: Reforming the International Trading System*, London and Atlantic Highlands, NJ, Zed Books

Burkey, S (1993) *People First: A Guide to Self-Reliant Participatory Rural Development*, London and Atlantic Highlands, NJ, Zed Books

Cairncross, F (1991) *Costing the Earth*, London, Business Books in association with *The Economist* Books

— (1995) *Green Ink: A Guide to the Environment*, London, Earthscan

Cameron, J and T O'Riordan (1994) *Interpreting the Precautionary Principle*, London, Earthscan

Capra, F (1983) *The Turning Point: Science, Society and the Rising Culture*, London, Flamingo

Carley, M (1994) *Policy Management Systems and Methods of Analysis for Sustainable Agriculture and Rural Development*, Rome, IIED/FAO

Carley, M and I Christie (1992) *Managing Sustainable Development*, London, Earthscan

Carson, R (1962) *Silent Spring*, New York, Houghton Mifflin

CAT (1995) *Clean Slate: The Journal of the Alternative Technology Association*, 16, Spring, Machynlleth, CAT Publications

Chambers, R (1983) *Rural Development: Putting the Last First*, Harlow, Longman

— (1986) "Putting the Last First", in P Ekins (ed) *The Living Economy*, London and New York, Routledge, pp305–21

— (1989) "Sustainable Rural Livelihoods: A Strategy for People, Environment and Development", overview paper for Only One Earth Conference on Sustainable Development organized by the International Institute for Environment and Development, April 1987

— (1992) "Sustainable Livelihoods: The Poor's Reconciliation of Environment and Development", in P Ekins and M Max-Neef (eds), *Real-Life Economics: Understanding Wealth Creation*, London and New York, Routledge, pp214–29

Clark, J (1991) *Democratizing Development: The Role of Voluntary Organizations*, London, Earthscan

Clarke, W C and R E Munn (eds) (1986) *Sustainable Development of the Biosphere*, Cambridge, Cambridge University Press

Clarke, R and L Timberlake, (1982) *Stockholm Plus Ten: Promises Promises? The Decade since the 1972 UN Environment Conference*, London, Earthscan

Claxton, G (1994) "Involuntary Simplicity: Changing Dysfunctional Habits of Consumption", *Environmental Values*, 3, pp71–8

Colby, M E (1991) "Environmental Management in Development: The Evolution of Paradigms", *Ecological Economics*, 3, pp193–213

Cole, H S D, C Freeman, M Jahoda and K L R Pavitt (eds) (1973) *Thinking about the Future: A Critique of "The Limits to Growth"*, London, Chatto & Windus

Commission for Social Justice/Institute for Public Policy Research (1994) *Social Justice: Strategies for National Renewal*, London, Vintage

Commission of the EC (1993) *Towards Sustainability: A European Community Programme of Policy and Action in Relation to the Environment and Sustainable Development*, Brussels, Commission of the European Community

Conroy, C and M Litvinoff (1988) *The Greening of Aid: Sustainable Livelihoods in Practice*, London, Earthscan

Conway, G R and E B Barbier (1990) *After the Green Revolution: Sustainable Agriculture for Development*, London, Earthscan

Costanza, R (1989) "What is Ecological Economics?", *Ecological Economics*, 1, pp1–7

Costanza, R (ed) (1991) *Ecological Economics: The Science and Management of Sustainability*, New York, Columbia

Crump, A (1991) *Dictionary of Environment and Development*, London, Earthscan

Dag Hammarskjöld Institute (1975) *What Now? Another Development*, Dag Hammarskjöld Institute, Uppsala, Sweden

— (1977) *Another Development: Approaches and Strategies*, Uppsala, Sweden, Dag Hammarskjöld Institute

Daily, G C, P R Erlich, H A Mooney and A H Erlich (1991) "Greenhouse Economics: Learn Before You Leap", *Ecological Economics*, 4, pp1–10

Daly, H E (1973) *Towards a Steady State Economy*, New York, W H Freeman

— (1980) *Economics, Ecology and Ethics*, San Francisco, W H Freeman & Co

— (1991a) "From Empty-World Economics to Full-World Economics: Recognizing an Historical Turning Point in Economic Development", in R Goodland, H E Daly, S El Serafy and B von Droste (eds) *Environmentally Sustainable Economic Development: Building on Brundtland*, Paris, UNESCO

— (1991b) "Elements of Environmental Macro-Economics", in R Costanza (ed) *Ecological Economics: The Science and Management of Sustainability*, New York, Columbia

— (1992a) *Steady-State Economics* (2nd edition), London, Earthscan

— (1992b) "UN Conferences on Environment and Development: Retrospect on Stockholm and Prospects for Rio", *Ecological Economics*, 5, pp9–14

— (1994) "Fostering Environmentally Sustainable Development: Four Parting Suggestions for the World Bank", *Ecological Economics*, 10, pp183–7

Daly, H E and J B Cobb Jr (1990) *For the Common Good: Redirecting the Economy towards Community, the Environment and a Sustainable Future*, London, Greenprint

Daly, H E and R Goodland (1992) *An Ecological-Economic Assessment of Deregulation of International Commerce under GATT*, Washington DC, Environment Department, The World Bank

Davidson, J and D Myers with M Chakraborty (1992) *No Time to Waste: Poverty and the Global Environment*, Oxford, Oxfam

de la Court, T (1990) *Beyond Brundtland: Green Development in the 1990s*, London and Atlantic Highlands, NJ, Zed Books

Devall, R (1990) *Simple in Means, Rich in Ends*, London, Greenprint

Diamond, I and G F Orenstein (eds) (1990) *Reweaving the World*, San Francisco, Sierra Club Books

Dobson, A (1990) *Green Political Thought*, London and New York, Routledge (second edition, 1995)

Douthwaite, R (1992) *The Growth Illusion: How Economic Growth has Enriched the Few, Impoverished the Many, and Endangered the Planet*, Hartland, Devon, Green Books

Doyal, L and I Gough (1991) *A Theory of Human Need*, Basingstoke, Macmillan Educational

Dube, S C (1988) *Modernization and Development: The Search for Alternative Paradigms*, London and Atlantic Highlands, NJ, Zed Books

Durning, A (1992) *How Much is Enough? The Consumer Society and the Future of the Earth*, London, Earthscan Worldwatch Environmental Alert Series

Eagan, D J and D W Orr (eds) (1992) *The Campus and Environmental Responsibility*, San Francisco, Jossey-Bass

Easterlinn, R A (1974) "Does Economic Growth Improve the Human Lot? Some Empirical Evidence", in P A David and M W Reder (eds) *Nations and Households in Economic Growth*, New York, Academic Press

*Ecologist, The* (1972) *Blueprint for Survival*, Harmondsworth, Penguin

— (1993) *Whose Common Future? Reclaiming the Commons*, London, Earthscan

— (1995) *Too Many for Whom? "Population Control" and the Environment*, London, Earthscan

Edwards, M, and D Hulme (eds) (1992) *Making a Difference: NGOs and Development in a Changing World*, London, Earthscan

Ehrenfield, D (1978) *The Arrogance of Humanism*, London, Oxford University Press

Ehrlich, P (1989) "The Limits to Substitution: Meta-Resource Depletion and a New Economic-Ecological Paradigm", *Ecological Economics*, 1, pp9–16

Ehrlich, P and A Ehrlich (1990) *The Population Explosion*, London, Hutchinson

Ekins, P (ed) (1986)*The Living Economy*, London and New York, Routledge

— (1989) "Trade and Self-reliance" in *The Ecologist*, vol 19, No 5, pp186–90

— (1992a) *A New World Order: Grassroots Movements for Global Change*, London and New York, Routledge

— (1992b) "Sustainability First", in P Ekins and M Max-Neef (eds) *Real-Life Economics: Understanding Wealth Creation*, London and New York, Routledge

Ekins, P and M Max-Neef (eds) (1992) *Real-Life Economics: Understanding Wealth Creation*, London and New York, Routledge

Ekins, P, M Hillman and R Hutchinson (1992) *Wealth Beyond Measure*, London, Gaia Books

Elkington, J and J Hailes (1988) *The Green Consumer Guide*, London, Gollancz

Elkington, J, P Knight and J Hailes (1991) *The Green Business Guide*, London, Gollancz

Elliot, J A (1994) *An Introduction to Sustainable Development*, London and New York, Routledge

Engel, J R (1990) "The Ethics of Sustainable Development", in J R Engel and J G Engel (eds) *Ethics of Environment and Development: Global Challenge, International Responses*, London, Belhaven

Engel, J R and J G Engel (eds) (1990) *Ethics of Environment and Development: Global Challenge, International Responses*, London, Belhaven

ENTEC (1993) *The ENTEC Directory of Environmental Technology: European Edition*, London, Earthscan

Esteva, G (1992) "Development", in W Sachs (ed) *The Development Dictionary*, London and Atlantic Highlands, NJ, Zed Books

Freire, P (1972) *The Pedagogy of the Oppressed*, Harmondsworth, Penguin

French, H (1995) "Forging a New Global Partnership", in L R Brown (ed) *State of the World*, New York, W W Norton

Fromm, E (1979) *To Have or to Be*, London, Abacus

Galbraith, J K (1993) *The Culture of Contentment*, London, Penguin

Galtung, J (1980) "Self-Reliance: Concepts, Practice and Rationale", in J Galtung, P O'Brien and R Preiswerk (eds) *Self-Reliance: A Strategy for Development*, London, l'Ouverture Publications for the Institute of Development Studies, Geneva

— (1986) "Towards a New Economics: On the Theory and Practice of Self-Reliance", in P Ekins (ed) *The Living Economy*, London and New York, Routledge, pp97–106

Galtung, J, P O'Brien and R Preiswerk (eds) (1980) *Self-Reliance: A Strategy for Development*, London, L'Ouverture Publications for the Institute of Development Studies, Geneva

Gandy, M (1994) *Recycling and the Politics of Urban Waste*, London, Earthscan

Garioch, R (1975) *Two Men and a Blanket*, Edinburgh, Southside

Geddes, P (1992) "Life and its Science", *Edinburgh Review*, 88, Summer

George, S (1976) *How the Other Half Dies: The Real Reasons for World Hunger*, London, Penguin

— (1988) *A Fate Worse than Debt*, London, Penguin Books

— (1992) *The Debt Boomerang*, Boulder, CO, Westview

Georgescu-Roegen, N (1971) *The Entropy Law and the Economic Process*, Cambridge, Harvard

Ghabbour, S (1992) Book review of "Caring for the Earth", *Environmental Values*, 1, pp171–3

Ghai, D (ed) (1991) *The IMF and the South: The Social Impact of Crisis and Adjustment*, London and Atlantic Highlands, NJ, Zed Books

Glaeser, B (ed) (1984) *Ecodevelopment: Concepts, Projects, Strategies*, Oxford, Pergamon Press

Glynn, A and V Bhaskar (eds) *The North, The South and the Environment*, London, Earthscan

Goldsmith, E (1990) *5000 Days to Save the Planet*, London, Hamlyn

Goodland, R (1992) "The Case that the World has Reached its Limits", in R Goodland, H E Daly, S El Serafy and B von Droste (eds) *Environmentally Sustainable Economic Development: Building on Brundtland*, Paris, UNESCO

Goodland R and H E Daly (1993) "Why Northern Income Growth is not the Solution to Southern Poverty", *Ecological Economics*, 8, pp85–101

Goodland, R, H E Daly and S El Serafy (eds) (1992) *Environmental Sustainable Economic Development: Building on Brundtland*, Paris, UNESCO

Goodland, R, H E Daly and S El Serafy (eds) (1993) *Population Technology and Lifestyle: The Transition to Sustainability*, Washington, DC, Island Press

Gordon, J (1994) *Canadian Round Tables and Other Mechanisms for Sustainable Development in Canada*, Luton, LGMB

Gore, A (1992) *Earth in the Balance: Forging a New Common Purpose*, London, Earthscan

Gray, R (1994) "Corporate Reporting for Sustainable Development: Accounting for Sustainability in AD 2000", *Environmental Values*, 3, pp17–45

Green College Centre for Environmental Policy and Understanding (1993) *Sustainable Development Seminar, Green College, Oxford, 18–20 March 1993*, Oxford, Green College Centre

Group of Green Economists, The (1992) *Ecological Economics: A Practical Programme for Global Reform*, London and Atlantic Highlands, NJ, Zed Books

Grubb, M (1994) *Renewable Energy Strategies for Europe*, London, Earthscan

Grubb, M, M Koch, A Munson, F Sullivan and K Thomson (1993) *The Earth Summit Agreements: A Guide and Assessment*, London, Earthscan and Royal Institute of International Affairs

Hancock, G (1989) *Lords of Poverty*, London, Macmillan

Harcourt, W (ed) (1994) *Feminist Perspectives on Sustainable Development*, London and Atlantic Highlands, NJ, Zed Books

Hardin, G (1968) "The Tragedy of the Commons", *Science*, 162, pp1243–8. Reprinted in A Markandya and J Richardson (eds) (1992) *The Earthscan Reader in Environmental Economics*, London, Earthscan

— (1991) "Paramount Positions in Ecological Economics", in R Costanza (ed) *Ecological Economics: The Science and Management of Sustainability*, New York, Columbia

Harrison, B W (1990) "The Power of Anger in the Work of Love: Christian Ethics for Women and Other Strangers", in A Loades (ed), *Feminist Theology: A Reader*, London, SPCK

Harrison, P (1992) *The Third Revolution: Environment, Population and a Sustainable World*, London and New York, IB Tauris

Hawken, P (1993) *The Ecology of Commerce: How Business can Save the Planet*, London, Weidenfeld & Nicholson

Hayter, T (1989) *Exploited Earth: Britain's Aid and the Environment*, London, Earthscan in association with Friends of the Earth

Henderson, H (1986) "TOES 85", in P Ekins (ed) *The Living Economy*, London and New York, Routledge

Hewett, J (ed) (1994) *European Environmental Almanac*, compiled by IEEP, London and published in association with WWF, London, Earthscan

Higgins, R (1980) *The Seventh Enemy: The Human Factor in the Global Crisis*, London, Pan Books

Hildyard, N (1993) "Foxes In Charge of the Chickens", in W Sachs (ed) (1993) *Global Ecology: A New Arena of Political Conflict*, London and Atlantic Highlands, NJ, Zed Books

Hinrichsen, D (1987) *Our Common Future: A Reader's Guide*, London, Earthscan

Hirsch, F (1977) *The Social Limits to Growth*, London, Routledge & Kegan Paul

Holmberg, J (ed) (1992) *Policies for a Small Planet*, London, Earthscan

Holmberg, J and R Sandbrook (1992) "Sustainable Development: What is to be Done?", in J Holmberg (ed) *Policies for a Small Planet*, London, Earthscan

Holmberg, J, S Bass and L Timberlake (1991) *Defending the Future*, London, Earthscan/IIED

Holmberg, J, K Thomson and L Timberlake (1993) *Facing the Future: Beyond the Earth Summit*, London, Earthscan

Hopson, B, and M Scally (1981) *Lifeskills Teaching*, London, McGraw-Hill

Hueting, R (1986) "An Economic Scenario for a Conserver Economy", in P Ekins (ed) *The Living Economy*, London and New York, Routledge, pp242–56

— (1990) "The Brundtland Report: A Matter of Conflicting Goals", *Ecological Economics*, 2, pp109–18

Hueting, R, P Bosch and P de Boer (1991) *Methodology for the Calculation of Sustainable National Income*, Netherlands Central Bureau of Statistics

Hughes, P, and W Lea (1993) *The Earth Summit One Year On*, House of Commons Research Paper 93/71

ICC (1992) *Business Charter for Sustainable Development*, Paris, International Chamber of Commerce

ICDSI (1982) *Common Security: A Programme for Disarmament*, London, Pan Books

ICIDI (1980) *North–South: A Programme for Survival*, London, Pan Books

— (1983) *Common Crisis*, London, Pan Books

IIED (1994) "Participatory Methods for Development in Scotland: Lessons from the South", *Haramata, Bulletin of the Drylands: People, Policies and Programmes*, 24, July, London, IIED, pp18–20

Illich, I (1981) *Shadow Work*, Boston and London, Marion Boyars

Imber, M (1993) "Too Many Cooks? The Post-Rio Reform of the United Nations", *International Affairs*, 69, pp55–70

IPCC (1990) *Scientific Assessment of Climate Change* (Report of Working Group 1, with accompanying policy-makers' summary), World Meteorological Organization, Geneva

IUCN (1980) *World Conservation Strategy: Living Resources Conservation for Sustainable Development*, Gland, Switzerland, IUCN

IUCN/IIED (1993) *National Sustainable Development Strategies*, (draft), Gland, Switzerland, IUCN

— (1994) *Strategies for National Sustainable Development: A Handbook on their Preparation and Implementation*, London, Earthscan

IUCN/UNEP/WWF (1991) *Caring for the Earth: A Strategy for Sustainable Living*, Gland, Switzerland, IUCN

Jackson, B and Marks (1994) *Poverty and the Planet: A Question of Survival*, London, NEF

Jacobs, M (1991) *The Green Economy: Environment, Sustainable Development and the Politics of the Future*, London and Concord, MA, Pluto Press

Jacobs, P and D A Munro (1987) *Conservation with Equity: Proceedings of the Conference on Conservation and Development – Implementing the World Conservation Strategy, Ottawa, 31 May–5 June 1986*, Cambridge, UK, IUCN

Jacobs, P, J Garner and D A Munro (1987) "Sustainable and Equitable Development" in P Jacobs and D A Munro, *Conservation with Equity: Proceedings of the Conference on Conservation and Development – Implementing the World Conservation Strategy, Ottawa, 31 May–5 June 1986*, Cambridge, UK, IUCN

Jiggins, J (1994) *Changing the Boundaries: Women-Centred Perspectives on Population and the Environment*, Washington, DC, Island Press

Johansson, T B (ed) (1993) *Renewable Energy: Sources for Fuels and Electricity*, London, Earthscan

Johnson, H and H Bernstein (eds) (1982) *Third World Lives of Struggle*, Oxford, Heinemann International

Johnson, S P (1993) *The Earth Summit: The United Nations Conference on Environment and Development (UNCED)*, London, Graham & Trotman

Jones, C A (1983) *The North–South Dialogue: A Brief History*, London, Pinter

Jordan, A (1993) *The Global Environmental Facility*, Working Paper, GEC 92–37, Centre for Social and Economic Research on the Global Environment, University of East Anglia, Norwich

Juma, C (1989) *The Gene Hunters: Biotechnology and the Scramble for Seeds*, London and Atlantic Highlands, NJ, Zed Books

Keen, S (1992) *Fire in the Belly: On Being a Man*, London, Piatkus

Kemp, D D (1994) *Global Environmental Issues: A Climatological Approach*, London and New York, Routledge (second edition)

Kidron, M and R Segal (1987) *The Book of Business, Money and Power*, London, Pan Books

Kirkby, J, P O'Keefe and L Timberlake (1995) *The Earthscan Reader in Sustainable Development*, London, Earthscan

Körner, P, G Maass, T Siebold and R Tetzlaff (1986) *The IMF and the Debt Crisis: A Guide to the Third World's Dilemma*, London and Atlantic Highlands, NJ, Zed Books

Lang, T and C Hines (1993) *The New Protectionism: Protecting the Future against Free Trade*, London, Earthscan

Lappé, F M and J Collins (1988) *World Hunger: 12 Myths*, London, Earthscan

Lappé, F M and R Schurman (1989) *Taking Population Seriously: The Missing Piece in the Population Puzzle*, London, Earthscan in association with WWF

Laszlo, E (1989) *The Inner Limits of Mankind: Heretical Reflections on Today's Values, Culture and Politics*, One World Publications, London

Leggett, J (ed) (1990) *Global Warming: The Greenpeace Report*, Oxford, Oxford University Press

Lele, S M (1991) "Sustainable Development: A Critical Review", *World Development*, 19, pp607–21

Leopold, A (1987) *A Sand County Almanac, and Sketches Here and There*, New York, Oxford University Press (first published 1947)

LGMB (1992) *Agenda 21: A Guide for Local Authorities in the UK*, Luton, LGMB

— (1993a) *A Framework for Local Sustainability: A Response by Local Government to the UK Government's First Strategy for Sustainable Development*, Luton, LGMB

— (1993b) *The European Community's Fifth Environmental Action Programme: A Guide for UK Local Authorities*, Luton, LGMB

— (1995) *Sustainability Indicators Research Project: Consultants' Report of the Pilot Phase*, Luton, LGMB

Litvinoff, M (1990) *Earthscan Action Handbook: For People and Planet*, London, Earthscan

Loening, U (1992), seminar presentation, Centre for Human Ecology, University of Edinburgh

Lone, Ø (1992) "Environmental and Resource Accounting", in P Ekins and M Max-Neef (eds) *Real-Life Economics: Understanding Wealth Creation*, London and New York, Routledge

Lovejoy, T (1980) "A Projection of Species Extinction", in G O Barney (ed) *The Global 2000 Report to the President*, Harmondsworth, Penguin

Lovelock, J E (1979) *Gaia: A New Look at Life on Earth*, Oxford and New York, Oxford University Press

— (1988) *The Ages of Gaia: A Biography of our Living Earth*, Oxford and New York, Oxford University Press

— (1991) *Gaia: The Practical Science of Planetary Medicine*, London, Gaia

Lutz, M (1992) "Humanistic Economics: History and Basic Principles", in P Ekins and M Max-Neef (eds) *Real-Life Economics: Understanding Wealth Creation*, London and New York, Routledge

— (ed) (1994) *The Future Population of the World: What Can We Assume Today?*, London, Earthscan in association with IIASA

McCaig, E and C Henderson (1995) *Sustainable Development: What it Means to the General Public*, Edinburgh, Scottish Office Central Research Unit

McConalogue, P (1995) "Inspired by Love and Anger", *Coracle*, Glasgow, Iona Community, January, pp6–7

McCormick, J (1991) *British Politics and the Environment*, London, Earthscan in association with WWF

McCoy, M and P Mc Cully (1993) *The Road from Rio*, International Books WISE

McHale, J and M C McHale (1979) *Basic Human Needs: A Framework for Action*, New Brunswick, NJ, Transaction Books

McNeely, J A (ed) (1994) *Conserving the World's Biological Diversity*, Washington, DC, Island Press

MacNeill, J (1989) "Strategies for Sustainable Economic Development", *Scientific American*, 261, pp105–13

McRobie, G (1981) *Small is Possible*, London, Jonathan Cape

Maddox, J (1972) *The Doomsday Syndrome*, New York, McGraw-Hill

Makhijani, A (1992) *From Global Capitalism to Economic Justice*, London and Atlantic Highlands, NJ, Zed Books

Markandya, A and J Richardson (eds) (1992) *The Earthscan Reader in Environmental Economics*, London, Earthscan

Maslow, A (1970) *Motivation and Personality*, New York, Harper & Row (2nd edition)

Max-Neef, M (1991) *Human Scale Development: Conception, Application and Further Reflections*, London and New York, Apex Press

— (1992) *From the Outside Looking In: Experiences in "Barefoot Economics"*, London and Atlantic Highlands, NJ, Zed Books

Meadows, D H (1991) *The Global Citizen*, Washington, DC and Covelo, Island Press

— (1992) *Beyond the Limits*, London, Earthscan

Meadows, D H, D L Meadows, J Randers and W W Behrens (1972) *The Limits to Growth*, London, Pan Books

Meadows, D L (ed) (1977) *Alternatives to Growth*, Cambridge, MA, Ballinger

Merchant, C (1980) *Death of Nature: Women, Ecology and the Scientific Revolution*, San Francisco, Harper Collins

Middleton, N, P O'Keefe and S Moyo (1993) *Tears of the Crocodile: From Rio to Reality in the Developing World*, London and Boulder, CO, Pluto Press

Milieu Defensie (1992) *Action Plan: Sustainable Netherlands*, Amsterdam, Vereniging Milieudefensie (Friends of the Earth Netherlands)

Miller, G Tyler (1991) *Sustaining the Earth*, Belmont, CA, Wadsworth Publishing Company (third edition)

— (1992) *Living in the Environment: An Introduction to Environmental Science* (Seventh edition), Belmont, CA, Wadsworth Publishing Company

Mishan, E J (1967) *The Costs of Economic Growth*, London, Weidenfeld & Nicolson (revised edition, 1993)

— (1969) *Economic and Technological Growth: The Price We Pay*, London, Staples

— (1977) *The Economic Growth Debate: An Assessment*, London, George Allen & Unwin

Moore, J A (1985) "Science as a Way of Knowing: Human Ecology" *American Zoologist*, 25, pp483–637

Morgan, R (1994) *Planet Gauge: The Real Facts of Life*, London, Earthscan in association with WWF

Myers, N (1985)*The Gaia Atlas of Planetary Management*, London, Pan Books

Naess, A (1990a) *Ecology, Community and Lifestyle: Outline of an Ecosophy*, Cambridge, Cambridge University Press

— (1990b) "Sustainable Development and Deep Ecology", in J R Engel and J G Engel (eds), *Ethics of Environment and Development: Global Challenge, International Response*, London, Belhaven

— (1993) "Beautiful Action: Its Function in the Ecological Crisis" *Environmental Values*, 2, pp67–71

NEF/WWF (1995) *New Directions for the Structural Funds: Indicators for Sustainable Development in Europe*, London, NEF

NEPP (1989) *To Choose or to Lose*, The Hague, Netherlands, SDU Uitgeverij

Norberg-Hodge, H (1992) *Ancient Futures: Learning from Ladakh*, London, Rider

Norgaard, R B (1988) "Sustainable Development: A Co-evolutionary View" *Futures*, 20, pp606–20

— (1994) *Development Betrayed: The End of Progress and a Co-Evolutionary Revisioning of the Future*, London and New York, Routledge

Opschoor, H and J van der Straaten (1993) "Sustainable Development: An Institutional Approach" *Ecological Economics*, 7, pp203–22

O'Riordan, T (1981) *Environmentalism*, London, Pion (second revised edition)

— (1988) "The Politics of Sustainability", in R K Turner (ed) *Sustainable Environmental Management: Principles and Practice*, London, Belhaven in association with the Economic and Social Research Council, pp29–50

— (1993) "The Politics of Sustainability", in R K Turner (ed) *Sustainable Environmental Economics and Management: Principles and Practice*, London, Belhaven, pp37–69

Orr, D W (1992a) *Environmental Literacy: Education and the Transition to a Postmodern World*, Albany, NY, State University of New York Press

— (1992b) "Pascal's Wager and Economics in a Hotter Time", *Ecological Economics*, 6, pp1–6

— (1994) *Earth in Mind: On Education, Environment, and the Human Prospect* Washington, DC and Covelo, Island Press

Parikh, J et al (1991) *Consumption Patterns: The Driving Force of Environmental Stress*, Bombay, Indira Gandhi Institute of Development Research

Pearce, D W (ed) (1991) *Blueprint 2: Greening the World Economy*, London, Earthscan

— (ed) (1994) *Blueprint 3: Measuring Sustainable Development*, London, Earthscan

— (ed) (1995) *Blueprint 4: Sustaining the Earth: Capturing Global Value*, London, Earthscan

Pearce, D W and D Moran (1994) *The Economic Value of Diversity*, London, Earthscan

Pearce, D W and K Turner (1990) *Economics of Natural Resources and the Environment*, London, Harvester Wheatsheaf

Pearce, D W, A Markandya and E B Barbier (1989) *Blueprint for a Green Economy*, London, Earthscan

Peet, J (1992) *Energy and the Ecological Economics of Sustainability*, Washington DC and Covelo, Island Press

Pepper, D (1986) *The Roots of Modern Environmentalism*, London and New York, Routledge

Pereira, W and J Seabrook (1991) *Asking the Earth: Farms, Forestry and Survival in India*, London, Earthscan

Pezzey, J (1989) *Economic Analysis of Sustainable Growth and Sustainable Development*, Washington, DC, World Bank Environment Department Working Paper No 15

— (1992) "Sustainability: An Interdisciplinary Guide", *Environmental Values*, 1, pp321–62

Pickering, K T and L A Owen (1994) *An Introduction to Global Environmental Issues*, London and New York, Routledge

Pitt, D and S Nilsson (1994) *Protecting the Atmosphere: The Climate Change Convention and its Context*, London, Earthscan

Plant, J (ed) (1989) *Healing the Wounds: The Promise of Eco-feminism*, London, Greenprint

Ponting, Clive (1991) *A Green History of the World*, London, Sinclair Stevenson

Porritt, J (1984) *Seeing Green: The Politics of Ecology Explained*, Oxford, Blackwell

— (ed) (1991) *Save the Earth*, London, Dorling Kindersley

Pretty, J N (1995) *Regenerating Agriculture: An Alternative Strategy for Growth*, London, Earthscan

Pretty J N and Chambers, R (1993) *Towards a Learning Paradigm: New Professionalism and Institutions for Agriculture*, Brighton, Institute of Development Studies, University of Sussex, discussion paper 334

Proops, J (1989) "Ecological Economics: Rationale and Problem Areas", *Ecological Economics*, 1, pp59–76

Pugwash Council (1990) *The Pugwash Conferences on Science and World Affairs*, London, Pugwash Council

Quarrie, J (ed) (1992) *Earth Summit 1992*, London, Regency Press

Raghavan, C (1990) *Recolonization: GATT, The Uruguay Round, and the Third World*, London and Atlantic Highlands, NJ, Zed Books

Rahman, A (1993) *People's Self-Development: Perspectives on Participatory Action Research*, London and Atlantic Highlands, NJ, Zed Books

Read, P (1993) *Responding to Global Warming: An Integrated Long-Term Strategy*, London and Atlantic Highlands, NJ, Zed Books

Redclift, M (1987) *Sustainable Development: Exploring the Contradictions*, London, Methuen

Reed, D (ed) *Structural Adjustment and the Environment*, London, Earthscan in association with WWF

Rees, W E and M Wackernagel (1992) "Appropriated Carrying Capacity: Measuring the Natural Capital Requirements of the Human Economy", unpublished discussion draft presented to the second meeting of the International Society for Ecological Economics, Investing in Natural Capital, Stockholm, August

Repetto, R (ed) (1985) *The Global Possible: Resources, Development and the New Century*, New Haven, CT, Yale University Press

Rich, B (1994) *Mortgaging the Earth: The World Bank, Environmental Impoverishment, and the Crisis of Development*, Boston, Beacon Press

Richardson, D and C Rootes (eds) *The Green Challenge: The Development of Green Parties in Europe*, London and New York, Routledge

Rietbergen, S (ed) (1994) *The Earthscan Reader in Tropical Forestry*, London, Earthscan

Riddell, R (1981) *Ecodevelopment*, Aldershot, Gower Publishing

Robertson, J (1978) *The Sane Alternative: A Choice of Futures,* Ironbridge, Shropshire, J Robertson (Revised and expanded edition 1993, Oxford, J Robertson)

— (1989) *Future Wealth: A New Economics for the 21st Century*, London, Cassell

Robinson, M (1992) *The Greening of British Party Politics*, Manchester, Manchester University Press

Roddick, J (1993) *Scottish Academic Network for Global Environmental Change (SANGEC) Bulletin*, Autumn/Winter, University of Glasgow

Rolston, H (1990) "Science-Based versus Traditional Ethics", in J R Engel and J G Engel (eds) *Ethics of Environment and Development: Global Challenge, International Response*, London, Belhaven

Rowley, J and J Holmberg (1992) "Living in a Sustainable World", in J Holmberg (ed) *Policies for a Small Planet*, London, Earthscan

Rowntree Foundation, Joseph (1995) *Inquiry into Income and Wealth*, chaired by Sir Peter Barclay, vol 1; vol 2, *A Summary of the Evidence by John Hills*, Joseph Rowntree Foundation, York

Royal Commission on Environmental Pollution (1994) *Transport and the Environment*, 18th Report of the Commission, London, Royal Commission on Environmental Pollution

Ruckelshaus, W D (1989) "Towards a Sustainable World", *Scientific American*, 261, pp114–20

Ryan, J C (1992) *Life Support: Conserving Biological Diversity*, Washington, DC, Worldwatch Institute

Sachs, W (1992a) *The Development Dictionary*, London and Atlantic Highlands, NJ, Zed Books

— (1992b) "Bygone Splendour", in P Ekins and M Max-Neef (eds) *Real-Life Economics: Understanding Wealth Creation*, London and New York, Routledge, pp156–61

— (ed) (1992c) "Poor not Different", in P Ekins and M Max-Neef (eds) *Real-Life Economics: Understanding Wealth Creation*, London and New York, Routledge, pp161–5

— (ed) (1993) *Global Ecology: A New Arena of Political Conflict*, London and Atlantic Highlands, NJ, Zed Books

Sale, K (1980) *Human Scale*, London, Secker & Warburg

— (1985) *Dwellers in the Land: The Bioregional Vision*, San Francisco, Sierra Club Books

Sandbrook, R (1993) "From Stockholm to Rio", in J Quarrie (ed) *Earth Summit 1992*, London, Regency

Savory, A (1988) *Holistic Resource Management*, Washington, DC and Covelo, Island Press

Schatan, J (1987) *World Debt – Who Is to Pay?*, London and Atlantic Highlands, NJ, Zed Books

Schmidheiny, S with the The Business Council for Sustainable Development (1992) *Changing Course: A Global Business Perspective on Development and the Environment*, Cambridge, MA, MIT Press

Schneider, B (1988) The Barefoot Revolution: A Report to the Club of Rome, London, Intermediate Technology Publications

Schumacher, E F (1973) Small is Beautiful: A Study of Economics as if People Mattered, Abacus edition, London, Sphere Books. (First published 1973, London, Blond & Briggs)

Scientific American (1989) Managing Planet Earth, September issue

Seabrook, J (1990) The Myth of the Market: Promises and Illusions, Bideford, Green Books

— (1993) Pioneers of Change: Experiments in Creating a Humane Society, London and Atlantic Highlands, NJ, Zed Books

Seager, J (1990) The State of the Earth, London and New York, Routledge

Sharp, R (1992) "Organizing for Change: People, Power and the Role of Institutions", in J Holmberg (ed) Policies for a Small Planet, London, Earthscan

Shiva, V (1989) Staying Alive: Women, Ecology and Development, London and Atlantic Highlands, NJ, Zed Books

— (1991) The Violence of the Green Revolution: Third World Agriculture, Ecology and Politics, London and Atlantic Highlands, NJ, Zed Books

— (1993) Monoculture of the Mind: Biodiversity, Biotechnology and "Scientific" Agriculture, London and Atlantic Highlands, NJ, Zed Books, with Third World Network

Shrader-Frechette, K (1985) "Environmental Ethics and Global Imperatives", in R Repetto (ed) The Global Possible: Resources, Development and the New Century, New Haven, CT, Yale University Press, pp97–129

Simon, J L (1981) The Ultimate Resource, Princeton, Princeton University Press

Skolimowski, H (1995) "In Defence of Sustainable Development", Environmental Values, 4, pp69–70

Slesser M, J King, C Revie and D Crane (1994) Non-Monetary Indicators for Managing Sustainability, Edinburgh, Centre for Human Ecology, University of Edinburgh

Smith, J W (1991)The High Tech Fix: Sustainable Ecology or Technocratic Megaprojects for the Twenty-first Century, Aldershot, Academic Publishing Group

South Centre, The (1993) An Interdependent World: Responses to "The Challenge to the South", London and Atlantic Highlands, NJ, Zed Books

— (1993) Whose Brave New World? Prospects for the South, London and Atlantic Highlands, NJ, Zed Books

South Commission, The (1990) The Challenge to the South, Oxford, Oxford University Press

Sterling, S R (1990) "Towards an Ecological World View", in J R Engel and J G Engel (eds) Ethics of Environment and Development: Global Challenge, International Responses, London, Belhaven

Tarnas, R (1991) The Passion of the Western Mind: Understanding the Ideas that have Shaped Our World View, New York, Harmony Books

Tart, C (1986) Waking Up: Overcoming the Obstacles to Human Potential, Boston, New Science Library

Therivel, R et al (1993) Strategic Environmental Assessment, London, Earthscan

Timberlake, L and L Thomas (1990) When the Bough Breaks: The Plight of Children in the Third World, London, Earthscan

Tolba, M K (1987) Sustainable Development: Constraints and Opportunities, Guildford, Butterworth Scientific

Trainer, F E (1985) *Abandon Affluence! Sustainable Development and Social Change*, London, Zed Books
— (1989) *Developed to Death: Rethinking Third World Development*, London, Greenprint
Turner, R K (ed) (1988) *Sustainable Environmental Management: Principles and Practice*, London, Belhaven in association with the Economic and Social Research Council
— (ed) (1993)*Sustainable Environmental Economics and Management: Principles and Practice*, Belhaven, London
UK Government (1994a) *Biodiversity: The UK Action Plan*, London, HMSO
— (1994b) *Climate Change: The UK Programme*, London, HMSO
— (1994c) *Sustainable Development: The UK Strategy*, London, HMSO
— (1994d) *Sustainable Forestry: The UK Programme*, London, HMSO
UN (1962) *The Development Decade: Proposals for Action*, New York, UN
UNDP (1991) *Human Development Report*, New York, Oxford University Press
— (1992) *Human Development Report*, New York, Oxford University Press
— (1994) *Human Development Report*, New York, Oxford University Press
UNICEF (1990) *The State of the World's Children*, New York, Oxford University Press
UNRISD (1970) *International Development Strategy*, Geneva, UNRISD
Vellve, R (1992) *Saving the Seed: Genetic Diversity and European Agriculture*, London, Earthscan
Verhelst T G (1990) *No Life without Roots: Culture and Development*, London and Atlantic Highlands, NJ
Vitousek, P M, P R Erlich, A H Erlich and P A Matson (1986) "Human Appropriation of the Products of Photosynthesis", *Bioscience*, 34, pp368–73
Wackernagel, M and W E Rees (1992) "Perceptual and Structural Barriers to Investing in Natural Capital", revised draft presented to second meeting of International Society for Ecological Economics, Investing in Natural Capital, Stockholm, August
Waddington, C H (1977) *Tools for Thought*, London, Cape
Wakeford, T and M Walters (eds) (1995) *Science for the Earth: Can Science Make the World a Better Place?*, Chichester, Wiley
Wallace, R R and B G Norton (1992) "Policy Implications of Gaian Theory", *Ecological Economics*, 6, pp103–18
Walsh, R and F Vaughan (eds) (1993) *Paths beyond Ego: The Transpersonal Vision*, Los Angeles, Jeremy P Tarcher/Perigee
Ward, B and R Dubos (1972) *Only One Earth: The Care and Maintenance of a Small Planet*, London, Penguin
Ward, D (1979) *Progress for a Small Planet*, Harmondsworth, Penguin
Waring M (1989) *If Women Counted: A New Feminist Economics*, London, Macmillan
WCED (1987), *Our Common Future*, Oxford, Oxford University Press
— (1987) *Food 2000: Global Policies for Sustainable Agriculture*, London and Atlantic Highlands, NJ, Zed Books
— (1987) *Energy 2000: A Global Strategy for Sustainable Development*, London and Atlantic Highlands, NJ, Zed Books
Weizsäcker, E U von (1994) *Earth Politics*, London and Atlantic Highlands, NJ, Zed Books

Weizsäcker, E U von and J Jesinghaus (1992) *Ecological Tax Reform: A Policy Proposal for Sustainable Development*, London and Atlantic Highlands, NJ, Zed Books

Wightman, A (1994) *The Greening of Rural Development*, Perth, Scottish Wildlife and Countryside Link

Wijkman A and L Timberlake (1984) *Natural Disasters: Acts of God or Acts of Man?* London, Earthscan

Wisner, B (1988) *Power and Need in Africa: Basic Human Needs and Development Policies*, London, Earthscan

Woodhouse, T (ed) (1986) *People and Planet: The Right Livelihood Speeches, 1980–85*, Hartland, Devon, Green Books

— (ed) (1990) *Replenishing the Earth: the Right Livelihood Speeches, 1986–89*, Hartland, Devon, Green Books

World Bank (1989) *World Development Report*, New York, Oxford University Press

— (1991) *The Challenge of Development: World Development Report*, Oxford University Press, New York and Oxford

Worster, D (1987) *Nature's Economy: A History of Ecological Ideas*, New York, Cambridge University Press

WRI (1992) *World Resources 1992–3: A Guide to the Global Environment*, Washington DC, WRI

WWF/NEF (1994) "Strategies for Sustainable Development Indicators for National Reports to the Commission on Sustainable Development and the EC Structural Funds Process", draft, London, WWF/NEF

# Index

# Other sustainable development publications from Earthscan

## Sustainability, the Environment and Urbanisation
*Edited by Cedric Pugh*

Sustainability literature and debate has tended to focus on 'green' issues, such as biodiversity, climate change and marine pollution. Much less attention has been paid to the 'brown' agenda: those issues, such as poor sanitation and water quality, air pollution and housing problems, which are particularly prevalent in Southern cities. *Sustainability, the Environment and Urbanisation* provides a comprehensive overview of the brown agenda, with case studies and examples from a number of Southern countries. Clearly written, with contributions from some of the leading experts in the field, the book will appeal to students on environment and development courses and all those concerned with the 'healthy cities' movement.

*Paperback £14.95 ISBN 1 85383 357 6 Hardback £35.00 ISBN 1 85383 362 2*

## The Earthscan Reader in Sustainable Development
*Edited by John Kirkby, Phil O'Keefe and Lloyd Timberlake*

A collection of the most accessible and authoritative readings on all the principal areas of sustainable development, providing the basic course material needed in all the relevant subjects, including economics, environmental studies, geography, politics, planning and social science.

*Paperback £14.95 ISBN 1 85383 216 2 Hardback £35.00 ISBN 1 85383 223 5*

## Sustainability: A Systems Approach
*Tony Clayton and Nicholas Radcliffe*

Sustainability affects most areas of human activity. Understanding it, and ways of achieving it, has to involve an understanding of the relatively new, but rapidly developing, science of complex adaptive systems and general systems theory. This book provides an introduction to, and thorough explanation of, this new field. It shows how the systems perspective is essential for the social sciences and for understanding sustainability, and includes practical guidance and case studies showing the application of the systems approach in the social and economic management of sustainability.

*Paperback £15.95 ISBN 1 85383 319 3 Hardback £35.00 ISBN 1 85383 314 2*